Winning Government Business

Gaining the Competitive Advantage

Winning Government Business

Gaining the Competitive Advantage

Steve R. Osborne, Ph.D.

MANAGEMENTCONCEPTS

Vienna, Virginia

𝆕𝆕𝆕
MANAGEMENTCONCEPTS
8230 Leesburg Pike, Suite 800
Vienna, VA 22182
(703) 790-9595
Fax: (703) 790-1371
www.managementconcepts.com

Printed in the United States of America

Library of Congress Cataloging-in-Publication Data

Osborne, Steven R., 1947–
    Winning government business: gaining the competitive advantage/
Steven R. Osborne.
        p. cm.
    Includes index.
    ISBN-13: 978-1-56726-106-6
    ISBN-10: 1-56726-106-X
    1. Public contracts—United States. 2. Proposal writing in public contracting.
    3. Letting of contracts. 4. Government purchasing—United States. I. Title.

HD3861.U6 O83 2002
658.8'04—dc21

                                                    2002071900

About the Author

Steve Osborne has an enviable record of leading successful business ventures and capturing new business. His 25 years of business development experience cover all branches of the military services, numerous federal government agencies, and a wide variety of commercial markets, both domestic and international. He has started and managed two medium-sized subsidiaries, held senior and executive management positions with three Fortune 200 aerospace and defense companies, and led teams in acquiring more than $2 billion in government contracts. For the last ten years, Dr. Osborne has served as President and Senior Consultant at Cornerstone Training, Inc., a proposal and business development consulting firm he founded.

Dr. Osborne's proposal experience includes major technical/management responsibility for more than 100 proposals spanning a broad spectrum of program types and clients. He has served in every role within the proposal development process: proposal manager, volume manager, strategy consultant, red team reviewer, and proposal writer/editor. Dr. Osborne has authored thousands of pages of proposal text, trained proposal/evaluation teams, and served as a professional proposal consultant to a host of e-companies that compete for government business. For the last 15 years, he has maintained a win rate of 90 percent for proposals he managed.

Dr. Osborne holds a Ph.D. from Arizona State University, where he also served on the faculty.

Table of Contents

List of Figures

Preface

In a 100-meter dash of world-class athletes, the margin of victory is inches and fractions of a second. Even in a grueling marathon, the difference between winning and losing often is measured in feet rather than meters or miles. Athletes appreciate the value of competitive advantage. Knowing that a modest performance enhancement can make the difference, they diligently seek an edge—that extra "something" that will speed them across the finish line ahead of the competition. Lighter weight shoes, clothing with less wind resistance, training regimen, diet, strength training, meditation—anything that might enhance performance is seriously considered.

This is a book about competition. The contestants, however, are not athletes but companies eager to capture business from the federal government. Nor is the field of battle a sports stadium; instead, it is the marketplace of new business. Despite obvious differences that distinguish these arenas of competition, some relevant parallels exist between the two.

For each competition, only one player emerges the winner. The winner of each respective contest is not necessarily the best, but merely the one whose performance was better than the other assembled competitors. And finally, the thin margin of performance that often separates victors and vanquished in athletic events is mirrored in the competition for government contracts.

The quest for that margin of victory is the subject of this book, and the battle for federal government business is its substance. My intent is to equip readers with the skills and knowledge they need to capture government business effectively and efficiently. Toward that end, the book provides an easy-to-read tutorial on the entire business and proposal development lifecycle. It is crammed full of tips, guides, recommendations, and examples to guide each stage of the new business development process. Yet, it is more than just another book on business and proposal development. It uniquely adopts, in analogous fashion, the mindset of the world-class athlete by searching out every conceivable opportunity to gain advantage over the competition—that something extra that enables one to edge ahead and win the contest. At every step, the book offers tried-and-true methods and tips that will enable readers to capture competitive advantage.

Perhaps of greater importance is the fact that the information, advice, and examples presented here are not academic. Their source is neither the pages of a textbook nor the outgrowth of untested theory. Instead, they are based on more than two decades of real-world experience, forged by the fires of battle and shaped by the unforgiving consequences of success and failure. Thus, the book's content is vouchsafed by a cumulative win rate of nearly 90 percent amassed over the last 15 years. Built upon a broad cross-section of customers, program types, and clients, this represents about $2 billion in new business—all captured using the knowledge shared in this book.

The intended audience is everyone who participates in the battle for new business. Gaining competitive advantage is not a task that can be assigned. It is a mindset—a business philosophy and an attendant process that will be most successful when they permeate the entire organization. Indeed, the book's content will most benefit capture team leaders, proposal managers, program managers, marketing personnel, and members of the proposal team. Yet senior and functional managers will likewise find value. Ultimately, they set the tone and direction for an organization. Hence, they must be onboard to support and approve processes and procedures that will enable their organization to capture competitive advantage and thus win federal contracts. And finally, those of you who provide proposal support will do well to understand the process and philosophy of your organization's new business initiatives.

The focus of the book is federal government procurements over $100,000 in value acquired through the competitive process. The guidance offered can also be applied to capture state and local government procurements to the extent that they follow the federal government's acquisition model. It also can be applied to cases where organizations bid as subcontractors to federal government prime contractors, but with the same caveat.

Any size organization can use the information in this book effectively to pursue government contracts. Whether you are a small business chasing a $300,000 contract or a major player vying for a multibillion dollar opportunity, the contents of this book will prove beneficial. However, one shoe does not fit all. The book's guidance will need to be scaled to accommodate the size of your organization and the type and value of business opportunities it pursues.

Finally, the book does not presume prior knowledge of proposal development or the government's method of evaluating bidders and awarding contracts. It can be read by neophyte and seasoned veteran alike. Each will benefit.

For the inexperienced, the book provides an end-to-end exposition of the business and proposal development process. Accordingly, it contains a wealth of information useful to build and improve processes, increase proposal win probability, and reduce bid costs. Again, all is underpinned by the concept of gaining competitive advantage and the goal of winning federal contracts.

For veterans, the book will verify and reinforce much of what they already know, yet still highlight some changes to enhance their organization's ability to capture new business. Perhaps this will ignite or reawaken a passion long dormant to implement what they know but do not currently practice.

BOOK PREVIEW

As a preview, the book consists of four parts. Overall, it provides information on topics ranging from learning how to navigate your way around a government RFP through attending a proposal debriefing after contract award—and everything in between. In each case, specific instructions are given to enhance proposal effectiveness and improve the efficiency of your bid and proposal process. Along the way, you will discover tactics and strategy about how to optimize the time allotted to prepare a winning proposal and avoid unnecessary rework due to false starts. These will soothe the sting of proposal work and allow you to stretch your bid and proposal dollars.

Part 1 of the book includes this introductory chapter, plus a walk through the structure of federal government RFPs and an overview of the government's source selection process. This will familiarize you with the lay of the land and the rules of the game.

Part 2 covers pre-proposal activities, stretching from strategic planning up until the time you receive the final RFP. The focus here is on performing the myriad activities necessary to position yourself strategically with your customer, develop a winning game plan, and accomplish the actions and planning required to capture a new piece of business. Key topics include pre-proposal marketing, making informed bid decisions, performing competitive assessments, fashioning an effective bid strategy, organizing the capture team, and handling customer interactions such as attending a pre-proposal bidders' conference or responding to a draft RFP.

Part 3 addresses in detail the proposal development phase, starting with receipt of the final RFP and ending with submittal of your proposal to the customer. It provides instructions, tips, guidelines, and examples of how to analyze a government RFP, create proposal management documents, build guides and templates to assist authors in preparing storyboards, develop proposal and section themes, analyze the features and benefits of your approach, develop and polish effective, hard-hitting proposal sections, perform proposal reviews to detect shortcomings and fine-tune the final product, and produce and deliver the final proposal. The focus throughout this portion of the book is on planning and preparing responsive, easy-to-read proposal narrative that convinces government evaluators that you are the best choice. A separate chapter addresses the basics of preparing the cost volume and provides some valuable insights into how to gain competitive advantage in this critical proposal area.

The final part of the book deals with post-proposal submittal activities. Essential guidance is provided to keep you from stumbling during this critical phase of the acquisition process. This includes how to prepare and deliver a program-winning oral presentation to your customer and how to respond effectively to customer inquiries concerning your submitted proposal. Additional topics address the value of using information gained from an evaluation debriefing from the government after contract award to improve future proposal performance, along with some necessary housekeeping chores required to close out the proposal.

Anyone who reads this book will be able to glean enough new insight to justify its cost and the time to read it. Those who choose to take it seriously will gain ample information to seize competitive advantage consistently and enjoy the spoils of victory far more frequently than they experience the sting of defeat.

Steve Osborne
July 2002

Part 1

The Foundations of Winning Proposals

Chapter 1

Winning New Business from the Federal Government

Each year the federal government procures products and services worth billions of dollars. In fact, the number is in the hundreds of billions. The sheer size of this market attracts the attention of hundreds of companies who compete for this vast source of potential revenue. If you are reading this book, you either work for one of those companies or you hope to join the hunt.

The only avenue available to those who seek to share in the spoils of federal spending is through the competitive process. Typically, bidders prepare a proposal in response to a request for proposal (RFP). Occasionally the government buys a product or service without competition, but those circumstances are rare. Mastering the complex set of skills required to prepare proposals, therefore, is a critical prerequisite to winning government business. For those companies that rely upon government contracts for their livelihood, proposal development is an essential survival skill. Everything else being equal, your ability to prepare proposals is the single most important factor in attaining new business from the government.

WHY PROPOSALS?

Proposal team members often ask why they have to write a proposal. After all, why can't the government buy things the same way the rest of us consumers do? They could decide what they need, survey the available products or services that fulfill that need, and pick the one they want. Actually, in a sense this is what the government does. They first define a need or requirement. Then they communicate the need to industry by posting a notice on the federal business opportunities website. (In the old days they would publish a notice in the *Commerce Business Daily*.) The government then releases an RFP or a Request for Quote (RFQ) that defines their need and provides instructions about how to bid. Once proposals or bids are received, the government evaluates them against a set of defined standards to pick a winner. For RFQs, they select the lowest-priced qualified bidder.

Proposals enable the government to evaluate offers and select the company they deem the best choice. Unlike consumers, the government is not supposed to just pick anyone they want. Instead, the evaluation process is highly regulated. It is intended to be fair and objective, with the goal of selecting the bidder that represents best value to the government.

The proposal process permits anyone who believes they are qualified to compete for government business. It is intended to give everyone a fair chance. It also is designed to maximize competition. Competition is good. It simulates innovation, promotes quality, and reduces cost. As taxpayers, and the beneficiaries of many government services, we should applaud the competitive process. Ultimately, it is in our best interest and the best interest of the country. Unfortunately, the federal government procurement process is controlled by a mind-boggling array of regulations and is implemented by an inefficient bureaucracy. That is truly the downside of the competitive process. Yet, it is a process we must navigate effectively if we want to acquire business from the government.

WHY IS PROPOSAL PREPARATION SO DIFFICULT?

There is an old saying that the only thing worse than *having* a government contract is *not having* a government contract. Part of this sentiment reflects the difficulty of acquiring business from the government, which typically entails the arduous task of preparing a proposal. Under the best of circumstances, proposal preparation is a serious challenge. Normally, the process is extremely difficult. Often it is nightmarish. During a difficult proposal, it is not unusual to hear someone threaten to quit and open a hardware store or bait shop just to avoid future proposals.

What makes proposals so difficult? Multiple factors contribute to the challenge. My candidates for the gremlins that contribute to proposal Hades include the following.

Puzzling RFP Structure and Content

To the uninitiated, a government RFP can appear to be a jumbled hodgepodge of regulations, requirements, contract deliverables, and instructions that defy human logic. Many RFP sections read more like a document you would expect to receive from your lawyer than an invitation to bid. Sorting through RFP sections and finding what is important can be a daunting challenge. It can be nearly impossible if you are not familiar with the various sections.

Inconsistent or Confusing RFP Requirements

Government RFPs often are assembled by committee. Separate groups prepare different RFP sections. Sometimes they do not coordinate their respective work efforts. Other times they cut and paste sections from old RFPs with different requirements. The result in either case is inconsistent or contradictory requirements. In yet other instances, an error in the RFP makes it impossible to perform the contract.

For example, a few years ago I was working on an RFP that required us to modify a series of flight simulators. Aircraft equipment kits required to perform the modification were to be provided by the government. Unfortunately, the RFP schedule for kit delivery was *after* the scheduled delivery dates for the simulators. It took us until the week before the proposal was due to get this issue resolved.

Reconciling inconsistent and poorly defined requirements is simply part of the job. Often this involves writing a question and submitting it to the government contracting officer—and then waiting for what you hope will be a clear answer.

Insufficient Time

A "blivit" is ten pounds of manure in a five-pound bag. Proposals have a similar quality, only the commodity is time instead of manure. (Some would argue that there is a correlation between the two). There never seems to be enough time to perform all the tasks required to prepare an effective proposal. Most federal procurements give bidders between 30 and 60 days to prepare and submit their proposal. It is not unusual for proposal teams to design a system, determine how to support it logistically, write a 300-page technical proposal, and prepare detailed pricing, including a lifecycle cost analysis for a 10-year contract, all in 45 days.

Federal procurement streamlining initiatives also place more of the burden on the bidder. Many RFPs now require bidders to prepare their own program management documents, like the statement of work, contract data requirements list (CDRL), product or performance specifications, and complicated management tools.

Time pressures are made worse by RFP amendments that require a major change in your proposal, or provide answers to questions that force a change in your technical approach. Although RFP amendments may include additional proposal preparation time, the time allotted may be insufficient to make the changes properly.

Time is the single biggest enemy of proposal teams. Its effective management is critical to a winning proposal effort. The only saving grace is the realization that your competition faces the same time pressures and challenges.

Many of the people assigned to work on proposals have regular day jobs. Consequently, they must juggle their normal daily workload with proposal demands. This can be very frustrating to employees torn between competing priorities. The short time fuse of most proposals only exacerbates this problem.

Lack of Proposal Skills and Experience

There is nothing in a normal work environment that prepares people to work on proposals. Proposals require a unique set of skills that are not easily acquired. Like most complex skills, they are best developed through experience. However, the average technical person will only work on a few proposals during their entire career. At best, they will enter the proposal fray once or twice a year. Few ever receive constructive feedback on their proposal performance. Hence, errors are propagated from proposal to proposal. Over time, poor proposal practices become institutionalized.

Most proposal team members receive little or no proposal training. Yet they are tasked with analyzing RFP requirements, preparing storyboards, identifying themes and discriminators, and writing complicated proposal sections that will convince the customer that their company should be awarded the contract. Technical personnel generally have sufficient writing skills to accommodate the business communication requirements of their job and communicate with their technical peers. Yet they often lack the peculiar blend and style of writing demanded by proposals.

RFPs routinely request bidders to present information in an illogical order and ask questions that seem peculiar to those not accustomed to government proposals. Consequently, proposal authors struggle to make sense of their assignment and become frustrated because they are asked to perform a task for which they are unprepared. Frequently, proposal authors work tirelessly for two or three weeks before their efforts are reviewed. Following an evaluation of their work, they are told they have failed to respond adequately to RFP requirements and their proposal sections must be completely redone.

Lack of Tools and Processes

The general lack of good proposal tools and formalized processes are additional factors that contribute to proposal difficulty. Tools include templates, examples, or aids that help proposal members perform their assigned tasks. These include things like an author guide that clearly shows the author what to address in his or her proposal section. Other helpful tools may include a style guide and proposal directive that identifies the required proposal format, specifies the writing style to be used, and sets standards for things like how to handle abbreviations, the preferred format for graphics, and how to refer to the team being proposed to perform the contract.

A formalized process consists of a series of well-defined, integrated stages of proposal development. Each stage has a defined product, and proposal team members are given detailed instructions about what will be accomplished during each stage and their role in the process. Hence, they know what is expected of them and when things are due. Having a proposal roadmap available helps ease proposal anxiety. It also enables proposal team members to understand the overall process and how the different stages fit together.

Many organizations lack a formalized proposal process. Each proposal follows a different course of events driven by the personality, style, and whim of the proposal manager. The absence of a formal proposal process only heightens the difficulty of proposal preparation. Proposal team members often are confused and frustrated because they do not know what is expected of them, or because they lack a clear picture of what is going to happen during the proposal preparation process.

WINNING

Except for procurements that allow multiple awards, the government competitive process is binary: There are only winners and losers; no silver or bronze medals are awarded. Few things are more disheartening than to slave over a proposal every day for two months, eat a metric ton of stale pizza, have your family forget what you look like, and drink 100 gallons of bad coffee, only to end up in the loser's circle. On the other hand, winning a major competition is an exhilarating experience.

Everyone wants to be a winner. Every proposal team begins by believing they will win or at least that they have a very good chance of winning. No one invests the resources required to prepare a government proposal with the intent of losing. You do not join the race just to get tired. You compete to win. The future success of your company and the careers of you and your fellow employees depend upon it.

If your organization is primarily or solely dependent upon government contracts, then planning for and preparing proposals is the most important business activity you will perform. In the words of the legendary football coach, Vince Lombardi, "Winning is not the most important thing, it is the only thing." Not only is winning the key, but you must be able to win consistently. Keeping work in your company's pipeline is a never-ending task, whether you work for a small company or a major behemoth.

Consider an organization with annual revenues of $24 million. Sustaining that revenue level requires $2 million of new business per month. However, you will not win everything you bid. If your maintain a win ratio of 25 percent, then you will need to bid for $8 million worth of new business each month. If you are more effective, winning 33 percent of your bids, then you only need to bid on $6 million in new business each month. Note that this is only to maintain your current revenue stream. You must bid for even more work if you want to grow.

The analogy holds for larger companies. A company with annual revenue of $240 million needs to bid on $60 million in new business each month to sustain current revenues based on a one-in-three win rate. It almost makes you feel sorry for the big guys, those with annual revenues of $20 billion or more. Well, almost.

It costs money to plan for and prepare a proposal. In fact, it can be quite expensive. Generally, it costs as much to prepare a losing proposal as it does to prepare one that wins. Money spent on losing proposals is money lost. It cannot be spent on other things the company may need. At some point, a poor win rate will undermine an organization's ability to sustain itself. Thus, the emphasis on winning is more than just talk. You must win to survive, and you must win consistently to stay afloat in the competitive waters of the federal government.

COMMON PROPOSAL MISTAKES

If winning is everything, then we will be well served to avoid making mistakes that limit our potential success. Over the last two-plus decades, I have worked on or managed well over 100 proposals. For more than 10 years I earned my living managing proposals for a wide variety of clients. Throughout this period I repeatedly witnessed companies make the same proposal mistakes. These mistakes tend to be common across companies regardless of size or type of business. They are expensive mistakes. Each undermines the ability to submit a winning proposal. Most of them result in the inefficient use of company resources.

Here are some common mistakes to avoid if you want to gain competitive advantage and win federal contracts:

- *Underestimating the difficulty of preparing a winning proposal.* Preparing a winning proposal is a complex, arduous process that requires adequate resources—people, time, tools, and facilities. Short-changing the process to save money is akin to spending dollars to save dimes.
- *Overestimating the ability of the proposal team.* Proposal teams require a broad mix of people and skills, even for small proposals. Two categories of people are needed: those who are experts for their assigned areas of proposal responsibility and those who are legitimate experts in proposal development. Don't make the mistake of using an inexperi-

enced proposal manager or selecting someone to lead the proposal just because he or she has great management skills or is a technical expert.

A related common mistake is having one person serve as both the proposal manager and the program manager. For small proposals, this may be possible from a workload standpoint, but it is still not wise. Proposal and program management require very different skill sets. Few people possess both. For large proposals, it is practically impossible for one person to handle the workload of both positions. Eventually one or the other is shortchanged.

- *Starting too late.* The development of a bid strategy and preliminary proposal planning and development must begin well in advance of the RFP. Waiting until the RFP is released to start your proposal puts you at a significant disadvantage. It exaggerates the problem of not having enough time to prepare the proposal and yields the competitive advantage to those companies who start early.

- *Using past winning proposals as a model for current efforts.* A proposal that was successful in winning a past contract is not necessarily a "good" proposal. It was just better than what the rest of the competition submitted for that procurement. Each procurement is different. Past proposals were probably written to a different set of requirements, a different group of competitors, and with a different bid strategy. Using past proposals as a template, or blindly using material from past proposals, can easily lead you down the wrong path. If you use information from past proposals, you must tailor and align it with the requirements of the current RFP and bid strategy.

- *Failing to develop or integrate bid strategy into the proposal.* Without a well-defined bid strategy, you have no basis for making important proposal decisions. Your proposal will lack a clear focus. Bid strategy should be the culmination of pre-proposal intelligence-gathering and decision-making that consider the competition, program requirements, and your company's capabilities. Amazingly, some companies expend enormous effort to develop and refine a bid strategy. Then they fail to ensure that the bid strategy is used to guide the proposal effort and is reflected in the final proposal product.

- *Inadequate review before submittal.* Practically every proposal undergoes some type of review before it is submitted to the government. However, these reviews produce dividends only if they are properly conducted and the results are used to correct proposal deficiencies. Experience suggests that effective proposal reviews are rare events. Too often they are conducted by people who do not possess the skills or insight they need to perform a useful review. Reviewers must be familiar with the RFP and your bid strategy—and they must conduct the review in the same manner as the government. Otherwise, review results may amount to little more than opinion. Direction given by an ill-informed review team may make the proposal worse than it was before the review.

- *Failure to show knowledge of customer or problem being solved.* Everything you need to know is not contained in the RFP. The material requested by the RFP must be couched and interpreted with respect to the needs, wants, fears, and desires of your customer. Moreover, your proposal must demonstrate a basic understanding of the requirement you are proposing to satisfy. You can prepare an adequate technical proposal and still miss the mark if you fail to demonstrate an understanding of the problem your customer needs to solve.

- *Failure to clearly address all RFP requirements.* Failing to clearly and completely address every RFP requirement makes your proposal nonresponsive. Failing to place your proposal response where government evaluators expect to find it likewise may cause your proposal to receive a poor score. This is the single most prevalent reason given by the government for why proposals lose. Some estimates indicate that as many as two-thirds of all government proposals are partially nonresponsive. With few exceptions, a nonresponsive proposal is a loser.

- *Features and benefits of proposed approach not articulated clearly.* Every product or service embodies features or characteristics that help define and distinguish it from other comparable products or services. As consumers we select those products whose features and benefits best match our needs or desires. For example, from the host of automobiles that offer reliable transportation, we select the one that has the benefits—speed, comfort, reliability, operating cost, looks, gadgets, etc.— we like the most. Faced with two proposals that offer an acceptable solution to their needs, the government will select the one that offers the greatest benefits. Highlighting the features of your proposed approach and the benefits these features offer the government is a key component of gaining competitive advantage and winning a government contract. Most proposals fail in this regard and thereby give away the competitive advantage in this critical area.

- *Proposal poorly written/hard to understand.* A well-known proposal consultant used to say, "A proposal should read like a dime novel." I agree. Well-written proposals that respond clearly to RFP requirements receive higher scores than their poorly written counterparts. Comparable technical material will be evaluated differently depending on how it is presented. If your proposal is difficult to read, or sounds like the operating manual for a personal computer, then you have missed an excellent opportunity to gain competitive advantage.

KEY CHARACTERISTICS OF WINNING BIDS

Winners of government contracts avoid common proposal mistakes. They also perform more parts of the proposal process better than their competitors. There is no simple formula for winning. Nonetheless, winning efforts tend to share common key characteristics. Figure 1-1 lists ten of those characteristics. These ten characteristics do not encompass everything you need to accomplish; they are just some of the major characteris-

Figure 1-1. Ten Characteristics of Winning Bids

WINNING BIDS

1. An effective marketing effort has been initiated well in advance of the proposal. Customer contacts have been made and a good understanding of customer requirements, fears, and desires has been developed before the RFP is released.
2. A bid strategy, or capture plan, has been developed to capture a selected piece of new business. This plan considers your existing technical capability, customer requirements, competitors, potential team members, and any significant aspects of the procurement that could impact your probable success.
3. The proposal team is assembled, proposal planning is complete, and key pre-proposal activities have been completed by the time the final RFP is released. The proposal team includes all the necessary personnel required to accomplish proposal preparation successfully, including an experienced proposal manager with demonstrated expertise.
4. The proposal team is empowered with the authority and responsibility to develop the proposal and has all the support and resources necessary to do the job
5. The proposal addresses every RFP requirement completely and clearly.
6. The bid strategy and previously gathered marketing intelligence are fully incorporated into the proposal.
7. The proposal focuses on the evaluation criteria delineated in the RFP.
8. Features of the proposed approach are highlighted. Their benefits to the customer are explained clearly. The technical proposal is written to minimize the evaluation of proposal risk by government evaluators.
9. The proposal is well-written and easy to understand by government evaluators.
10. The proposed cost is reasonable, competitive with other bidders, corresponds to the technical proposal, and fits within the government's funding profile.

tics of winning proposals. Achieving them does not guarantee that you will win, but it will dramatically improve your odds. At the same time, failing to meet these characteristics does not guarantee that you will lose, but it drastically reduces your odds.

KEYS TO WINNING CONSISTENTLY

Competing for government contracts can be very confusing. Sometimes you seemingly do everything right and you still lose. Other times you violate many of the characteristics of a winning proposal and you still win. I have led winning proposal efforts that failed to follow much of the advice given here. Breaking the rules, however, is not a good strategy. It certainly is not the road to consistent winning.

The apparent randomness of government contract awards has created a lot of myths and half-truths in the marketplace, giving rise in many cases to an air of cynicism among bidders. One viewpoint suggests that proposals are just an excuse the government uses to award contracts to whomever they please. After a losing effort, it is not uncommon to hear comments like, "they won because the customer likes them," "the XXX's bought in," "the procurement was wired for them," or "it was their turn to win." These are rationalizations intended to soothe the agony of defeat. Unfortunately, such rationalizations are almost never true. They militate against an intelligent, systematic analysis to determine the real reason you lost. If you discover why you lost and why your competitor won, you have an opportunity to learn from your mistakes. Otherwise, you are destined to repeat them in the future.

If you are serious about winning government contracts, then you need to understand a few harsh realities. First, if you lose it is because your competitor did something better. They were more clever or innovative, took more risk, accepted a lower profit margin, convinced the customer they had a better solution, or represented a lower risk approach. Second, the key to winning is doing more things *better* than the competition. You never know in advance what your competition will do well. If you want to win consistently, you need to do everything well.

Popular books on proposals suggest you can win if you will just follow a few simple rules. Indeed, rules about starting your proposal early, collecting good marketing intelligence, building good proposal storyboards, and integrating themes into your proposal are all important. Yet, you can follow all the rules and still lose. Remember, your competitors know the same rules.

Everything in a proposal is important. You must manage every detail with a focus on winning—starting with the first piece of marketing information and continuing until the contract is signed. Every contact you have with the customer, every phone conversation, every meeting, every question you ask and how you ask it, and every single aspect of your proposal all contribute to a winning or losing effort. Nothing is unimportant. The one thing you neglect or overlook may well be the one thing that determines whether you win or lose.

Winning and losing in the competitive arena of government contracts is determined by how well you play the proposal game. You will win if you do a better job of preparing your proposal and responding to the government's need than the rest of the competition. Your proposal does not have to be great. It just has to be better than the other proposals that are submitted. "Better" is a judgment the government makes based on your proposal, the quality of your relevant past performance, and how well you have positioned yourself with your customer. You may have a superior technical approach compared to your competition, but it will not matter if you fail to convince the government evaluators.

Never forget: It is not the most qualified team, the most technically qualified company, or the lowest cost that wins. It is the proposal that persuades the government that you are the "best" choice for the contract. I have managed proposals and won major contracts against companies that were far more qualified. I also have watched companies who possessed tremendous technical capability, and a superior technical approach, lose to far less capable competitors.

SOLVING THE PROBLEM

Given the difficulty and importance of preparing proposals, we must ask ourselves, "Is there any way to make this easier?" Are there some steps you can take to reduce the pain? The short answer to these questions is a resounding "yes." Much of the information contained in this book focuses on developing an effective, efficient proposal process. There is no magic cure to proposal drudgery. You will not find the "six steps to proposal bliss" contained in the chapters that follow. Nor will I promise to make proposals fun or easy. They can be fun, especially when you win, but they are never easy. Instead, this book includes some tips and guidelines, as well as detailed instructions, on how to master the proposal process. It will equip you with the information you need to:

1. Avoid common proposal mistakes
2. Overcome problems that plague proposal teams and create trauma
3. Create proposals that satisfy the ten characteristics of winning proposals.

GAINING THE COMPETITIVE ADVANTAGE

At its core, this is a book about preparing for and capturing new business. Yet it is far more than that. The book's entire focus is on gaining competitive advantage. It is not based on a magic formula. Nor does it rely on a few key activities that lead to success. Instead, it covers every aspect of the competitive process and provides instructions on how to gain the competitive advantage at every twist and turn along the way.

Every event, every action, and every decision during the proposal lifecycle affords an opportunity to gain or yield the competitive advantage. The information that follows will equip you with the knowledge you need to gain the competitive advantage, consistently win government contracts, and make good use of company bid and proposal resources.

Let the games begin!

Chapter 2

Anatomy of a Government RFP

My first encounter with a government request for proposal (RFP) occurred in 1978. Having just left the faculty of Arizona State University, I was familiar with sorting through reams of technical journal articles. Yet, I was totally unprepared for the trauma and confusion of finding my way through what appeared to be a disorganized collection of regulations, requirements, and instructions. Worse still, I had an important proposal assignment. Frankly, I did not have a clue of where to start or what to do. No one bothered to explain the organization, content, or importance of the various RFP sections. Instead I learned by trial and error (mostly error).

Since then, I have read hundreds of RFPs. I wish I could say the process has become simple and straightforward. It has not. Regardless of one's education, intelligence, experience, or technical competence, dissecting a government RFP is an arduous, painstaking undertaking. Nonetheless, the ability to navigate your way through an RFP effectively is a fundamental prerequisite to preparing a compliant, winning proposal. Having a roadmap and some basic understanding of the content of each RFP section can be a big help.

Fortunately, federal government RFPs follow a standard format. They consist of 13 separate sections, A–M, organized into four parts, as shown in Figure 2-1. Many RFPs also contain multiple attachments. Each attachment corresponds to one of the RFP sections. Most often, this will be Section C or J. Not all RFPs clearly label the four parts; do not let this confuse you.

A brief overview of each RFP part and section follows. If you are unfamiliar with RFP organization, grab an old RFP or one you are currently using, and follow along with this discussion. This will enable you to correlate the generic description of RFP sections to a real RFP, hopefully one with which you are familiar. However, a word of caution is necessary before we begin. Describing RFP organization is hideously boring. It will make you long for the opportunity to watch paint dry. Nonetheless, it is a required first step in understanding the government acquisition process.

Figure 2-1. Uniform Contract Format

SECTION	TITLE

PART I—THE SCHEDULE

A	Solicitation/contract form
B	Supplies or services and prices/costs
C	Description/specifications/statement of work
D	Packaging and marking
E	Inspection and acceptance
F	Deliveries or performance
G	Contract administration data
H	Special contract requirements

PART II—CONTRACT CLAUSES

I	Contract clauses

PART III—LIST OF DOCUMENTS, EXHIBITS, AND OTHER ATTACHMENTS

J	List of attachments

PART IV—REPRESENTATIONS AND INSTRUCTIONS

K	Representations, certifications, and other statements of offerors or respondents
L	Instructions, conditions, and notices to offerors or respondents
M	Evaluation factors for award

PART I—THE SCHEDULE

Sections A–H make up the schedule part of a government RFP.

Section A: Solicitation/Contract Form

Section A is the cover sheet for the RFP. It contains basic administrative information like the name and address of the procuring agency, a brief description of the procurement, when and where proposals are to be delivered, the solicitation number, and whether or not the RFP is for full and open competition. Some procurements are restricted to, or "set aside" for, specific business categories, like small or disadvantaged businesses. Restricted RFPs are so noted in Section A, along with the type of restriction. For example, small business set-asides will include a size standard based on revenue or number of employees. Most procuring agencies use Standard Form 33 as the RFP cover sheet. Regardless, Section A will contain the basic administrative information that governs the solicitation.

Section B: Supplies or Services and Prices/Costs

Section B identifies what the government intends to buy. It typically includes a brief description of the product or services required (e.g., item number, national stock number/part number, nouns, nomenclature) and the quantity to be purchased. Section B defines the products or services to be delivered to the government. Technical data or information required as a contract deliverable will be listed in Section B. Deliverable data most often are defined by a Contract Data Requirements List (CDRL) included as part of the RFP package or prepared by the offeror. A sample CDRL is provided in Figure 2-2.

Figure 2-2. Sample CDRL

CONTRACT DATA REQUIREMENTS LIST					Form Approved CMB No. 0704-0188		
Public reporting burden for this collection of informaiton is estimated to average XX hours per response, including the time for reviewing instructions, searching existing data sources, gathering and maintaining the data needed, and completing and reviewing the collection of information. Send comments regarding this burden estimate or any other aspect of this collection of information, including suggestions for reducing this burden to Department of Defense, Washington Headquarters Services, Directorate Reduction Project (0704-0188), Washington, DC 20503. Please DO NOT RETURN your form to either of these addresses. Send completed form to the Government Issuing Contracting Officer for the Contract. PR No. listed in Block E.							

A. Contract Line Item No.		B. Exhibit			C. Category		

D. System/Item				E. Contract/PR NO.		F. Contractor	

1. Data Item No.		2. Title of Data Item:				3. Subtitle:	

4. Authority (Data Acquisition Document No.)					5. Contract Reference	6. Requiring Office	

7. DD 250 Req	9. Dist Statement Required	10. Frequency	12. Date of First Submission			14. Distribution	
8. APP Code		11. As of Date	13. Date of Subsequent Submission		a. Addressee	b. Copies	
						Draft	Final
							Reg · Repro
16. REMARKS							
					15. TOTAL		

G. PREPARED BY							

DD Form 1423-2, JUN 90   Previous editions are obsolete   Page ___ of ___ Pages

Section B services or products typically are divided into Contract Line Item Numbers (CLINs). If the procurement will be purchased in lots, or if it includes options or multiple delivery orders, then a separate set of CLINs will cover each separate delivery or option. Figure 2-3 provides a sample Section B.

Section B provides the basis for developing your bid cost. In most instances, bid prices are placed in the allotted spaces in Section B and submitted with your proposal. The sample in Figure 2-2 illustrates a cost-plus type contract, with spaces for pricing information. Because this sample is a cost-type procurement, additional information is required about proposed fee.

Section B is not always divided into CLINs. In cases where there is no specific contract deliverable, the government may instead describe the services to be provided. The following Section B example, taken from an Envi-

Figure 2-3. Sample Section B

CLIN	SUPPLIES/SERVICES	QTY	UNIT	UNIT PRICE	TOTAL AMOUNT*
0002	Technical Data and Information ACRN:	1	LO		
0003	Conferences ACRN:	1	LO		
0012	Trainer Systems Analysis and Definition ACRN:	1	LO		
	COST PLUS INCENTIVE FEE				
	Target Cost				$
	Target Fee (8%)				$
	Target Cost plus Target Fee				$
	Minimum Fee (3%)				$
	Maximum Fee (13%)				$
	Share Ratio (80/20)				
	*Total amount is target cost plus target fee for this CLIN				

ronmental Protection Agency RFP, illustrates the purchase of services to be provided as a level of effort.

B.1 LEVEL OF EFFORT—COST REIMBURSEMENT TERM CONTRACT (EPAAR 1552.211-73) (APR 1984) DEVIATION

(a) The Contractor shall perform all work and provide all required reports within the level of effort specified below. The Government will order 11,000 direct labor hours for the base period which represents the Government's best estimate of the level of effort required to fulfill these requirements.

Subsequent Section B paragraphs further defined the effort and the parameters under which the effort would be procured.

Section C: Description/Specifications/Statement of Work

Contract deliverables defined in Section B are further described in Section C. Statements of work and product specifications are most often provided as attachments to this section. More detailed product or service descriptions, or documents that further define product parameters, also are typically provided as attachments. Otherwise the product description is contained within the narrative of Section C.

The following example corresponds to CLINs 0001 and 0002 from the Section B sample of Figure 2-1:

Item 0001 - The contractor shall design, develop, integrate, test and deliver the Engineering and Manufacturing Development (EMD) XYZ System in accordance with the requirements of Attachment 2, "XYZ Performance Specification"; Attachment 3, "Acquisition Logistics Support Specification"; Attachment 6, "XZY Detailed Specification"; and Attachment 7, "Statement of Work."

Item 0002 – The contractor shall provide engineering data in accordance with Exhibit A.

Note the references to specifications and statement of work contained in the description of Item (CLIN) 0001. Exhibit A referenced under Item 0002 above refers to a list of CDRLs. In this particular case, the offeror was required to propose the recommended CDRLs. In other cases, the government will provide a list of required CDRLs with the RFP. Or, they will simply reference a required report or technical document and then describe it either within Section C or in an attachment.

Section C also can contain clauses or directions concerning the manner in which services will be provided or specify procedures or equipment to be used. Such instances are most prevalent for service type contracts.

Section D: Packaging And Marking

Section D defines any required packaging, packing, or marking requirements for products to be delivered to the government. Otherwise, this RFP section is left blank. Here is a sample Section D:

> *Item 0001 and Option Items 0101, 0102, 0201, 0202, 0205, 0301, and 0302*
> *– The supplies to be furnished hereunder shall be commercially packed in accordance with ASTM D 3951-95. The contractor shall mark all shipments using best commercial practices.*

Section E: Inspection and Acceptance

RFP Section E defines the inspection, acceptance, quality assurance, and reliability required of delivered products or services. Section E also identifies the person or office responsible for accepting the product or service for the government and the place of inspection/acceptance. For example:

> *Item 0001 – Inspection of the XYZ System will be made at the contractor's facility in accordance with the requirements of Attachment 2, "XYZ Performance Specification"; Attachment 3, "Acquisition Logistics Support Specification"; Attachment 6, "XYZ Detailed Specification"; and Attachment 7, "Statement of Work." Acceptance of the XYZ System will be made by (to be designated by PMA-263) via a DD Form 250.*

Specific inspection or test procedures are often defined in an acceptance test plan or comparable documents. Test plans typically are defined by a CDRL and submitted to the government for review and approval before the scheduled test or inspection. Inspection and acceptance of delivered data are defined in the CDRL or via a referenced government standard.

For service-type contracts, like providing engineering services, government acceptance of those services may be governed by specific criteria that define availability, responsiveness, reliability, or quality requirements. Such requirements are provided in Section E.

Contract payments normally are contingent upon meeting the inspection and acceptance criteria contained in Section E. Therefore, it is important to pay close attention to these requirements (assuming you care about being paid).

Section F: Deliveries or Performance

Section F specifies the time, place, and method of delivery for contract deliverables defined in Section B. Delivery times can either be calendar days or elapsed time from contract award. Sometimes, a period of performance is tied to a particular program milestone. The following Section F example illustrates both time after contract award and time following a program event:

> *Item 0001* – *The contractor shall provide the XYZ System to the Government for testing no later than 180 calendar days after contract award. The contractor shall provide integration and test support for this system through the 90th calendar day following the Physical Configuration Audit of the XYZ System.*
>
> *Item 0002* – *The contractor shall provide engineering data for Item 0001 beginning 90 calendar days after contract award and continuing through the 90th calendar day following the Physical Configuration Audit of the VTUAV System as reflected in Exhibit A.*
>
> For service-type contracts, Section F specifies the period of performance. For example: *The period of performance of this contract shall be from February 24, 2003 through February 23, 2004 inclusive of all required reports.*

It is important to understand what constitutes delivery. A Section F clause that specifies a contract deliverable that is operationally available means that all the events necessary to fulfill the "operationally available" criteria must be completed. Otherwise, the deliverable may be judged late according to the schedule requirements of Section F.

In planning, all necessary program events must be accounted for. For example, suppose the government procures a flight simulator with a ready-for-training delivery of 24 months after contract at a specified Air Force base. According to the performance requirements of the RFP, this means the simulator must first pass an in-plant acceptance test before it is shipped to site. Once assembled on site, it must undergo another on-site acceptance test. In addition, the Air Force must certify the simulator as "ready for training."

In scheduling the project activities and the resources needed to perform them, consideration must be given to the time and cost of testing, transportation to site, and fixing any test discrepancies. Such considerations may appear to be intuitive or trivial, but you might be surprised how often such "simple" considerations are overlooked. This can result in late deliveries and cost overruns.

Section G: Contract Administration Data

Section G contains any required contract administration information or instructions other than those on the solicitation form (Section A). This section also may contain required accounting or appropriations data. This includes the procedures required to submit invoices and get paid for work completed. Section G also typically identifies significant government representatives, like the administrative contracting officer or the government quality assurance representative.

Section H: Special Contract Requirements

Section H includes special contract requirements that are not contained in Section I (Contract Clauses). These clauses typically deal with specific aspects of the procurement. If the procurement includes options in Section B, then this section will address how and when those options will be exercised.

Section H can span a broad variety of topics. They may include anything from conflict of interest clauses, how contractor performance will be evaluated, application of state and local taxes, identification of key personnel labor categories, compensation of overtime, the requirement for associate contractor clauses, or how award fee will be calculated for award-fee type contracts.

Proposal teams and managers often skip over Section H, leaving the review of this section to their contracts manager. This can be a mistake. Sometimes Section H has a significant impact on the technical aspects of the program.

PART II—CONTRACT CLAUSES

The second part of a government RFP consists of a single section.

Section I: Contract Clauses

Section I contains contract clauses required by law or by regulations that govern the procurement. It also contains any additional clauses expected to be included in the resulting contract, if these clauses are not required in any other section of the uniform contract format. Except for contracting experts, the information in Section I will be less than inspiring.

Most often Section I is just a list of federal acquisition regulations applicable to the procurement. A typical list will look something like this:

NUMBER	DATE	TITLE
52.202-1	OCT 1995	DEFINITIONS
52.203-3	APR 1984	GRATUITIES
52.203-5	APR 1984	COVENANT AGAINST CONTINGENT FEES
52.203-7	JUL 1995	ANTI-KICKBACK PROCEDURES
52.203-10	JAN 1997	PRICE OR FEE ADJUSTMENT FOR ILLEGAL OR IMPROPER ACTIVITY
52.203-12	JUN 1997	LIMITATION ON PAYMENTS TO INFLUENCE CERTAIN FEDERAL TRANSACTIONS

52.209-6	JUL 1995	PROTECTING THE GOVERNMENT'S INTEREST WHEN SUBCONTRACTING WITH CONTRAC-TORS DEBARRED, SUSPENDED, OR PROPOSED FOR DEBARMENT
52.215-2	JUN 1999	AUDIT AND RECORDS—NEGOTIATION
52.215-8	OCT 1997	ORDER OF PRECEDENCE-UNIFORM CONTRACT FORMAT
52.215-11	OCT 1997	PRICE REDUCTION FOR DEFECTIVE COST OR PRICING DATA—MODIFICATIONS
52.215-13	OCT 1997	SUBCONTRACTOR COST OR PRICING DATA—MODIFICATIONS

In other cases, Section I will provide the full text of the regulations referenced.

PART III—LIST OF DOCUMENTS, EXHIBITS, AND OTHER ATTACHMENTS

Like Part II, the third part of a government RFP is a single section. It includes other exhibits and attachments not referenced by other RFP sections.

Section J: List of Attachments

Not all RFPs will have a Section J. If it is included as part of the RFP, it should contain a list of the RFP exhibits and attachments, along with the title, date, and number of pages for each. Here is a sample Section J taken from an Environmental Protection Agency RFP:

J.1 LIST OF ATTACHMENTS (EP 52.252-100) (APR 1984)

Number	Attachment Title
1.	STATEMENT OF WORK
2.	TECHNICAL EVALUATION FACTORS
3.	TECHNICAL PROPOSAL INSTRUCTIONS
4.	COST PROPOSAL INSTRUCTIONS
5.	PAST PERFORMANCE QUESTIONNAIRE
6.	CLIENT AUTHORIZATION LETTER
7.	INVOICE PREPARATION INSTRUCTIONS
8.	DEFINITION OF LABOR CATEGORIES
9.	MINIMUM STANDARDS FOR CONTRACTORS' CONFLICT OF INTEREST PLANS

PART IV—REPRESENTATIONS AND INSTRUCTIONS

Part IV consists of three RFP sections: K, L, and M. Sections L and M are the heart of the RFP. They provide instructions on how to prepare your proposal and the criteria that will be used to evaluate proposals.

Section K: Representations, Certifications, and Other Statements of Offerors

Section K contains the representations and certifications required from bidders. These request information about your company and require you to certify that you comply with specific RFP and government requirements. These requirements include things like the company's taxpayer identification number, its classification as a small, woman-owned, or other special status business, and certifications that you comply with affirmative action practices. Typically your contracts manager will fill out this section of the RFP, which is returned as part of your proposal response.

Section L: Instructions, Conditions, and Notices to Offerors or Respondents

Section L of the RFP includes provisions and information not included in other RFP sections. More importantly, Section L tells you what information to include in your proposal, how to organize and prepare it, and how it should be delivered to the government. This may include proposal format instructions (e.g., font size, page margins) and how the proposal should be packaged (e.g., in three-ring binders). It also specifies the division of your proposal into separate volumes (e.g., technical, cost, past performance), identifies the number of copies of each volume to be delivered, and defines the delivery format in terms of hard copy or electronic media.

Many procurement agencies are moving to electronic evaluation systems and often require an electronic version of the proposal in addition to hard copies. Typically this is via floppy disc, CD-ROM, or Zip disc. Section L typically provides any special instructions about where and how to deliver your proposal.

As part of acquisition streamlining initiatives, many procuring agencies apply page limitations either to the entire proposal or to various sections. Failure to adhere to these restrictions can cause pages beyond the limitation to be returned unread. Moreover, when you exceed page limitations, you have demonstrated that you cannot follow simple instructions. In other cases, the procuring agency provides a recommended page limit. Although there is no formal consequence of exceeding these limitations, it is a good idea to stay within the recommended boundaries. Figure 2-4 shows

Figure 2-4. Sample Section L, Listing of Proposal Volumes

Volume	Title	Number of Copies	Max Pages
	Executive Summary	Original plus 1 copy	5
	Proposal Cross-reference Matrix	Original plus 1 copy	N/A
I	Technical Proposal	Original plus 1 copy	385
	Part A: Training Strategy		
	Part B: Design Approach		
	Part C: Specifications		
	Part D: Supportability		
II	Management Proposal	Original plus 1 copy	135
	Part A: Integrated Master Plan		
	Part B: Integrated Master Schedule		
	Part C: Statement of Work		
	Part D: Work Breakdown Structure	Original plus 1 copy	N/A
	Part E: Data Submissions	Original plus 1 copy	N/A
	Part F: Administrative		
	(Representations, Certifications, and Small Business Plans)	Original plus 1 copy	N/A
III	Past Performance	Original plus 1 copy	70
IV	Cost	Original plus 1 copy	N/A
	Part A: Cost Data		
	Part B: Labor and Material Estimates		

a sample Section L requirement for a multi-volume proposal with a page-count limitation.

Section L tells you what information to include in your proposal. This is the information the government will evaluate to determine who wins. Clearly, understanding the requirements of Section L is critical to preparing a winning proposal. The organization of Section L varies significantly between RFPs. Typically, this section provides specific instructions about how to prepare each proposal volume or section. These "instructions" include specific questions or topics that must be addressed, or information that must be provided as part of your proposal.

Careful attention to the requirements of Section L is absolutely essential to preparing a responsive proposal. As other parts of this book emphasize, the single greatest earmark of a losing proposal is failure to respond adequately to all RFP requirements. Section L defines these requirements. Unfortunately, understanding exactly what the government wants can be an overwhelming challenge. Often it seems like the government is asking for an incredible amount of information. Consider the following sample Section L requirement for software:

> *Describe the software development methodology, software quality assurance and software configuration management processes and procedures. Describe the content and format of software development folders, types and format of internally generated software documentation, software metrics and their use in software process improvement, the types and frequency of software quality auditing functions performed, system software requirements traceability, and software architecture in an object oriented design.*
>
> *Each offeror, as a separate and identifiable part of its technical proposal, shall submit a Quality Assurance (QA) program plan setting forth the offeror's capability for quality assurance.*
>
> *The offeror shall provide examples where they managed programs of similar size and complexity to the XYZ System. The offeror shall present their experience in utilizing Integrated Program Teams (IPTs) for system design, including system integration and system computer resources.*
>
> *Provide a description of the management and administrative organization available or to be established for the supervision, and assurance of expeditious and economical performance of the services required under the proposed contract, including a sample work structure chart by job classification and code.*

The number of volumes and amount of information requested varies enormously between RFPs and procurement agencies. Generally, development-type contracts require more information than service-type contracts. Specific proposal requirements also vary significantly between procuring agencies. However, at a minimum you will be required to provide information about your technical approach, cost, and your organization's past performance. In addition, some RFPs request an executive summary, plus proposal volumes as determined by the procuring agency. In many Department of Defense (DoD) RFPs, offerors are required to prepare and submit their own statement of work and CDRLs. For procurements that require the implementation of integrated product/process development procedures, an integrated master plan and/or integrated master schedule may also be required.

Section M: Evaluation Factors for Award

Section M describes how proposals will be evaluated. It identifies the areas or factors that will be considered in determining the "value" of each proposal and the relative importance of each area. In particular, the government must define the relative importance of cost to the other proposal areas. In fact, the government is required to state whether all evaluation factors other than cost or price are:

- Significantly more important than cost or price
- Approximately equal to cost or price
- Significantly less important than cost or price.

Normally, the procuring agency also will identify the particular regulations that will be used to conduct source selection. Such regulations include the Federal Acquisition Regulation (FAR), plus any supplemental regulations that implement the procuring agency's procedures. For example:

> *(a) The Government will perform source selection in accordance with FAR Part 15 and the EPA Source Evaluation and Selection Procedures in EPAAR Part 1515 (48 CFR Part 1515).*

Section M also will provide information about the relative importance of the various factors that will be used to evaluate your proposal. For example:

> *Proposals will be evaluated using the four factors, which are listed below. Technical is equal in importance to Past Performance and each is more important than the Cost/Price factor which is significantly more important than the Small Business and Small Disadvantaged Business Subcontracting Plan factor.*
> *A. Technical*
> *B. Past Performance*
> *C. Cost/Price*
> *D. Small Business and Small Disadvantaged Business Subcontracting Plan*

Typically, technical evaluation factors are further divided into subfactors, and the relative importance of each subfactor is provided. One approach is to list the subfactors in descending order of importance and provide a brief description of the important characteristics of each. Another approach is as follows:

> *The offeror's total proposal shall consist of four volumes as follows:*
> *Volume I - Technical*
> *Volume II - Management*
> *Volume III - Past Performance*
> *Volume IV - Cost*

The Government will evaluate each proposal in accordance with the Areas and Factors listed herein. The relative importance of the Areas is as follows:
A. Technical Area is more important than Management Area
B. Management Area is more important than either Past Performance Area or Cost Area
C. Past Performance Area and Cost Area are approximately equal.

Some procuring agencies use a point system to evaluate proposals. In these cases, the points allocated to each proposal requirement may be contained in Section M.

Criterion		*Weight*
I.	*Demonstrated Corporate Experience*	*200 Points*
II.	*Demonstrated Qualifications of Personnel*	*250 Points*
III.	*Quality of Program Management Plan*	*200 Points*
IV.	*Adequacy of QA/QC Program Plan*	*100 Points*
V.	*Past Performance*	*250 points*

Section M also should identify how cost and past performance will be evaluated. Typically, technical proposals are scored using either a point system or a rating scale. (Chapter 3 describes government source selection.) Cost and past performance information is not scored, but is evaluated using criteria listed in Section M. Cost is typically evaluated for reasonableness, realism, and completeness. In some cases, the government may perform a cost analysis to determine what they believe the most probable cost will be for each bidder based on its particular technical approach. Past performance information can be scored, but it is most often judged to determine the risk of selecting your company to perform the contract. In these cases, you will receive a risk rating—high, medium, or low—for each significant evaluation area or factor.

A clear understanding of the evaluation criteria of Section M is critical to preparing a winning proposal. The relative importance of evaluation areas can be used to help determine what aspects of your approach to emphasize and as a guide in determining page allocations for page-limited proposals. Section M evaluation criteria also can be used to clarify what is being asked for in Section L.

Become familiar with RFP sections and their respective content. Use this knowledge to maximize the effectiveness of time you spend extracting valuable information from government RFPs. In the process, you will gain a modest competitive advantage over your less astute competitors.

Chapter 3

Federal Government Source Selection

There are only two ways to acquire new business from the federal government: through a sole source award or through competition. Sole source awards are relatively rare. They occur only when time constraints or limited sources are available to the government. Sole source awards also are contrary to the government's desire to acquire the best deal possible. Therefore, the vast majority of government business is acquired through competition.

New business is competitively awarded based on either a sealed bidding process or through negotiated procurement. Sealed bids are used when the product or services to be procured are very well defined. This process allows the government to shop for the best price. The government solicits bids from qualified suppliers via an Invitation for Bid (IFB) or a Request for Quote (RFQ), and then awards a contract to the lowest qualified bidder.

Sometimes the government uses a two-step sealed bidding process. Offerors first provide the government with a technical proposal to verify that they are qualified to perform the contract. All qualified bidders then submit their prices, and the award goes to the lowest bidder. IFBs and RFQs follow the same uniform contract format as RFPs (described in Chapter 2). However, the specific RFP sections vary depending upon the nature of the procurement.

Source selection for a sealed bid acquisition is fairly simple: The low bid wins. If a two-step procedure is used, the government first evaluates the technical proposal using a binary—go/no go—scoring system, and then awards to the lowest qualified bidder.

Source selection procedures get far more complicated for competitive, negotiated acquisitions. Under this process, the government solicits proposals via an RFP and then evaluates those proposals to select the winner. Understanding the process the government uses to evaluate your proposal and arrive at a selection decision is critical to winning new business.

I do not know anyone who would enter a high-stakes poker game without first knowing the rules. Likewise, I cannot imagine a professional golfer competing in a tournament without first reviewing the course. Yet every day companies spend hundreds of thousands of dollars competing for government business without understanding the rules of the game. Sometimes they get lucky, just like gamblers. Or, they have a great game and win the tournament without any knowledge of the course. However, over the long haul, this lack of knowledge proves to be very expensive, and it yields competitive advantage to someone else.

If you want to win new business from the government consistently, you must understand how your proposal will be evaluated and how the government selects winners. Otherwise, you must rely upon luck or having a better day than the rest of the players.

THE FEDERAL ACQUISITION REGULATION

The Federal Acquisition Regulation (FAR) is the primary source of procurement regulations used by all federal agencies to acquire products and services. The FAR system became effective on April 1, 1984. It replaced the Federal Procurement Regulation (FPR) used by civilian agencies of the federal government, the Defense Acquisition Regulation (DAR) used by the Department of Defense (DoD), and the National Aeronautics and Space Administration Procurement Regulation (NASAPR) used by the National Aeronautics and Space Administration (NASA).

The FAR contains all of the provisions and clauses used in government contracting, including those that govern source selection. For example, negotiated acquisitions are governed by FAR Part 15; sealed bids by FAR Part 14. Some major procuring agencies (e.g., DoD, NASA, Department of Energy) implement the FAR with their own regulations or supplements. For example, DoD procurements are regulated by Defense FARs. Air Force procurements are then regulated according to Air Force Regulation (AFR) 70-15 for major procurements and AFR 70-30 for non-major acquisitions. Separate Air Force commands can further supplement these regulations.

Depending upon the particular procuring agency, up to four levels of regulations and supplements can be involved. However, there are two important points to keep in mind. First, the basic FAR cannot be violated because it governs all federal procurements. Second, you must be familiar with the specific source selection policy and process used by the agency to which you are bidding. The good news is that all agencies use a common source selection process. They vary only in the specific details used to implement this process.

Over the last decade, there has been a concerted effort to exploit the capability of the Internet and to streamline the overall acquisition process. Beginning in January 2002, the government established the federal business opportunities website (www.fedbizopps.gov) as the single source for federal procurement opportunities over $25,000. Many procuring agencies also maintain their own acquisition websites, and some agencies now allow bidders to deliver their proposals via e-mail.

The Federal Acquisition Streamlining Act (FASA) of 1994 repealed or substantially modified more than 225 provisions of law to reduce paperwork burdens and promote electronic commerce, especially for procurements under $100,000. FASA, which went into effect in 1995, streamlined the acquisition process for small threshold purchases and set in motion initiatives across procuring agencies to reduce the burden of procuring goods and services.

In addition to FASA, further modifications to government procurement occurred with the enactment of the Federal Acquisition Reform Act (FARA) of 1996. FARA implemented government-wide procurement reforms to promote greater efficiency and procurement uniformity among government agencies. Perhaps the most significant of these gave federal officials more latitude to award contracts based upon a contractor's performance or expertise rather than price.

Ongoing acquisition reform and streamlining initiatives seek to reduce the time and money spent in acquiring goods and services by relying on the competitive marketplace. Current trends include an added focus on past performance and performance-based service contracting. In addition, many agencies are adopting the concept of indefinite delivery/indefinite quantity (ID/IQ) contracts. Under this scheme, bidders compete for an "umbrella" or omnibus type contract. Winners of an ID/IQ contract either receive subsequent task orders sole source or compete among themselves for task orders. If you do not win an ID/IQ contract, you are not permitted to compete.

I cannot predict what trends will be prevalent at the time you read this book. I can, however, state unequivocally that acquisition policy in the federal government is dynamic. Therefore, it is important to keep up with the latest changes. These changes can dramatically impact how you approach the acquisition of new business and your ultimate success in such endeavors.

THE SOURCE SELECTION PROCESS

Competitive negotiation is formally called "source selection." Regulated by the FAR, this process involves the following steps:

1. The RFP is prepared and publicized by the government on the federal business opportunities website. Once approved, a final RFP is released to industry.
2. Bidders submit technical and cost proposals to the procuring organization and make an oral presentation, if required.

3. Proposals are analyzed and evaluated by government evaluators against stated criteria and unstated standards. An award can be made at this stage without discussions, based upon the decision of the contracting officer.
4. Potentially successful proposals are identified and included in the "competitive range" (shortlist) based upon price and other factors. Bidders outside the competitive range are eliminated from further competition (and are notified in writing).
5. Unless an award is made without discussions, oral or written discussions are conducted with those offerors in the competitive range to clarify their bid and to eliminate proposal deficiencies.
6. Those offerors are given an opportunity to submit a best and final offer (BAFO).
7. BAFOs are evaluated. A contract award is made to the bidder whose proposal is judged to be most advantageous to the government based on the stated evaluation criteria.
8. Unsuccessful bidders are notified promptly in writing, and debriefings are held with offerors who request them.

The source selection process has traditionally been dominated by weapons procurement. Hence, formal source selection procedures of the U.S. Air Force frequently serve as a model for other federal agencies as well as international governments. The following discussion is based on this model. Some terminology differences exist between agencies and in the specific application of evaluation procedures. This is especially true for NASA and Department of Energy procurements. Nonetheless, the overall process is common across agencies.

Source Selection Organization

Source selection is performed by a formal source selection organization. The size and specific composition of this organization vary depending upon the size, importance, and complexity of the procurement. Evaluation areas are defined in RFP Section M, and the division of those areas provides a likely view of the source selection organization.

Figure 3-1 shows a representative source selection organization for a major procurement. The ultimate source selection decision is made by the source selection authority (SSA). The SSA is supported by a source selection advisory council (SSAC) and a source selection evaluation board (SSEB). Led by a chairperson, the SSEB is divided into major areas that correspond to the criteria that will be used to evaluate proposals. At a minimum, the SSEB will include separate teams to evaluate technical and cost/contract criteria. Typically, the technical evaluation team will be further subdivided into teams that correspond to evaluation factors and subfactors. The example shown in Figure 3-1 is divided into three technical areas: logistics, technical, and management.

The source selection organization for a non-major procurement or streamlined acquisition is the same as shown in Figure 3-1, except that the advisory council and the evaluation board are collapsed into a single organization, often called a source selection evaluation team (see Figure 3-2). This evaluation team performs the roles of both. Otherwise, the basic roles and responsibilities of source selection members remain the same. Individual evaluation panels or teams are still responsible for evaluating individual proposals. For non-major acquisitions, the procuring contracting officer (PCO) may serve as the source selection authority.

Each portion of the source selection organization has well-defined roles and responsibilities, as described below.

Source Selection Authority

The SSA is responsible for the acquisition. He or she makes the final selection decision and ensures that the selection process is conducted properly. Additional SSA responsibilities include:

Figure 3-1. Representative Source Selection Organization for a Major Acquisition

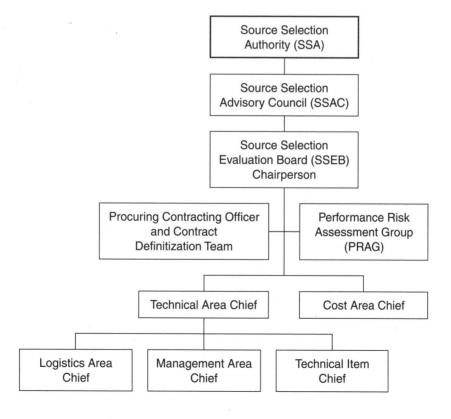

Figure 3-2. Representative Source Selection Organization for a Non-Major Acquisition

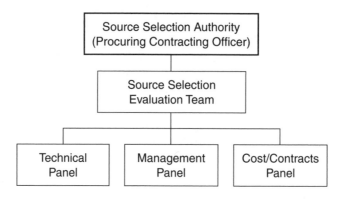

- Approves the acquisition plan or source selection plan used to guide source selection
- Appoints the chairperson and members of the advisory council
- Approves competitive range determinations and elimination of offerors from the competitive range
- Authorizes release of the RFP and approves execution of the contract.

Source Selection Advisory Council

The advisory council consists of senior government personnel who advise the SSA on how to conduct the source selection. They also perform a comparative analysis of the results of the evaluation performed by the SSEB. They report their results to the SSA and may make a selection recommendation.

Additional roles of the SSAC include:

- Develop the evaluation criteria contained in Section M and assign relative weights to these criteria
- Appoint the chairperson and members of the SSEB
- Review and weight the findings of the SSEB
- Approve the RFP.

Procuring or Principal Contracting Officer

The procuring or principal contracting officer (PCO) oversees source selection to ensure that the process complies with applicable acquisition regulations. He or she serves as a staff advisor to the SSA, SSAC, and SSEB and may chair the SSAC. The PCO also is responsible for contract terms and conditions, conducts negotiations with offerors, and serves as a single point of contact for bidders once the RFP is released. In addition, the PCO:

- Ensures that the evaluation criteria in the source selection plan are properly reflected in the RFP
- Makes competitive range recommendations
- Decides whether or not to conduct discussions and how they should be conducted
- Leads the contract team, which conducts discussions with bidders.

Source Selection Evaluation Board

Led by a chairperson, the SSEB is responsible for evaluating proposals. Separate teams evaluate technical, cost/contract, and past performance areas. Evaluators evaluate each proposal against objective standards and do not compare proposals against one another. Typically a team leader responsible for overseeing a particular portion of the evaluation leads each evaluation team. The evaluation board prepares an evaluation report for each bidder, which is provided to the advisory council. The SSEB chairperson oversees day-to-day evaluation processes and coordinates the evaluation between the SSEB and the SSAC, as well as between separate evaluation teams.

Overview of Source Selection Process

The source selection process actually begins at the time the government determines it has a need. This need is eventually translated into a RFP document. Different aspects of the need are described in the various RFP sections (as described in Chapter 2). As the RFP is being developed, the government also begins building an acquisition or source selection plan. This plan defines how the source selection will be conducted. As the RFP is being developed, the procuring agency may release draft portions for industry review and comment. The agency also may host a bidders' conference to provide an overview of the procurement and to answer questions.

Once the final RFP is approved, it is released to industry. Interested bidders prepare a proposal in response to the RFP and submit it to the government at the prescribed time and place. After proposals are received, they are checked to see if they meet submittal requirements. For page-limited proposals, the government counts the pages. If the proposal exceeds the limit, pages over the limit are removed from the back of the proposal and returned to the bidder. Proposals are logged in and locked in a secure place for safekeeping. Typically, source selection is conducted in a secure location. Proposals must be checked in and out and are treated as confidential documents. No one outside the source selection team is allowed access to the proposals

The evaluation team is instructed on how source selection will be conducted. This includes security, schedules, work hours, rules of conduct, evaluation procedures, proposal scoring systems, evaluation criteria, and how to document source selection results. The proposal is divided among the various evaluation teams. For example, the technical team sees only the technical proposal. They do no get to see cost data or past performance information.

The teams then begin evaluating proposals. Only one proposal is evaluated at a time. Again, this is intended to preclude comparing proposals from different bidders. The order of evaluation is determined randomly. At least two people typically evaluate each factor, although the number may be much larger. On large proposals, and depending on the availability of evaluators, factor teams evaluate only that section of the proposal that deals with the factor they are evaluating. On smaller proposals, they may evaluate larger sections of the proposal or the entire technical proposal for their area.

Proposals are evaluated at the lowest level of evaluation criteria. Typically this is at the factor or subfactor level. Section M contains the evaluation criteria and lists those areas, factors, and subfactors that make up the evaluation. The evaluation process is different for the technical, cost, and past performance portions of the proposal.

TECHNICAL EVALUATION

Evaluators read their assigned proposal sections to determine what is being offered. Then they compare this with the corresponding evaluation standards. Evaluators do not compare your proposal with the proposals submitted by other bidders. Instead, they compare it with the evaluation standards and assign it a score or rating. This rating is based on how well the proposal meets the criteria contained in the standards.

Evaluation standards typically are developed by the advisory council and approved before the RFP is released. These standards serve several purposes. First, they provide an objective and uniform basis for evaluating all proposals. That is, each proposal is scored against a set of objective standards rather than compared to other proposals. Therefore, every proposal is evaluated against the same criteria. Second, standards provide the basis for evaluating proposal responses. That is, evaluators compare your proposal response to the evaluation standard and assign it a rating or score based on the type of scoring system being used.

Standards establish the minimum level of compliance, with respect to a defined requirement, that must be offered for a proposal to be considered acceptable. They can be qualitative or quantitative.

Quantitative standards often are numerical values that reflect a minimum requirement. For example:

AREA: *Technical*
FACTOR: *Computer Capability*
SUBFACTOR: *Modem Speed*
Description: *This factor is defined as the data transmission speed required to operate in an efficient manner.*
Standard: *The standard is met when the modem operates at a speed of 56K baud in accordance with Statement of Work paragraph 1.2.3.4.*

Qualitative standards are more subjective. They require the evaluator to determine by degree the extent to which the standard is met. For example:

AREA: *Management*
FACTOR: *Program Management Plan*
Description: *The proposed Program Management Plan will be evaluated for its adequacy to correlate and organize contractor resources and any subcontractor efforts to fulfill the requirements of the Statement of Work and ensure timely, high-quality, cost-effective performance of work activities.*
Standard: *The standard is met when the proposal:*
a. Defines a system to track and monitor individual Work Assignment and overall contract costs and level of effort to ensure performance within budgetary constraints and scheduled deadlines.
b. Has a demonstrated plan for managing work assignments, including the strategy for managing work assignments with quick turn-around "rapid response" deadlines and expected responsibilities of all prime contractor and any subcontractor personnel.
c. Describes an overall organizational structure which clearly delineates the responsibilities, lines of authority, and proposed staff levels, including the proposed Project Manager and span of control mechanisms.

Standards are developed to the lowest level of each evaluation factor and subfactor contained in Section M. Unfortunately, standards usually are confidential. So neither you nor your competitors will know what they are. However, a careful review of Section M provides a good deal of insight concerning probable standards.

Winning proposals respond effectively to evaluation criteria and the underlying evaluation standards.

Scoring Systems

As previously stated, evaluators read your proposal and determine the extent to which it meets, exceeds, or fails to meet the standard. Procuring agencies use a variety of scoring systems to evaluate technical proposals. The Air Force uses a scoring system based on color codes. Some DoD agencies use a rating system, and yet other federal agencies use a point scoring system. Despite these variations, all accomplish the same objective: to determine the extent to which the standard is met.

Figure 3-3 illustrates the Air Force color scoring system. It uses four colors—blue, green, yellow, and red—to denote cases where requirements are exceeded, met, not met but correctable, and unacceptable, respectively.

Other color rating systems add a fifth category to distinguish between proposals that merely exceed requirements and those that significantly exceed requirements. Point scoring systems provide yet a finer distinction between how well requirements are met. The relationship between different systems is shown in Figure 3-4.

There are pros and cons for each system. Generally, the finer-grain scoring systems result in more variability between individual evaluators. In some cases, evaluators use a simple "plus, check, and minus" system to denote proposals that exceed, meet, or do not met requirements. They use this system to evaluate proposals at the lowest level. Then they sum the ratings at the subfactor level and translate the results into a factor score using a more fine-grain system.

Regardless of the system being used, evaluators score your proposal at the lowest level of evaluation criteria. Scores for subfactors are combined to determine a factor score. Factor scores are then combined to determine an area score.

Figure 3-3. Air Force Evaluation Scoring System

COLOR	RATING	DEFINITION
Blue	Exceptional	Exceeds specified performance or capability in a beneficial way to the Air Force and has a high probability of satisfying the requirement; no significant weaknesses.
Green	Acceptable	Meets evaluation standards and has good probability of satisfying the requirement; any weaknesses can be readily corrected.
Yellow	Marginal	Fails to meet minimum evaluation standards; has a low probability of satisfying the requirement; has significant but correctable deficiencies.
Red	Unacceptable	Fails to meet a minimum requirement; deficiency requires major revision to the proposal to make it correct.

Figure 3-4. Different Scoring Systems and Their Relationships

Color System	Rating System	Point System
Blue — Exceptional	Outstanding	10
		9
	Highly Satisfactory	8
		7
Green — Acceptable	Satisfactory	6
		5
		4
Yellow — Marginal	Marginal	3
		2
		1
Red — Unacceptable	Unsatisfactory	0

Technical evaluators also identify proposal strengths and weaknesses. Strengths are proposed products, services, or approaches that exceed the evaluation standard. Weaknesses are areas where what is offered fails to meet the evaluation standard.

Risk

There are two types of risk. One is based on your proposed approach—proposal risk—and one is based on your past performance. Technical evaluators assess proposal risk if it is included in the RFP as an evaluation consideration (not all agencies assess proposal risk). Performance risk is evaluated separately by a different group of evaluators.

Proposal risk is the uncertainty associated with a bidder's proposal. Government technical evaluators charged with scoring your technical proposal also assess the amount of risk associated with your proposed approach. Normally this is accomplished by assigning a proposal risk rating of high, moderate, or low. The following are standard definitions used to evaluate proposal risk:

- **High**: Likely to cause significant serious disruption of schedule, increase in cost, or degradation of performance even with special contractor emphasis.

- **Moderate**: Can potentially cause some disruption of schedule, increase in cost, or degradation of performance. However, special contractor emphasis will probably be able to overcome difficulties.
- **Low**: Has little or no potential to cause disruption of schedule, increase in cost, or degradation of performance. Normal contractor effort will probably be able to overcome difficulties.

Summary of Technical Evaluation

Evaluators read your proposal and compare it to the evaluation standards. They assign a score to each subfactor and identify any associated strengths or weaknesses. They also judge the risk associated with your proposal and assign it a risk rating of high (H), moderate (M), or low (L). Evaluation results for subfactors are combined to determine a composite evaluation for each factor.

It is important to note that a poor score for a single subfactor can overweigh a good score for the other subfactors. In fact, an unacceptable rating at any level can result in the entire factor being judged as unacceptable. The key point here is: There are no unimportant or trivial proposal sections. Everything counts. Sometime the "little things" can kill you. I can recount many instances where bidders shot themselves in the foot by overlooking or underemphasizing a proposal section they viewed as trivial or unimportant. Imagine proposing the best engineering solution and losing the competition because your safety write-up missed the mark. It happens every day.

Bidders repeatedly lose programs because their competitors submitted a better proposal. More often than not, the difference between winning and losing is small. The advice I always give is to treat every part of the proposal as if it were the single factor that determines whether or not you win the competition. There is a natural tendency to emphasize the most heavily weighted evaluation factors. Indeed, that is important. Yet if you neglect the less highly weighted factors, then you stand a very good chance of losing, especially if your competitors know better.

Figure 3-5 illustrates a case where a poor rating on a single subfactor pulled down the overall score for the factor being evaluated. In this case, an evaluation of "yellow" was assigned to one of four subfactors, while the other three subfactors received a "green" rating. When evaluators summed up the subfactors to arrive at a factor score, they assigned a "yellow" to the entire factor.

PAST PERFORMANCE EVALUATION

The government views a bidder's performance on past contracts as one indicator of its ability to successfully perform the work being solicited.

Figure 3-5. Illustration of Combining Subfactor Scores

Offeror: Company C

	Y
FACTOR: LOGISTICS SUPPORT T.3	L
Subfactors	
	Y
Proposed Approach and Resources to Maintain the System T.3.1	L
Ability of the Logistics Suport Plan to Support Logistics Function T.3.2	G
	L
	G
Capability of Inventory Control System T.3.3	L
	G
Qualifications and Skill Mix of Logistics Personnel T.3.4	L

B = Blue G = Green Y = Yellow H = High M = Moderate L = Low

With few exceptions, an evaluation of past performance is required for negotiated, competitive procurements. In fact, past performance continues to grow in importance as a source selection criterion. It is not uncommon to see past performance account for one-fourth or one-third of the entire evaluation criteria.

The government's contract team evaluates past performance. Some agencies used a special group, referred to as a performance risk assessment group (PRAG), to perform this evaluation (see Figure 3-1). The specific method used to evaluate your past performance must be included in the RFP, typically in Section M.

The assessment of performance risk is based on information about your performance on other current and recent relevant contracts. A variety of methods is used to collect this information. In most cases, the government requests information about past contracts. Sometimes a questionnaire is included in the RFP. Bidders are required to send the questionnaire to their past or current customers, who complete the questionnaire or interview and return it to the procuring agency. In addition, members of the contract team may contact the program manager or contracting officer from your past contracts, as well as the government agency that audited your cost proposal.

Many RFPs require bidders to submit a separate past performance proposal volume. Here they list those recent programs that are most relevant to the work they are bidding on. Typically, this volume requires administrative information about past contracts and points of contact for people who administered and managed the contract. Sometimes, bidders are given the opportunity in the past performance volume to summarize these efforts and show how they are relevant to the proposed effort.

Government contracts personnel review and evaluate your past and current contract performance and read your past performance volume. Past performance typically is treated as a risk area and rated as high, moderate, or low. However, some agencies use a point system to evaluate past performance. The following is a typical performance risk rating system:

- **High (H)**—Based on the offeror's past performance and systemic improvement record, substantial doubt exists that the offeror will successfully perform the required effort.
- **Moderate (M)**—Based on the offeror's past performance and systemic improvement record, some doubt exists that the offeror will successfully perform the required effort.
- **Low (L)**—Based on the offeror's past performance and systemic improvement record, essentially no doubt exists that the offeror will successfully perform the required effort.

The outcome of the past performance assessment is combined with the results of the technical evaluation. For every technical evaluation criterion, each proposal receives a rating based on how well it meets the RFP requirement, a risk rating of the proposed approach, and a risk rating based on past performance. This is supplemented by a list of strengths and weaknesses and a brief narrative that summarizes the evaluation results.

You cannot change your past performance. Nonetheless, you can help yourself in this area. First, make absolutely sure that all the information contained in your past performance proposal (e.g., names, addresses, phone numbers, contract numbers) is correct. Double-check the accuracy of this information. If you mail out questionnaires, follow up to ensure that they were received. Check again to see if they were submitted to the government on time.

If you have the chance to provide a summary or narrative of past efforts, make sure that the relevance of the past effort is clearly explained. If you have had problems on past contracts, be honest. Identify the problem and explain what you did to fix it or recover from a bad situation. This is extremely important. The government does not expect bidders to be perfect. Problems are a normal occurrence in government programs. Whether or not you have had problems is not the main issue; it is how you dealt with them that counts the most.

There is no substitute for an unblemished record of on-schedule and below-cost performance. However, in the absence of a perfect history, do everything you can to achieve the best possible past performance rating. Actually, even if you have a perfect record, you should still do everything possible to maximize your past performance evaluation. If you are proposing key personnel who have performed on successful contracts in the past, make sure you highlight this information in your proposal. The past performance of key people also impacts your ability to successfully perform the proposed effort. This can be especially beneficial if the agency to which you are bidding knows the key person proposed, or if the past effort is a good match with the requirements of the proposed effort.

COST EVALUATION

Cost is not scored, but it is evaluated. It also can receive a risk rating based on your past cost performance and the risk associated with your proposed approach. The cost you bid is not necessarily the same as your evaluated cost. The government may adjust your proposed cost to arrive at what they call "most probable cost to the government."

If the government views your approach as risky, or if they do not accept as legitimate your basis of estimate, they may add cost to what you bid. Under these circumstances, you could bid the lowest cost but still lose on cost because of government adjustments. The RFP must specify how cost evaluations will be conducted. So, pay close attention to this information and use it to prepare your cost proposal. In addition, some RFPs require a complete cost volume. Follow the cost volume instructions provided in RFP Section L and take care to provide clear and convincing bases of estimates for all proposed costs (see Chapter 13).

The role of government cost evaluators is to determine if your bid price is fair and reasonable. Specific cost analysis techniques are defined in FAR 15.404, and they are normally delineated in the RFP.

Generally, the government reviews your proposed price to determine if it is realistic, reasonable, and complete. Cost realism means that the costs in your proposal are judged to be realistic for the work to be performed, reflect a clear understanding of the requirements, and are consistent with the various elements of your technical proposal. Here is the important point: The *only* information available to determine the cost realism of your bid is what you provide in your cost proposal. Do a poor job of presenting and explaining your proposed costs, and you risk having the government increase your bid price. Likewise, if the government detects an imbalance in your pricing. Unbalanced pricing exists when, despite an acceptable total evaluated price, the price of one or more contract line items is significantly over- or understated based on cost or price analysis techniques.

Cost realism is more important for cost-reimbursable type contracts, but it also may be applied to fixed-price contracts with incentive or award fees. Cost completeness refers to whether or not your cost proposal addresses all program requirements and elements.

If the government determines that your bid prices are unrealistic or materially imbalanced, you can be eliminated from the competition before you have a chance to correct the prices.

COMPETITIVE RANGE

If the government decides to award a contact without discussions, then there is no reason to determine a competitive range. Otherwise, based on the ratings of each proposal against all evaluation criteria, the contracting officer establishes a competitive range, which consists of the most highly rated proposals. If your proposal is judged to be outside the competitive range, you are eliminated from the competition at that point.

Elimination can be due to deficiencies that, in the judgment of the government, would require a substantial change to correct your proposal. Or, the government may have more qualified proposals than they can reasonably and efficiently evaluate. So, they eliminate those at the bottom of the competitive range. In either case, the contracting officer will notify you if you are eliminated.

The remaining bidders are then permitted to clarify any ambiguous parts of their proposal and address any weaknesses, omissions, or deficiencies identified by the government. Typically, each bidder is provided a list of questions or issues to which they must respond in writing. Most often this takes the form of amended proposal sections, but it can include written responses to specific government questions. Once these "discussions" are complete, bidders are then allowed to adjust their proposed costs based on changes to their proposal. This is accomplished by a request for a best and final offer (BAFO). Once all the new proposal information is received, each proposal is evaluated a second time using the same evaluation criteria as before.

COMPARATIVE ANALYSIS OF PROPOSALS

Members of the SSEB do not select the winner. They evaluate proposals according to the evaluation criteria and standards but do not compare proposals. Evaluation results for cost, technical, and past performance are summarized by each of the evaluation teams and passed to the SSAC or its equivalent. Most procuring agencies combine the past performance and technical evaluation results to produce a composite score for each evaluation factor and area that includes proposal and performance risk ratings.

The advisory council also applies factor weightings to determine the actual weighted rating of technical factors. Most evaluation teams do not know the specific weights given to subfactors or factors except for procurements that use a point system. They may know that one subfactor is more important than another, but usually they do not know the actual weighting.

Figure 3-6 provides a sample display of technical evaluation results for three companies. The technical area consists of three evaluation factors of equal importance. The technical score is shown in the upper right-hand corner, performance risk in the lower left-hand corner, and proposal risk in the lower right-hand corner. The technical area score is a composite of the factor scores. Cost is the bid cost, with cost performance risk shown in the lower left-hand corner.

The evaluation of each proposal is summarized, along with associated strengths and weaknesses. The SSAC combines, weighs, and discusses the evaluation results of each proposal. Typically, the technical evaluation is completed first. Cost is then added and compared across bidders. Tradeoffs are made among technical merits, risk, cost, and strengths and weaknesses. As shown by the example in Figure 3-6, trying to determine a winner can be very difficult and involves some subjective judgment.

As shown in the example, Company C bid a low-risk technical approach and proposed the lowest price, but its logistics support approach is mar-

Figure 3-6. Sample Summary Evaluation Sheet

	Company A		Company B		Company C	
TECHNICAL		G		G		Y
	L	M	M	H	L	L
System Design T.1		B		G		G
	L	H	L	H	L	M
Management T.2		G		G		G
	M	L	M	M	L	L
Logistics Support T.3		Y		G		Y
	L	L	M	M	L	L
COST	12.2M		10.0M		9.8M	
	L		L		M	

B = Blue G = Green Y = Yellow H = High M = Moderate L = Low

ginal and its cost performance is only moderate. Company A proposed a superior system design, but its approach was evaluated as high-risk and it bid the highest price. Its past performance risk is generally low, as is its cost performance. Company B proposed an acceptable technical approach with an intermediate price, but its overall proposal risk was rated high. Strengths and weaknesses, not shown in the example, would be discussed by the source selection evaluation team, along with any contractual considerations, such as if one bidder asked for a deviation or waiver of required contract terms.

Sometimes just one poor evaluation score can cost you the award. The one marginal rating of Company C might keep it from winning. An acceptable rating in logistics would have made it a likely winner—an acceptable technical solution with low risk and the best price. Part of the tradeoff process is to determine if the superior system design proposed by Company A is worth the higher risk and price. This is where strengths and weaknesses noted by the evaluation team become critically important.

Once the advisory council completes its analysis, it presents its results to the source selection authority. The SSAC summarizes the pros and cons of each proposal and makes a source selection recommendation (if the source selection authority has previously requested one).

FINAL SOURCE SELECTION

The final decision is made by the SSA. The advisory council presents its analysis of the bids, including the tradeoffs among different evaluation criteria, and answers questions. For Air Force procurements, the SSAC prepares a proposal analysis report (PAR). Other agencies may use a different format, but they tend to include the same type of information.

The PAR contains source selection administrative data and a description of each proposal within the competitive range. The PAR also identifies strengths, weaknesses, and risks for all areas, factors, and subfactors except for cost. The outcome of the cost analysis and the reasonableness, realism, and completeness of each bidder's cost proposal is compared and explained. Proposal and performance risks are discussed, along with the confidence that risks can be accommodated. Any contractual considerations are discussed, and significant issues are identified. The PAR also summarizes any issues significant to the source selection decision.

The SSA weighs the evaluation results and makes the final source selection decision. The contract is awarded to the winner, and losers are notified. Debriefings are provided to bidders, and the source selection process is complete.

A lack of understanding about how the government selects winners and losers is remarkably prevalent among companies who compete for government business. The consequences of such ignorance are calamitous. Contracts are lost and bid and proposal resources wasted because proposal teams failed to understand how their proposals would be evaluated. Capture the competitive edge by becoming a savvy bidder. Become familiar with the source selection process your customer uses. Stay abreast of current trends in government acquisitions and streamlining initiatives. Visit your customer's contracts department. Ask contracting officers what you can do in your proposal to make their source selection job easier.

Know the rules of the game if you want to be a successful player. Exploit this largely untapped source of information to gain competitive advantage and win federal contracts.

Part 2
The Pre-Proposal Phase

Chapter 4
Strategic Business Planning

"If you do not know where you are going, any road will get you there." This paraphrase from Lewis Carroll's novel *Through the Looking Glass* applies equally well to organizations. If an organization does not know where it wants to go, any set of activities will get it there.

Actually, most organizations do have some idea where they want to go. They may want to grow annual sales and earnings, increase market share, or just win a key competition. Unfortunately, most companies fail to articulate their ideas clearly. Even worse, they fail to develop clear plans to achieve their objectives. Captured by the tyranny of daily business, serious planning for the future is overcome by more immediate issues. Like Alice, the character in the Carroll novel, they are destined to meander through an undefined maze of business activities, never quite knowing where they are or specifically where they are going.

In a business sense, knowing where you are going is referred to as strategic planning. This is a process of envisioning the future of your company and then building a plan to achieve that future. Strategic planning goes beyond just planning for the future. Done properly, it can help an organization *create* its future. Strategic planning differs from typical long-range planning. Practically every organization has a business plan. But planning to keep doing the same thing in the future, only better, is not strategic planning.

Strategic planning goes beyond mere long-range planning. Instead, it requires an organization to take a hard look at its products and services, the environment in which it competes, and the business ingredients necessary to succeed. Strategic planning is a process concerned with making decisions today that will affect the organization in the future. Essentially, strategic planning addresses three basic questions:

1. Where does the organization want to go?
2. What is the environment in which the organization operates and competes?
3. How will the organization get to where it wants to go (i.e., what actions are required)?

PART OF BUSINESS ACQUISITION PROCESS

Developing a strategic business plan is an important part of the overall business acquisition process. It provides a framework within which business and marketing decisions can be made rationally. It also helps focus an organization's resources. Bid decisions, allocating internal research and development funds, marketing emphasis, development of new procedures or processes, teaming or partnering with other companies, future employee skill requirements, and a host of other business decisions should be made within the boundaries and direction established by the strategic plan. Moreover, these decisions can be based on a shared set of values and a common understanding of what the organization is trying to achieve. Proper strategic planning enhances an organization's effectiveness and efficient use of its resources—again, all aligned by an established future direction defined clearly by a set of business objectives.

Effective strategic planning requires the approval and participation of senior management and other key people in the organization. It also requires "buy in" from employees and stakeholders. Consequently, it is important to keep everyone informed during the planning process and to solicit input from employees and stakeholders. Everyone in the organization needs to be aware of the basic strategic plan and to understand the direction the organization is pursuing. Otherwise, they will be unable to coordinate their work efforts to support the plan.

Developing a strategic plan to be placed in a desk drawer where it gathers dust is simply a waste of valuable resources. To be effective, the strategic plan must be used to manage the organization. Key business decisions should be made in concert with the goals and objectives delineated in the plan. Management indecision, inconsistent and parallel activities, and general organizational chaos often are due to a lack of strategic planning or a failure to effectively communicate the plan to all employees.

Strategic planning is a dynamic, ongoing activity. It is iterative. Business conditions and priorities change; the strategic plan should reflect this evolution. At specified intervals, progress against the plan is reviewed. Feedback from these reviews is then fed back into the planning process.

STRATEGIC PLANNING AS A COMPETITIVE ADVANTAGE

Given the relative importance and utility of strategic planning, you might mistakenly assume that it is a core business practice. In truth, it is not. Many organizations operate without the benefit of a true strategic business plan. Many of these same organizations are successful, at least for a season. Strategic planning, therefore, is not an absolute essential for business success. Books on business and proposal development rarely address it. Indeed, you could skip this chapter and still gain all the essential information you need to capture business from the federal government. Nonetheless, this book is about gaining competitive advantage. Over the long haul, those companies that plan and manage strategically fare better than their counterparts who fail to practice strategic planning. That is why we are addressing the topic of strategic planning here.

The first step in gaining competitive advantage is to develop and implement a strategic plan. If your organization has an existing plan, then you are ahead of the game. If not, you may want to initiate the process or try to convince management to get started. The world will not end if you fail. Nor will humanity cease to exist because you do not have a strategic plan. Yet, those who practice strategic planning will gain an edge in the race to capture government business.

The following sections of this chapter summarize the strategic planning process. This is not intended to be a comprehensive treatment of the subject. Instead, it is provided to familiarize or refresh readers with the basics. If you decide to develop a strategic business plan, you will need more information than is contained here. You might also consider hiring a professional consultant to help you through the process.

DEVELOPING A MISSION STATEMENT

The first step in developing a strategic business plan is to formulate a mission statement. A company's mission statement defines its business mission. It defines the reason the company exists. Four basic questions must be addressed:

1. What functions does the company perform?
2. Who are the customers for whom these functions are performed?
3. How (i.e., by what means) does the organization perform these functions?
4. Why does the organization exist?

Answers to these questions are distilled into a relatively short statement—100 to 150 words—that succinctly defines the mission of the organization. An effective mission statement is an organization's best effort to define its future state in terms of products/services, customers, and the organization's distinctive attribute or approach to products or customers.

What

The first question concerns the function served by the organization. There is a natural tendency to define "what" in terms of tangible products or services. A more fruitful approach is to define your organization's function according to customer needs. Consider the following.

One of my clients builds flight simulators for military aircraft. They could view their function as providing flight simulators to military customers. But their customers do not have a need for flight simulators. Instead, they have a need to produce trained pilots who possess the skills required to fly sophisticated military aircraft safely and effectively.

Defining organizational function in terms of customer needs will help you avoid restricting your offerings to current product lines. It also will enable you to be more creative and innovative in how you satisfy those needs. Focusing on customer needs can be a safeguard against product stagnation and obsolescence. For example, having my client define their function as training pilots versus providing flight simulators opens new vistas for how they accomplish that function. Instead of just offering flight simulators, they might offer a mix of training devices and training materials, or they might consider embedding some training systems into the aircraft itself.

Being sensitive to meeting the needs of customers enables an organization to respond to new contingencies in the marketplace and advances in technology, as well as to envision new ways of meeting those needs. A very real difference exists between a company that sees itself as a pretzel company and one that sees itself as a provider of snack foods.

As another illustration, consider the difference in orientation between a personal computer manufacturer and an organization whose function is to meet the computational needs of its customers. The first view is limiting. The second sets broad horizons.

Who

Identifying the "who" part of the business equation is the second part of building a mission statement. Which market or market segment is your organization targeting? Markets can be segmented in many ways. Saying that the federal government is your market is too broad to be useful. Some organizations may segment this market by agency. Others will segment it by function, such as information technology. No organization is large enough to supply the needs of everyone. Therefore, it is important to define clearly the segment of the total potential customer base that is your organization's primary market.

Different market segments embody different needs. The needs of the Department of Defense are different from those of the Department of Justice. Clarity about market segments will enable the organization to be more sensitive to the needs of that segment and to focus its resources on its prime targets. At the same time, avoid defining too narrow a segment; you may miss some valuable opportunities.

How

The third question addressed by the mission statement concerns how the organization will meet its objectives. "How" may refer to a special competency unique to the organization, a particular application of technology, an emphasis on quality, a marketing strategy, or the manner in which services will be provided. For example, you may elect to be the low-cost provider of a particular product or service. Or, you may emphasize innovative, technology-driven solutions. Still further, you may provide products that are highly reliable, offer services provided by experienced professionals, or want to capitalize on a unique technical competency.

The "how" portion of the mission statement must match reality. If you plan to be the low-cost supplier, then you must either currently measure up to this statement or put in place plans to do so. Moving to become the low-cost supplier can be part of your strategic plan, along with the actions required to achieve that goal.

Why

The final component of the mission statement involves defining "why" the organization exists. Many organizations feel compelled to include a statement that reflects the values of the organization in their mission statement. Others do not. The "why" portion is optional. It should be included only if it adds clarity to the stated mission of the organization. "Why" statements probably have greater value and relevance for companies providing products that impact health and safety, or those providing services that address human needs.

Value of the Mission Statement

A well thought-out mission statement provides the organization with a valuable tool. It clearly charts the future direction of the organization and establishes a basis for organizational decision-making. This will enable employees to align their efforts with organizational goals and to apply their energies to accomplishing the organization's mission.

Developing an effective mission statement can be a very difficult task, however. It will require multiple iterations, refinements, and edits before it is right. Once a draft statement is available, post it publicly and solicit recommendations from employees. You may be surprised at the insight of employees not involved in the process. This also will help employees accept the final mission statement, which every employee should be able to recite from memory.

STRATEGIC BUSINESS MODELING

Strategic business modeling is the process of defining what is required to accomplish the organization's mission and how progress toward that goal will be measured. It is a way of stating concretely the desired future of the organization. The business modeling process includes defining the success the organization wants to achieve, how success will be measured, what will be done to achieve success, and the organizational culture. All the elements of the strategic business model must be consistent with the organization's mission statement. Alternatively, it may be necessary to adjust the mission statement in light of decisions made during the strategic business modeling process.

Strategic business modeling consists of four major elements:

1. Identifying the lines of business (LOB) the organization will engage in to accomplish its mission
2. Establishing measures or indicators to assess progress in each LOB
3. Identifying the strategic activities required to realize the organization's vision of the future
4. Assessing the organizational culture necessary to support achievement of its objectives.

Lines of Business

An important ingredient of strategic planning is to identify LOBs that will enable the organization to achieve its desired future. An LOB is a product or service offering that is distinct from other products or services, or significantly different in terms of the market segment it serves. An LOB analysis begins by assessing current products and services. However, do not restrict your thinking to current LOBs; they may not be the ones that take you where you want to be. Instead, determine what future LOBs will enable your organization to achieve its goals.

The strategic planning team should identify those businesses they want the organization to pursue. If a new LOB is identified, then it must be compared with the mission statement to ensure consistency. Moreover, selecting a new LOB should be based on current capabilities of the organization, the contribution of that LOB to organizational measures of success, and the fit of the new LOB within the existing product line.

Part of the LOB analysis is to determine the mix of products and services the organization wants to offer in the future. For each LOB, you should determine its relative size in terms of expected sales and profits. You also need to identify marketing resources and any investment required. The purpose of the LOB analysis is to determine the ideal mix of products and services required to achieve the goals of the organization. This may require an adjustment to the current mix, the deletion of a current product, or the addition of a new LOB. A business plan for each LOB must be prepared, including a list of advantages and disadvantages associated with that LOB. If possible, the business plan should cover a five-year period.

Once a business case is prepared for each LOB, the role of the strategic planning team is to determine which LOB to pursue and the relative contribution of each to the organization's success. These must be realistic decisions based on an accurate estimate of the market potential for each LOB. This requires knowledge of market conditions, competitors, and potential sales.

The output of the LOB analysis is a determination of the organization's future mix of products and services. In addition, the LOB analysis identifies the expected contribution of each LOB, the resources required to achieve that contribution, plus any other special considerations. Again, the final determination of LOBs should be compared to the mission statement to ensure consistency.

Strategic Success Indicators

Once an organization has set its sights on the future, it must select a way of assessing its progress. Strategic success measures need to be selected for each LOB and for the overall organization. Success measures typically are a mix of financial figures and "soft" indicators. Financial measures can be sales, profits, return on investment, market share, cash flow, or any number of indicators to assess the organization's financial success (see Figure 4-1 for some examples). Soft measures refer to the human factor. They might include customer satisfaction or employee morale.

Other measures can be added to standard indicators. These can include the percentage of competitive proposals won, the number of new products introduced, or on-time delivery of products and services for existing government contracts. The selected measures must be clear, quantifiable, and trackable. They also must relate meaningfully to the future success your organization is trying to achieve.

With respect to soft measures, I often hear people say that you cannot measure customer satisfaction on government contracts. I disagree. Most Department of Defense agencies evaluate contract performance annually and issue a report. For Air Force contracts, this is called a Contract Perfor-

Figure 4-1. Sample Strategic Success Indicators

Indicator	Annual Target to Be Achieved
Sales	$400 million
Earnings	8.5% of sales
Cash Flow	Positive by this date
Return on Investment	22%
Research and Development Expenditures	6% of sales
General and Administrate Rate	16% of direct labor
Overhead	125% of direct labor
Percent of Competitive Proposals Won	40%
Ratio of Bid and Proposal Cost to Contract Value	5%
Equipment Availability	98%
Contract Performance	All ratings good or excellent
Percent of On-time Delivery of Contract Deliverables	98%
Customer Satisfaction	Average of 8 on 10-point scale
Employee Satisfaction	Average of 7 on 10-point scale
Annual Employee Turnover	Less than 10%

mance Assessment Report. The information is subsequently used as one criterion in awarding future contracts.

Performing work for a government agency that does not regularly evaluate contract performance does not restrict you from soliciting that information. In fact, I highly recommend that you devise a method to regularly assess the satisfaction of your customers, even if they do not formally evaluate contract performance. I also suggest that you periodically assess the morale and satisfaction of employees. Employee morale can have an enormous impact on the success of your organization. Often a dime spent to improve morale will reap a dollar's worth of increased productivity.

Strategic Activities

Strategic activities define the steps required to achieve the goals and objectives of the strategic plan. These activities can be short-term, focused activities. Alternatively, they may be long-range and far-reaching processes. Examples include:

- Winning a key contract as a way of entering a new business area or maintaining dominance in that area
- Improving product reliability
- Obtaining certification in a key process
- Increasing the size and sophistication of the marketing organization
- Establishing a long-term partnership with another company
- Implementing an earned value management system to improve cost tracking
- Revamping employee compensation to promote teamwork and improve employee morale.

Assessing Necessary Culture

A final component of strategic business modeling involves the organization's culture. Often omitted, it concerns the culture necessary to support the attainment of business objectives. Cultural issues include organizational structure, the organization's attitude toward risk, how management decisions are made, and employee morale issues. Changes to an organization's current LOBs may require corresponding changes to its culture. If so, these need to be included in the strategic business plan.

ORGANIZATIONAL PERFORMANCE ASSESSMENT

Another one of my favorite quotes is, "If you do not know where you are going, a map will not do you any good." The first portion of the strategic planning process involves determining where you want to go. To get there, you first need to determine your starting point. An organizational performance assessment provides this information. It is a focused analysis of the current performance of the organization. Four factors are considered. Two focus on the internal organization, evaluating its current *strengths* and *weaknesses*. The other two factors look outside the organization, evaluating *opportunities* and *threats*. Taken together, the factors form the acronym "SWOT."

The internal assessment examines the organization's current performance in terms of basic indices such as sales, earnings, cash flow, return on investment, growth (sales and personnel), quality, technology, operations, and service. The measures used to assess performance should be the same measures you will use to assess progress toward the objectives listed in your strategic business plan. For example, if you plan to increase sales 15 percent per year for the next five years, then your performance assessment should include an evaluation of current and past sales.

If practical, review organizational data for the last several years. If you want to increase your proposal win rate, or the ratio of bid cost to contract value, then you need to assess current and past performance in these areas. As part of the organizational performance assessment, you also need to list weaknesses that may hinder efforts to achieve your strategic objectives.

The external assessment examines opportunities and threats outside the organization that could impact future success. These may include competitors, suppliers, markets and customers, economic trends, changes in procurement practices, labor market conditions, and government regulations. Planning to expand into software development and integration as a new LOB, for example, could be significantly affected by the availability of software engineers. Likewise, it may be difficult to increase sales in a market that is expected to shrink over the next five years.

A SWOT analysis should be performed for each separate LOB. Figure 4-2 provides a sample form for recording SWOT information.

COMPETITOR ANALYSIS

A detailed assessment of competitors is an integral component of this step of the strategic planning process. Competitors are companies who compete for contracts in the markets represented by your current or proposed LOBs. Clearly, competitors represent a serious threat to many strategic objectives, especially those related to increased sales, market share, or new markets. A realistic assessment of your competitors for each LOB is essential input to the strategic planning process. It also is information that must be updated regularly and used to support decisions throughout the business acquisition lifecycle.

GAP ANALYSIS

Once completed, the results of the performance assessment should be compared with the objectives of the strategic plan. The difference between where you are and where you want to go is the "gap." Gap analysis defines differences between current and desired performance. This analysis then leads to the development of specific strategies to close the "gaps." These are time-phased plans that define clearly the actions and resources required to achieve strategic objectives in light of current performance.

Figure 4-2. Sample Form to Record Results of SWOT Analysis

LINE OF BUSINESS ANALYSIS WORKSHEET			
LOB Description:			
Strength	**Weakness**	**Opportunity**	**Threat**
Ways to Exploit Strengths:			
Ways to Mitigate Weaknesses:			
Ways to Capture Opportunities:			
Ways to Counter Threats:			

Sometimes the gap between current and desired performance is too great. In these cases, it may be necessary to reevaluate the strategic objective. Four basic approaches are available to close the gap:

1. Increase the timeframe allotted to achieve the objective
2. Reduce the size or scope of the objective
3. Reallocate resources as a means of achieving the objective
4. Obtain new resources if possible.

DEVELOPING AND IMPLEMENTING ACTION PLANS

The output of the gap analysis phase is a set of action plans for each LOB. The collective set of action plans is reviewed to ensure that they are mutually consistent and to determine an overall grand strategy for the organization. Each action plan should contain milestones, a set of success measures, and a budget, if required. Each action plan should be assigned to the person responsible for implementing it and for tracking and reporting progress.

The functional and operational units of the organization should review the overall strategic plan and the corresponding set of action plans. In many cases it will be necessary to develop a more detailed operational plan to achieve the specifics contained in the action plan. For example, part of the strategic plan is likely to include future sales and earnings. Supporting this strategic objective will require a business plan and sales forecast along with any collateral plans to acquire new business. These might include increasing marketing staff or allocating research and development funds to design a new product.

Progress toward strategic objectives must be measured and reported regularly. The strategic planning team should meet at least quarterly to review progress and annually to review the overall strategic plan. Everyone in the organization needs to be familiar with the strategic objectives of the organization, and the strategic plan must be used as the basis for day-to-day management decisions.

Knowing where you are going and why are critical ingredients to long-range business success. Lacking this essential business focus causes organizations to waste precious resources on fruitless pursuits. Like a ship without a compass, they occasionally sail on high seas, but too often blow into a bad port. Organizations need a solid foundation upon which to base important business decisions, especially those related to the acquisition of new business.

Gain competitive advantage by building a strategic plan. Establish it as the foundation upon which business decisions are made. Use it to guide your organization effectively into a successful future.

Every shred of evidence suggests that companies that practice strategic planning outperform their directionless counterparts.

Chapter 5

Long-Term Positioning

The starting point for long-term positioning is your strategic business plan. If you do not have a plan, then your business plan and sales forecast will have to fill the bill. As the words imply, long-term positioning refers to activities performed long before the government prepares an RFP. These are activities designed to put your organization in a position to achieve its business goals. Long-range positioning comprises two key tasks: (1) building a strong relationship with your customers and (2) collecting marketing intelligence about future procurements, customers, and competitors. This information must be fed back into the organization, where it can be stored and evaluated to guide future bid efforts.

The role of marketing in the long-range development of new business parallels yesteryear's wagon train scout. In the old West, scouts rode out ahead of the wagon train. Their job was to collect and report information necessary to ensure that the wagon train arrived at its destination safely. They had to "scout" the trail to assess its suitability, locate alternate routes when necessary, and identify potential dangers.

In a similar vein, marketing personnel go out ahead of the organization. They gather information to qualify potential business opportunities and confirm the viability of goals and objectives contained in the business plan. They also look for potential dangers that threaten the successful achievement of business goals. Dangers might include changes in program requirements that reduce your competitive advantage, program delays or potential cancellations, technical and acquisition trends that could adversely affect future success, or competitors positioning themselves to capture business you have targeted.

A healthy marketing organization is one that promotes a continuous flow of market information into the strategic business development process. This information is used to develop, refine, and implement strategic marketing initiatives. It also is used to better define potential business opportunities, make bid decisions, and develop bid strategies.

DEVELOPING CUSTOMER RELATIONSHIPS

A key role of marketing is to develop good customer relationships. Marketing personnel are business ambassadors. Their job is to favorably represent your company and its capabilities. They work to create a sense of acceptance and trust that enhances the effective flow of information between the customer and your company. Although it is led by marketing, this role should not be marketing's sole province. Other people who represent technical, contract, financial, and program interests should also be used, when appropriate, to foster positive customer relations.

Customer relationships are achieved primarily through personal site visits. However, regular phone calls, letters, copies of company brochures, product announcements and press releases, advertising, presentations at trade conventions, and participation at trade shows offer multiple opportunities to develop relationships. Take care to coordinate these activities so that they all communicate a consistent message. Moreover, this message should be a direct outgrowth of your strategic business plan. Integrated and coordinated marketing activities can produce valuable results.

Visits by Senior Management

I am always amazed at how seldom senior management visits their government customers and counterparts. This suggests to the government that management is not interested and probably not involved in the oversight of programs administered by their agency. Senior management also is deprived of special insights that can be gained by meeting with their customers. This is information they may never hear from their own employees. It could also represent information about what is happening at the agency that could prove useful for future marketing efforts.

At least annually, a senior manager from your company, preferably your president or a division leader, should pay a call on any agency with which you have a contract and any agency with which you want to do business in the future. A word of caution is warranted concerning visits by senior management: Managers must be briefed on the status of current programs and any existing problems before they visit. Otherwise, they may appear uninformed and uninvolved. This could not only embarrass your management, but it will create a negative impression with your customer. The primary purpose of these visits is to impress the agency favorably and to demonstrate the interest and involvement of senior management.

Annual Briefing of Your Company Capabilities

At least once a year, you should schedule a presentation of your company capabilities to each procuring agency with which you plan to do business in the future. If you have existing contracts with an agency, do not assume that they are aware of your capabilities. Chances are that many who work there do not know. Many people are compartmentalized within their own program or area of interest. Moreover, personnel turnover tends to be high for most federal agencies.

Make sure you are aware of the status of your current programs so you do not get "ambushed" during the presentation with a comment or question about a problematic program. The presentation should identify your capability, what you are doing to improve this capability, and how it can be used to satisfy agency requirements or needs. Although this is a marketing presentation, the emphasis should be on technical and management capability. Sometimes it is necessary to give two briefings—one geared toward your customer's senior management and the other geared toward the rest of the working-level technical and management staff. If so, tailor each presentation to the expected audience.

Customers Versus Users

It is important to distinguish between customers and users. Typically, your customer will be a procuring agency that has acquisition responsibility. The customer prepares the RFP, conducts source selection, picks a winner, and manages and administers the resulting contract. However, the user of the product or service often is not the same as the procuring agency.

Users are the ultimate recipients of the product or service procured. They may help prepare the RFP and participate in source selection, but they do not select the winner. For example, the Aeronautical Systems Division of the Air Force buys aircraft for the Air Force. The users of those aircraft are not the same as the people who procure them. Hence, some of your long-range positioning may need to take place with potential users. So the term "customer" really refers to both customers and users.

COLLECTING MARKET INFORMATION

Collecting information about forthcoming contracts, customers, and competitors provides valuable input into the long-range positioning process. It is essential to planning and developing an effective bid strategy.

Identifying Your Customer's Long-Range Needs

Successful marketing needs to look beyond programs already identified by the customer. This involves assessing current or future problems that your customer faces and determining potential solutions that your company can offer. There is no easy way to explain how to accomplish this important marketing activity. It requires a perceptive observer—someone who thoroughly understands the customer's mission and can recognize potential trends that threaten its successful accomplishment. Changes and trends that could impact your customer include: staffing levels, budget, agency or user policy, expansion or contraction of mission scope, emphasis placed on technical areas (e.g., increased awareness and desire for better logistics support, plans to guard against obsolescence), and technology trends.

The key is to identify customer needs early. Then work with your customer to develop a solution that will both solve their problem and enable you to gain competitive advantage. For example, you might tailor a solution that favors your company's capabilities and strengths.

Understanding your customer's "wants and desires" also creates potential opportunities. These may not be hard-and-fast program requirements. Nevertheless, if the customer truly wants something, then you should be in a position to capitalize on that want or desire. I do not mean this in a negative way, like a "snake oil" salesman, but as the reasonable response of a supplier who is sensitive to the desires of customers and willing to help achieve those desires.

Monitoring your customer's long-range needs includes paying attention to the early stages of the acquisition cycle. Needs go away, are ignored, or eventually are defined as requirements. The process differs among customers and procuring agencies, but each one has a defined process. Military needs, for example, are translated and defined in documents like an operational requirements document. Again, marketing needs to be on the leading edge of developing requirements to define business opportunities and then to nurture those opportunities. Nurturing involves developing innovative solutions for those requirements and influencing requirements in a way that gives your company a competitive advantage. Developing innovative solutions or a special technical capability may represent an area where you want to allocate independent research and development (IR&D) funds as a way to gain the upper hand on the competition.

Most federal procuring agencies provide annual presentations of their procurement plans for the next three to five years. Many post these plans on the Internet and update them either quarterly or semiannually. Procurement plans clearly offer a rich source of information for long-range market positioning. However, if marketing is doing its job, you should have this information long before it finds its way into a formal presentation.

Helping Your Customer Articulate Program Needs and Sell a Program

Sometimes customers know their needs, but they do not know how to formulate or articulate them sufficiently. By building a close working relationship with your customer, you may position your company to help translate a need into a bona fide requirement and program. Assistance can take the form of stating the need in a way that suggests potential solutions, brainstorming to articulate the need, or reviewing available products or technology to solve the need. Providing this type of assistance will help you build a great relationship with your customer. It also affords you valuable insight into how to respond to this need once it becomes a requirement and a formal RFP.

In some cases, you may need to help your customer "sell" a program. This may include defending the need and showing its benefits. Support here might include helping conduct a cost-benefit, lifecycle cost, or feasibility analysis, preparing a presentation to defend the need, or using your contacts to help support a customer program. Incidentally, this type of support is completely above-board, legal, and ethical. There are no regulations or laws against helping a government customer develop or defend a need or requirement. However, you cannot expect any favors from the government in return. That *is* against the law. The insight you gain by understanding the background and thought process your customer has gone through to define a need, and working with him or her to solve that need, will pay huge dividends in the long run. This type of information and level of understanding cannot be achieved by reading the RFP or attending a bidders' conference.

Helping your customer does not always have to be self-serving. Providing assistance, even if it equally benefits other competitors, will eventually yield a dividend. Sometimes such assistance does more to positively impress a customer than doing something that is in your company's best interests.

Becoming Familiar with Your Customer's Procurement Practices

The federal government procurement process is fairly standardized, as discussed in Chapter 3. Each procuring agency implements the process according to specialized regulations and according to its own unique procedures and requirements. Every agency is different. In addition, procurement practices and trends change. Part of long-range positioning is to understand how the procurement agency implements the acquisition process and how it conducts source selection. This information is important input into the proposal planning and preparation phases of the bid and proposal lifecycle. Everyone on the proposal team needs to understand the process.

Here is an example of how procurement practices can affect your success. In the mid 1980s, one of the major federal procuring agencies tended to select the lowest bidder who was technically compliant with all RFP requirements. Following an initial review of all proposals, they would issue clarification requests and deficiency reports to each bidder who was within the competitive range. Each bidder responded to these requests, amended its proposal accordingly, and subsequently submitted its final price in response to a BAFO request from the procuring agency. Price was the deciding criterion. Therefore, clever bidders often bid just below what they believed was technically compliant. If a bidder erred on the low side technically, the government let them know by issuing a deficiency report. The bidder then adjusted the technical approach just enough to meet the requirement. These processes allowed bidders to "low ball" their initial bid and then use feedback from the government to adjust it to a minimally acceptable level.

The winner in these competitions was the company who had played the game the best. Knowing the rules and practices of the procuring agency was essential to winning. Today, there is a growing tendency for the government to make awards without discussions. This practice requires a very different approach than in the days when you knew you would get a chance to change both your technical proposal and your bid price.

For the last decade, there has been a growing trend for the government to award contracts based on "best value." This means that the government does not necessarily award to the lowest technically qualified bidder. Instead, they weight the value to the government of what is proposed and pick the bidder who represents the best value—technical, price, risk, and schedule—to the government. Some agencies actually practice this selection process; others just pay it lip service. Knowing the difference is vital to successful bidding.

Bidding for a contract without knowing the history and practices of the procuring agency is akin to competing in an athletic contest without knowing the rules. You may win, but you will have to be very good or very lucky. Imagine a baseball game in which you are out after only two strikes instead of three, or where you are ejected from the game for smashing a line drive over the left-field fence. Learning the rules after the fact will prove to be a painful experience.

Likewise, failing to know your customer's formal and informal practices places you at a competitive disadvantage. Contract types, procurement practices, and what customers expect to see in your proposal change over time and from agency to agency. Staying abreast of these trends and practices, coupled with an understanding of a procurement agency's history, will enable you to capture an advantage over your less informed brethren.

Identifying Future Programs

As soon as enough data are available, you should begin developing a profile for each program opportunity. Initially, you may not have very much information. Over time, however, you can fill in the details. Program information is used to support sales forecasts and to support bid and proposal planning, including bid strategy. Initially, the following information should be collected:

- Customer/procuring agency
- Brief statement of need/requirements
- Program requirements/deliverables
- Budget and phasing of funds
- Period of performance
- Procurement schedule
- Likely competitors
- Unique or notable aspects of the procurement.

This information should be maintained in a business acquisition database, as described below, and updated as new information becomes available.

As a program becomes better defined, it becomes even more important to identify any customer technical or business trends that could affect the procurement. Customers have biases just like everyone else. They may favor a particular manufacturer, product, or specific software authoring language, or they may decide to standardize using one manufacturer's product to reduce the cost of logistically supporting multiple products. Similarly, customers may be enthralled with a particular technology or technological approach. Knowing these trends and biases can help you gain competitive advantage. Not knowing them might make the difference between winning and losing.

Building and Maintaining a Long-Range Schedule of Upcoming Procurements

Identify as early as possible the expected milestones and dates for future procurements. This is important information for planning purposes. Continually update schedule information for procurements within 12 months of an expected RFP release. Milestones can include budget approval or requirements approval, draft and final RFP release dates, bidders' conferences, contract award, and any other milestone dates that could impact program planning.

Identifying Potential Competitors and Building Competitor Profiles

Winning government business is all about competition. Imagine a professional boxer jumping into the ring for a title fight without knowing anything about his opponent. That would be crazy. It is equally crazy to spend bid and proposal resources if you do not thoroughly know your competitors. How will you beat them if you do not know their strengths and weaknesses and their likely approach for the current procurement? Information about your competitors is vital to developing a bid strategy. Quite simply, the more you know about your competitors, the better.

Interestingly enough, many companies know relatively little about their competition. This puts them at a competitive disadvantage. Avoid this mistake by collecting as much information as you can about your primary competitors. One way to accomplish this task is to build and maintain a profile for each primary competitor. The specific information to be collected needs to be tailored to your particular industry and the areas in which you compete. Nonetheless, the following categories of information provide a good starting point:

- *Competitor name/division*—If this is a division of a larger company, provide some information on the parent company.
- *Description of products and services*—List the products and services offered by the competitor and provide a brief description of each. Include any relevant information that could be used in the future to determine a bid strategy against this competitor.
- *List of current contracts*—Provide a list of current contracts held by the competitor and a brief description of each contract: procuring agency, users, deliverables, period of performance, value, any special features or work effort, plus anything that might provide insight into the capability of the competitor. If possible, organize current contract information by product line or service area.
- *Strengths and weaknesses*—Strengths and weaknesses should be listed at the company level and for each product line and service area. Separating strengths and weaknesses into categories will facilitate future use of competitor information. General categories include technical, cost, key personnel, past performance, customer/political, and "other." Technical factors should be divided in a way that corresponds to the particular products and services offered.

Tapping Sources of Competitor Information

Collecting useful competitor information is easier said than done. It is hard work and a never-ending challenge to keep the information current. Out-of-date or inaccurate information on competitors is worse than no information at all. Common sources of competitor information include copies of existing contracts, customer contacts, subcontractors and suppliers, personal contacts, trade journals, press releases, company brochures, annual reports, your employees who have previously worked for the competitor, and the competitor's employees. Many companies today maintain websites full of good information. Take advantage of the ease of the Internet to collect this information.

Request a copy of each current contract from the procuring agency and maintain a file of contracts for each competitor. Contracts can be obtained from the contracting office of the procuring agency. Submit a written request of the contract by name and contract number. This information must be released as directed by the Freedom of Information Act. Sometimes, contracting officers will let you make a copy of the existing contract without a formal request. This is faster and easier than making a written request. Much of the information you need to complete the competitor profile can be found in copies of existing contracts. In particular, contracts contain pricing information that will enable you to estimate your competitor's bid rates.

The customer also is a rich source of competitor information. They administer and monitor the contracts being performed by your competitors. Customers have first-hand experience and a sense of what competitors do well and what they do poorly. This is valuable information in developing your list of competitor strengths and weaknesses. However, you will need to be tactful in gaining competitor information from the customer. Incidentally, your customer also is a good source of information concerning your company's strengths and weaknesses.

Your competitor's regular subcontractors and suppliers are another source of information. First, just knowing who they are will tell you something about your competitor's technical approach. In addition, suppliers have first-hand information about your competitors, but from a different vantage point. Some of your competitor's suppliers may be the same ones you use or work with regularly.

Building a Strategic Marketing Database

Information about markets, programs, customers, and competitors is worthless unless it is used. All too often marketing collects mountains of data, but never shares it with anyone. Many of the people who might otherwise apply this information to make bid decisions and develop bid and proposal strategies are not provided access. This is a waste of time and effort.

Marketing information should be reviewed and evaluated by a team charged with the acquisition of new business. The composition of this team should include at least one member from each of the following areas: technical or engineering, marketing, proposal management, contracts, finance, and program management (if your company has a program management group). These should be experienced people selected for their areas of expertise and ability to develop business strategies. For small companies, one person may cover multiple areas. Do not wait until the last minute before you involve technical, contracts, and finance personnel in the decision-making process. Every bid strategy and proposal response will require their unique expertise and insight.

One way to share marketing information is to establish a bid and proposal (B&P) library or database. This is sensitive and proprietary information. It must be protected, and access should be regulated. Most companies have computer systems connected via a local area network. It is fairly simple in these cases to set up a directory with access restricted to a list of authorized individuals or to protect access via a password.

ESTABLISHING A BID AND PROPOSAL LIBRARY

Opportunities to gain competitive advantage often lurk in unlikely locations. For example, building and maintaining a robust B&P library is one way to gain the upper hand on your less astute competitors.

For proposal managers, time is the most precious commodity. Anything that maximizes the time available to prepare a proposal has greater worth than gold. Ready access to relevant B&P information is among the best ways to avoid wasting time searching for it. The information can be data required to prepare your proposal, information that helps reduce proposal development time or improve content quality, or competitor data to assist in bid strategy development. Reducing "lost time" tracking down information translates into more time available to develop your proposal. Optimizing this time via an effective B&P library potentially will enable you to gain advantage over competitors. It also will seriously reduce the frustration associated with chasing down information that should be within hand's reach.

For example, preparing a past performance volume should be a simple, straightforward task. Rarely is that the case. More often, endless hours are wasted contacting contract and program managers to obtain the required information for each individual contract. Another typical example is the time spent looking for past proposal write-ups that can be applied to the current proposal.

A well-maintained, readily accessible library can be a valuable asset. Yet, it is an advantage that most companies either overlook or fail to exploit fully. Inexpensive computers and the ease of storing vast amounts of information enable the efficient development and maintenance of electronic libraries or databases.

I highly recommend you give top priority to establishing and maintaining a B&P library if you do not already have one. If you must start from scratch, don't try to establish everything at once. Lay out a reasonable plan and schedule. Start small and expand over time. The key is to get started.

An effective bid and proposal library should contain the following:

- Copies of previous proposals
- Proposal database organized by topic
- Graphics database organized by topic
- Résumés for key personnel
- Past and current performance database
- Lessons-learned database
- Competitor database
- Marketing information database.

Copies of Previous Proposals

Maintain a complete file for each proposal you prepare regardless of whether or not it resulted in a win. Keep a copy of the RFP, any communication between the customer and bidders, questions you asked and the customer's answers, copies of evaluation notices, slides for any oral presentation given, and a copy of the evaluation debriefing. By keeping the whole proposal file, you can go back and review the entire bid or any segment. If you organize this database by customer, then you can review past RFPs and other communications to establish trends in how the customer asks for information and conducts the overall solicitation process. Knowing what customers expect and how they conduct their business can be an effective planning tool.

Proposal Database

The proposal database contains sections of previous proposals organized by topic. This is the same information contained in the previous proposals database. However, it is organized topically for easy reference. Capture team leaders can then access information through index terms or file headings and quickly find what they need. You can hyperlink the index to individual files to further enhance the search. This technique is particularly valuable when time is of the essence and you need to pull information together quickly on a variety of proposal topics.

Using information from past proposals can be a great timesaver. This is especially true for write-ups on processes, like systems engineering or configuration management, which tend to remain constant across programs. However, every RFP is different. The writing requirements for the same topic may vary enormously between solicitations. Inexperienced proposal authors may not recognize this difference and simply plug old write-ups into the new proposal. Therefore, I recommend restricting access to this database to members of the capture team. They can draw relevant information from the proposal database and make it available to other proposal members, with the appropriate cautions concerning its applicability to the present proposal.

Actually, I prefer to have authors build detailed writing outlines before giving them access to past proposal information. This encourages them to formulate a response specific to RFP requirements first and then use past proposal information to help with the writing task.

Graphics Database

The graphics database is the same as the proposal database, except that instead of proposal narrative, it contains copies of proposal graphics. Like the proposal database, it should be organized topically for easy reference. Drawing a graphic from the database and modifying it to fit the requirements of the current proposal will save time and money.

Having a graphics database available also helps proposal authors envision ways to express complex ideas or concepts graphically. Again, hyperlinking the graphics index to individual graphics will enhance the ability to search the file.

Résumés for Key Personnel

This database reflects the needs of each individual company or division. If you bid regularly on programs that require résumés for key personnel, then maintaining a database of current résumés will prove to be a great timesaver. Likewise if bid opportunities you pursue typically require a description of key personnel experience, rather than a full résumé. For these cases, develop a one-page summary résumé for key personnel in your organization and have each person update his or her résumé annually. Alternatively, if the programs you chase rarely ask for résumés, then the effort to create and maintain a résumé database is probably not worthwhile.

Rather than asking for personnel résumés, some service-type programs request job descriptions for each technical position covered by the contract. If you routinely respond to RFPs with these requirements, then build and maintain a database of standard job descriptions. These descriptions should be developed with participation from your human resources department. Include basic information on minimum education and experience plus a brief summary of the tasks performed by people covered by the description. Also, identify the level of supervision given or received for each description.

Past and Current Performance Database

Chasing down information required to prepare a past performance section typically consumes far more time and energy than necessary. Information about the organization's past and current programs should be standardized and readily available. Building and maintaining a database for this purpose will significantly enhance your proposal development efforts. Moreover, many government agencies place considerable emphasis on past performance as an evaluation factor. Being able to respond quickly and accurately to this important aspect of proposal development is well worth the effort required to maintain a past performance database.

Build a standard format for past and current performance information. Most agencies require a common set of administrative data. In addition, you will want to include other relevant program information. In building the rest of your database format, consider the following topics as candidates:

- Brief program description
- List of key program personnel
- List of major subcontractors and their program roles
- Any significant technical, schedule, or cost challenges
- Extraordinary achievements (e.g., solving an especially difficult technical problem, performing ahead of schedule or under budget)
- Any customer problems encountered and actions taken to fix them
- Periodic updates of program progress.

Program progress should be updated quarterly, at least semiannually, for each active program being performed by your organization. Set up a system to automatically remind program managers when progress updates are required.

Maintain a copy of past performance proposal write-ups in this database. These often can be used with relatively little tailoring. I also recommend that you maintain in this database copies of any customer evaluations of contract performance. Many government agencies perform an annual contract assessment and provide a copy to the contractor. These are especially valuable because they represent your customer's assessment of contract performance. This is the information that will be provided to the procuring agency for a past performance evaluation, if such an evaluation is part of the source selection process. Clearly, you need to be aware of this information in preparing the past performance section of your proposal.

Lessons-Learned Database

At the end of each proposal effort, summarize the lessons learned by the proposal capture team. You also can solicit input from other proposal members. Maintain lessons learned in a database. This information can be used to detect trends that should be addressed. It also can be used to help train prospective proposal managers and as a periodic refresher for veterans. The maxim that "those who ignore history are destined to repeat it" probably applies in this case.

Competitor Database

Maintaining up-to-date information about competitors is critical. It is practically impossible to build an effective bid strategy without competitor data. If you cannot make a reasonable estimate of what your competitors will do, then making a no-bid decision may be the better part of valor.

As discussed, several categories of data should be maintained in this database. First, include any competitor assessment you have completed. Second, maintain an active file for each competitor to keep track of contracts they have won, press releases, or any other type of information that will help you understand the competition. Finally, try to obtain copies of your competitors' proposals whenever possible. You can request a copy of the winning proposal by exercising your rights under the Freedom of Information Act (FOIA). However, in most cases, the proposals you receive through this process will contain little relevant information. Contractors normally are allowed to cross out any information they consider proprietary, so you can guess the outcome. Nonetheless, the effort to get a copy of their proposal is still worth the effort. Occasionally, you get lucky.

Alternatively, you always should be able to get a copy of the contract. Often a simple request to the government contracting officer will produce a copy. Otherwise, you can get a copy via the FOIA route. At a minimum, the contract will display CLIN prices. This will enable you to perform a cost analysis of the winning bid. Comparing competitor costs to what you bid, integrated with your understanding of program requirements, will at least provide some insights into pricing strategy.

Marketing Information Database

Maintain a copy of current and past marketing presentations. Such information can be used as input to proposal volume and section introductions. By reviewing recent customer presentations, proposal authors can reinforce the marketing message in the proposal. Moreover, they can avoid putting contradictory or inconsistent information in the proposal. This may sound trivial.

Yet, it is not terribly unusual for marketing to tell your customer one thing, only to have the proposal say something vastly different.

Value of B&P Library

An effective B&P library will pay for itself many times over in terms of both time and money. For it to be effective, however, someone must keep the library updated. For a small organization, this will require a part-time person. For some large organizations, maintaining your B&P library may require a full-time person. In either case, developing and maintaining a B&P library represents an excellent return on investment.

The road leading to winning federal contracts starts long before a bid opportunity is fully defined. Start early to position yourself strategically with the customer. Take a long-range view of developing creative, cost-effective solutions that go beyond the immediate program needs of customers. Help your customers define program requirements and assist them in defending their program if necessary. Ensure that customers are fully aware of your technical and program capabilities. Demonstrate high-level corporate interest by having senior management periodically visit customers. Take every action to become the favored contractor long before the formal procurement process begins.

Know your competition. Maintain an ongoing program to collect information about competitors. Use these data to provide timely support for bid decisions and as input into developing bid strategies.

Build and maintain the currency of a comprehensive bid and proposal library. Use this asset to reduce bid costs and to maximize the time and data available to prepare your proposal. Fewer activities will yield a higher return on your bid and proposal dollars.

Chapter 6

Pre-Proposal Phase

There is no clear demarcation between long-range positioning and the pre-proposal phase of the business acquisition lifecycle. In fact, the two phases overlap. Long-range positioning is an ongoing activity. Its focus is more general in nature, but it feeds information into the pre-proposal phase. The pre-proposal phase is specific to a single program. It is entered once sufficient information exists to make a bid decision and to begin formulating a bid strategy. This may occur 12 months or more before a formal RFP is released.

More often than not, the seeds of victory or defeat are sown during this phase. This is when the government transforms its need into a formal RFP. It also is during this period that the government decides how to conduct the competition, build a source selection plan, identify source selection members, and interact with prospective bidders to inform them about the forthcoming procurement. Concurrently, potential bidders must evaluate the program to determine if it merits an investment of their bid and proposal resources. If so, they must develop and implement a bid strategy and begin planning for the proposal itself. This also marks a period of heightened customer contact and a more focused collection of marketing information.

Those companies who start early and do a good job of planning and strategizing prior to RFP release gain competitive advantage. Those who start late and squander this time enter the competition at a significant disadvantage. The choice between these two options should be intuitive, but it is not. Nothing in life is free. Effort expended during the pre-proposal phase costs money. In an attempt to conserve bid and proposal resources, some organizations postpone these activities until later, i.e., once an RFP is released.

Unfortunately, such efforts to save money most often yield a double dose of disaster. First, starting late increases the probability of losing. Either key pre-proposal activities do not get done, or they are accomplished too late or so hastily that they fail to contribute positively. Second, starting late practically never reduces total bid cost. In fact, just the opposite occurs. Trying to make all the necessary decisions and accomplish all the work in less time leads to the inefficient use of resources. This only increases the cost compared to performing the same effort over a longer time period.

Making good use of bid and proposal resources is a prudent business practice. Yet, spending valuable resources on a losing effort is foolish at best. If starting early does in fact cost more, then it should be weighed against the value of increasing win probability. Ultimately, you will find that it makes more sense to follow a path that leads to a higher rate of success. Typically, that means starting early.

MAKING BID DECISIONS

No one can afford to chase every possible business opportunity. Nor should anyone want to. Bid and proposal resources tend to be scarce. They should be applied only to those opportunities with a reasonable probability of success. The decision to pursue a particular contract opportunity, therefore, needs to be a conscious, well-thought-out effort.

A bid decision should be made once enough information is available. This marks the point when an organization decides either to pursue a program or to forgo the opportunity. A positive bid decision also normally means that the organization will allocate and spend bid and proposal funds.

Information about forthcoming procurements tends to be spread over time. Things like specifications, contract terms, competitors, and competing opportunities also change during this period. Therefore, it may be necessary to make multiple bid decisions.

A three-tier bid decision system works for most procurements. The first tier is a preliminary decision to pursue a contract. A "pursue" decision in this case means that the organization will continue to collect information until enough information is available to make another bid decision, or until a set time in the future. It also means that a limited budget will be allocated.

The second tier or gate occurs when sufficient information exists to make a formal bid decision. The type of information necessary to support this decision level is provided below. A third-tier decision occurs once the final RFP is released.

The final decision is primarily to validate an earlier bid decision. It verifies that nothing has changed that would undermine the earlier decision or significantly reduce win probability. This rarely happens. Nonetheless, if something has happened that would seriously undermine your ability to win, then it is better to cut your losses than to spend additional funds on a losing effort. Reversing a previous decision to bid is always difficult. Money has already been spent and plans put in place. Yet continuing to pursue an effort that falls below your normal bid criteria is bad management. It is better to take the money you would have spent and apply it to another opportunity with a higher probability of success.

Bid Decision Criteria

If you are going to make a bid decision, it follows logically that you will need a set of criteria upon which to base this important decision. The following questions provide some typical criteria. They also highlight the type of information that must be available to make an informed decision.

Does the opportunity fit within your strategic business plan, and is it consistent with your organization's mission statement and marketing plan? This is a go/no-go criterion. You only pursue opportunities that are consistent with the organization's overall strategic plan. One of the values of having a mission statement is to screen potential opportunities. If a new program is outside the scope of your mission statement, you do not bid on it. As an extreme example, if your organization's mission is to be a world leader in software integration, then you would not decide to bid on a contract to build bazookas. Actually, having a strategic plan and mission statement normally would allow the screening and elimination of irrelevant opportunities during the long-range planning phase.

A common mistake is to bid on contracts well outside the scope of the organization's mission. This often happens when few new business opportunities are available or when the business base of the organization is declining. Succumbing to this temptation is shortsighted. Lean times demand restraint and discipline to preserve scarce bid and proposal resources. This also is the wrong time to try and branch into a new line of business just because an opportunity presents itself. The successful pursuit of new lines of business is the purview of strategic planning, not the happenstance of rash decisions to acquire new business.

If the opportunity being considered meets the go/no-go criterion, then address the following areas.

- *Opportunity background.* Is this opportunity funded? Do you understand the problem being solved by the customer? Do you have a clear grasp of the technical and program requirements? Do these requirements match your organization's expertise?
- *Relationship/reputation with the customer.* Are you currently performing work for the customer, or have you performed work for them in the past? If so, what is your reputation with the customer? Can you overcome any poor past performance efforts? If you do not have any performance experience with the customer, have you ensured that the customer knows you and is aware of your capability to perform the required work?
- *Technical capability.* Does your company possess the necessary technical capability to successfully perform the contract? Do you have more technical experience than competitors, or a technical advantage, in this area? Is your staff better trained or educated? Can you come up

with an innovative solution to the customer's requirements? Note that there is a difference between having the required capability addressed by this criterion and whether or not the customer is familiar with that capability. The customer *must believe* that you possess the required technical capability.

- *Subcontractors.* Do you need to add subcontractors to your team to overcome a real or perceived weakness? Will a qualified subcontractor enhance the value of your team in terms of customer relationships or technical capability?
- *Marketing intelligence.* Have you done a good job positioning yourself with the customer? Do you know their needs, fears, and desires? Have you collected up-to-date information on competitors? Does anyone have the "inside track" with the customer, or is the procurement "wired" for a competitor?
- *Competition.* Who are the likely competitors for this procurement? What are their strengths and weaknesses compared to program requirements? What is the reputation of the competitors with this customer? What relevant experience do competitors possess?
- *Pricing.* Can you present a credible, competitive price to the customer? Are your labor rates, overhead, and general and administrative (G&A) costs competitive for this type of procurement and for this customer? Do you have any capability, experience, or insight that will give you a price advantage?
- *Personnel/proposal resources.* Will sufficient personnel and proposal resources be available to prepare a winning proposal? Will other proposal efforts overlap with this one? If so, will you still have the necessary resources available to prepare an excellent proposal? Do you have a stable of contract labor or consultants who can effectively cover any shortfall in proposal resources?

Considering all relevant criteria, what is the realistic probability your organization will win the procurement? Be honest with yourself. Assess the competition realistically. If you cannot impartially assess your ability to win at 50 percent or greater, then you probably are better off passing on this opportunity.

Bid Decision Evaluation Form

One way to assess bid criteria is to rank each relevant area on a scale from 1 to 10. Figure 6-1 provides a sample rating scale that includes candidate bid criteria. (Bid criteria can be adjusted, if necessary, to meet your organization's specific requirements.) Procurements that achieve a minimum threshold score are considered legitimate bid opportunities. Two options are available for those that fall below the threshold: (1) abandon the bid opportunity, or (2) try to identify actions that would improve the bid

Figure 6-1. Bid Decision Evaluation Form

BID AREA	BID AREA SCORING CRITERIA										RATING
	Negative			Neutral				Positive			
	1	2	3	4	5	6	7	8	9	10	
Background Opportunity	Unfamiliar with customer needs; cannot meet requirements.			Generally understand customer and may meet requirements.				Fully understand customer and completely meet requirements.			
Customer Reputation	Poor past performance. Problems exist with customer.			Neutral or no past performance. Relationship neither positive nor negative.				Good past performance and strong customer relationship.			
Technical Capability	Not qualified to perform.			Capable of performing technically.				Technically superior. Have unique capability.			
Subcontractor	Subcontractors detracting.			Subcontractors have no impact.				Subcontractors substantially enhancing.			
Marketing Intelligence	Surprised by the RFP. Little contact with customer.			Generally familiar with what is going on.				Inside track. Excellent knowledge.			
Personnel/ Proposal Resources	Sufficient personnel and resources not available to support the proposal.			Sufficient resources available but need to be supplemented.				The best and the brightest are available.			
Competition	Competitor has significant advantage.			No one has an advantage.				Superior positioning. Have significant advantage.			
Pricing	Must cut corners to be competitive. Price credibility problem.			Responsive and generally competitive.				Have pricing advantage and within known limits.			
TOTAL SCORE:											
AVERAGE SCORE: Total Points Divided by Number of Bid Areas											
Comments:											

rating enough to meet the threshold. If you choose the latter path, then the bid opportunity should be evaluated again after the corrective action has been put in place.

Evaluating bid opportunities by scoring them against a predetermined set of criteria has several advantages. First, the process yields a fairly objective method for making bid decisions. Opportunities either meet or fail to meet the bid threshold. Second, the process of assigning a score to a bid decision area requires each evaluator to seriously consider the factors that contribute to a favorable or unfavorable score. This level of "thinking" often is neglected unless the bid decision process forces it. Third, the bid evaluation exercise highlights the need for information necessary to score bid decision areas credibly. This need in turn serves as a catalyst. It stimulates the organization to collect, organize, and use information to make informed bid decisions. It will be very difficult, for example, to evaluate the competition on a scale of 1 to 10 if you do not have available information on competitors. Fourth, if you have competing bid opportunities and have funds to pursue only one of them, then you could select the one with the highest bid score. Finally, scoring bid opportunities will enable you to compare the overall score with the outcome of the bid.

Theoretically, higher bid scores should correlate positively with bid success. Some simple recordkeeping will allow you to correlate bid decision scores with success or failure and may enable you to modify your bid process to work to your advantage in the future.

Bid Committee

A key consideration in making a bid decision is who will perform the evaluation and who will make the bid decision. Ultimately, a senior decision-maker will have to approve the bid decision, especially if B&P resources are going to be spent on its pursuit. I favor using a bid committee with a fixed core membership supplemented with additional members based on specific program requirements.

The composition of the bid committee needs to be tailored to the unique requirements of each organization. Typical committee membership might include representation from marketing, proposal management, contracts, pricing, program management, and relevant technical disciplines. Ideally, the committee chairperson would be the person responsible for approving the bid decision. Otherwise, a senior manager from marketing or proposals should chair the committee.

Each committee member individually completes the bid decision evaluation form. The committee then meets to discuss individual ratings and determine consensus. A composite rating that exceeds the threshold score indicates a favorable decision to bid the program in question. If the bid committee is not empowered to make the bid decision, then the outcome of the committee process can be used as the source of a presentation made to decision-makers.

CUSTOMER CONTACT PLAN

A commonly used marketing strategy is to develop and implement a customer contact plan during the pre-proposal phase. This is simply a plan to visit key customer personnel before the final RFP is released. The plan includes the names of customer and user representatives to be visited, when visits should be made, and the person in your organization who will make or lead the visits. The purpose of these visits is to collect information to help you develop a bid strategy and to support proposal planning.

Target customer personnel who will likely serve as members of the source selection team: the government program manager, contracting officer, lead engineering and technical personnel, key users, potential members of the source selection advisory council, etc. Customer contacts should not be used to make a marketing presentation. These are opportunities to identify customer wants, fears, and desires, plus any biases that could influence your proposal approach.

Customer contacts should be made by your program manager and appropriate members of your technical and contracts staff, depending upon the specific person you are meeting with. For example, your technical managers should meet with their government counterparts, your contracts manager with the government contracting officer, and so on. Marketing can assist with these meetings but should not take the lead role.

Plan each visit. Make a list beforehand of the information you want to collect and the topics you want to discuss. Let the customer do most of the talking. Take good notes and document the results of each visit.

Figure 6-2 shows a simple form that can be used to list customer names and decision-makers and to build a customer contact plan.

PRE-PROPOSAL CONFERENCES

Customers frequently hold pre-proposal conferences. The purpose is to provide an overview of the upcoming contract, get input from potential bidders, and answer any questions in an open forum so that all interested parties can hear the answers. The style and format of such conferences run the gamut. Most often they are held before the final RFP is released. In some cases, the customer will release a draft RFP before the conference and use the conference as a means to solicit comments about the draft and to answer questions concerning the procurement.

There are some general rules of thumb concerning conduct at pre-proposal conferences. Every interaction with your customer is important. How

Figure 6-2. Sample Forms to Record Customer Information and Build Contact Plan

Customer Team:

Name	Position	Phone Number	Responsibility

Customer Decision-Makers:

Name	Position	Bias/Priority	Comments

Customer Contact Plan:

Customer Name	Lead Person	Issue/ Requirement	Estimated Meeting Date	Meeting Objective

they perceive you and your organization is important. Their impression can bias, positively or negatively, how they respond subsequently to your proposal. So, be on your best behavior. Avoid any hint of arrogance. Be friendly. Act interested. Do not ask a question for which any qualified bidder should know the answer. In fact, I generally recommend that you refrain from asking questions at a public conference. Your role at a proposal conference is to listen and to learn, not to talk or give away information.

Observe who attends. These are potential competitors. Listen carefully and take good notes. This may provide you with some useful information beyond what you can find in the RFP. Pay attention to the type of questions asked and who is asking them. Judging by the questions being asked, how many of those present are serious competitors? How many are from competitor organizations? Likewise, listen carefully to the customer's answers. Try to discern any customer concerns about the cost, schedule, quality, or feasibility of satisfying their need. Chat with other bidders. Listen for clues about their reactions to the solicitation or potential team relationships between attendees. Be noncommittal about your own intentions or ideas. If possible, get a list of attendees. Customers often distribute these or post them on their websites.

Sometimes, customers schedule a one-on-one session where they meet individually with each bidder. Always take advantage of these opportunities. Typically, the information exchanged in a one-on-one session is confidential and will not be shared with other bidders. If in doubt, ask.

These sessions offer an excellent chance to interact with the customer and probably members of the source selection team. Prepare questions in advance and review them before the meeting. *Never* be confrontational with your customer, disagree strongly with what they have to say, or show your frustration or anger with aspects of the impending procurement. Also, do not use this opportunity to give a marketing pitch. Focus on collecting information you need to build a bid strategy or to clarify a point about the contract.

To the extent practical, express your understanding of the customer's needs and the capability of your team to meet those needs. Try to demonstrate that you will be easy to work with and are competent to perform the contract.

Again, take good notes and pay attention to the body language of customer attendees. Sometimes there is more information in a facial expression than in the verbal answer. At a minimum, two people from your organization should attend so you have one person free to take notes. Ideally, the person responsible for capturing the bid should lead the meeting for your company.

PROPOSAL PLANNING

Preliminary proposal planning should be accomplished before the final RFP is released. Start early so you can forecast needed resources. If the customer releases a draft RFP, this should include enough information to build a good initial plan. Proposal planning covers three major elements: schedule, resources, and budget.

Build a preliminary proposal schedule. Identify key milestones for the completion of draft proposal sections, reviews, and final products for the technical and cost proposals. Include ample time to produce the final product, subject it to a quality control check, and deliver it to the customer.

Resources cover people, facilities, systems, and whatever else you will need to prepare your proposal. The earlier you can forecast personnel requirements, the better. Proposals compete for resources just like every other function. Work with functional managers to identify personnel who possess the requisite skills and preferably people who have some proposal savvy. Make sure managers understand the timeframe during which people will be required and the scope of the assignment. If possible, get a commitment that once they are assigned, personnel will not be pulled off the proposal for another purpose. Swapping out personnel during proposal preparation can be disastrous. At best, it causes a break in continuity with a corresponding loss of time—a most precious commodity for proposals.

Build a matrix showing the required labor categories or skills and the time period they will be required. This can serve as a good checklist, and it will prove valuable in estimating the proposal budget.

In addition to personnel, you should identify any required facilities and systems necessary to prepare the proposal. Use your organization's proposal center or area, if you have one. Otherwise, locate the proposal team in a common area. This greatly enhances team communication. Leaving people in their regular offices generally is a bad idea. There are too many distractions and interruptions. Eventually you will have to seclude the proposal team if you hope to prepare a winning proposal.

If a separate group in your company is responsible for proposal publication, then coordinate future needs with the department manager. Again, this will enable adequate planning and prevent any unwanted surprises.

Also identify any special systems or processes necessary to prepare your proposal. These might include unique application software tools not normally available to employees, access to pricing systems, or special packaging. Many procuring agencies now require an electronic copy of your proposal via either floppy disc or compact disc. If so, make sure you have a CD "burner" and someone who knows how to use it.

Someone in your organization will probably want to know how much preparing the proposal is going to cost. Use information about resources and schedule to prepare a proposal budget. You may already have a preliminary budget established as part of your annual planning process. If so, update it with the specific information you used to identify resources. Include contingency funds in the budget to accommodate slips in schedule or extensions to the proposal. Also add a little money for things you forget. There is always something that slips through the cracks and unforeseen problems that require money to fix. Include costs for outside services, including consultants.

If you have people who normally charge their time directly to a contract, they will need a charge number to work on the proposal. Set up a charge number and make a list of everyone authorized to charge his or her time against that number. This information will be necessary to track charges to the proposal budget. It is essential if you plan to monitor and manage the proposal budget.

Update your proposal plan once you receive the final RFP.

COMMENTING ON DRAFT RFPS

Some procuring agencies release a draft RFP and ask bidders to comment on the draft and ask questions about the procurement. The customer uses these comments and questions as input to amend the final RFP. Normally, comments/questions and the customer's answers are provided to all potential bidders. So, be careful about what you ask because this information may be shared with your competitors.

Have the proposal team read the draft RFP and make notes. Make sure that at least one person reads the entire RFP. Note inconsistencies, missing information, and apparent ambiguities, and write candidate questions/comments. For each, identify the RFP reference—section number, title, and page number. Compile all the questions and then assemble the proposal team. Go through each question in detail to determine which questions will be submitted to the customer.

Like pre-proposal conferences, there are some general rules that should be followed in responding to a draft RFP. Again, you want to use this opportunity to positively impress the customer. Here are some recommended guidelines:

- Do not ask questions that display your ignorance, give competitors insight about your approach, reveal information you do not want everyone else to have, or address an issue that could produce an unwanted answer. If an RFP ambiguity can be used to your advantage, do not ask for clarification.
- If you make a recommendation, then explain its benefit to the customer. Be careful not to give the appearance of making a recommendation that is beneficial solely to your company. That will appear to be self-serving. You *should* make recommendations that give you an advantage; just frame them so they do not appear that way.
- Be sure that the clarity and quality of submitted questions match the same standards you use for final proposal material. Confusing questions will likely lead to irrelevant or confusing answers. Typographical and grammatical errors suggest a lack of attention to detail and connote inattentiveness.
- Do not use inflammatory language or cast questions in a way that appears to question the intelligence, decision-making ability, or integrity of the customer. Customers do dumb things all the time; let one of your competitors point out their shortcomings.
- Use a casual writing style that communicates respect. For example, "RFP section A states the transition period is 60 days, whereas Section B indicates the period is 90 days. Please clarify the correct transition period," is preferable to, "Why are the transition periods different for Section A and B? Only one can be correct."

It is okay to point out inconsistencies in the RFP or even disagree with an RFP requirement. Just do it gracefully and in a manner that does not appear to be argumentative.
- Organize questions/comments according to RFP section. Separate administrative comments concerning RFP typos, numbers out of sequence, missing information, etc. This will facilitate review by the customer.

WRITING PROPOSAL SECTIONS AGAINST THE DRAFT RFP

Starting early is prudent. Preparing an initial cut at your proposal using the draft RFP is a common practice and one I recommend. However, some caveats are in order.

You must have a good sense of how much the final RFP will change. Otherwise, a wholesale change in proposal requirements between the draft and final will frustrate your proposal team and waste a lot of money. A good knowledge of your customer and their typical practices in preparing draft and final RFPs is your best weapon. Beware of schedule slips in the release of the final RFP—they often forecast major RFP changes. When in doubt, focus on those RFP requirements that are least likely to change.

Starting early is one of the single most important contributors to proposal success. This advantage needs to be balanced against the downside risk of changing RFP requirements and conserving bid and proposal resources.

PROPOSAL TEAM TRAINING

An easy way to gain competitive advantage is to equip the proposal team with the skills and knowledge they will need to accomplish their proposal tasks successfully. Training the proposal team in some of the basics will significantly reduce their frustration level. It also will produce a windfall of increased productivity.

You have at least three options available for proposal training. First, you can send people to a professional proposal-training seminar. Several companies offer excellent proposal seminars. The downside of this approach is cost and timing. Second, you can bring in a consultant to train the proposal team. This approach enables you to control the training schedule. Finally, you can build and conduct your own proposal training, perhaps using the services of a proposal consultant to construct the course. (The information contained in this book provides the essential ingredients of a proposal course if you choose to go that route.)

The most effective proposal training is delivered during the pre-proposal phase, once you have a draft RFP. Using the draft as a training tool will make training relevant. It also enables training exercises to be structured so that they contribute to actual proposal development. Plan to spend two or three days training the proposal team.

If you build your own training, you can organize it to correspond with each step of the proposal development process. Here are my candidate proposal training topics:

- RFP organization—what is contained in each section (Chapter 2)
- Basic government source selection—what proposal teams need to know (Chapter 3)
- RFP analysis (Chapter 9)
- Building proposal storyboards and proposal outlines (Chapter 10)
- Basics of proposal themes, discriminators, features, and benefits (Chapter 10)
- Proposal writing and editing (Chapters 11 and 12)
- Basics of preparing the cost volume (Chapter 13)
- How to conduct proposal reviews (Chapter 14).

Even if you do not have a draft RFP available, the pre-proposal phase is still the best time to conduct proposal training. Having a draft RFP is a bonus that facilitates the relevance and carry-over value of training.

Each topic described in this chapter affords an opportunity to gain or yield competitive advantage. The pre-proposal phase marks a time of increased customer contact. Make the most of these contacts to favorably impress your customer and collect information to support bid strategy development and proposal planning. Use this information to make informed bid decisions. Avoid chasing opportunities with a low win probability. Plan and implement activities to position your organization effectively for the forthcoming procurement. Develop a preliminary proposal plan, train the proposal team, and write a first draft of your proposal. Get a head start on the competition—and keep it.

Chapter 7

Bid Strategy

If you decide to pursue a bid opportunity, then you *must* address the key question of how you plan to win. The operative word here is "plan." Those who develop a systematic set of actions focused on capturing a future procurement gain competitive advantage. Those who fail to develop a plan or bid strategy rely on luck. Or, they wrongfully imagine that they will win for some other reason, like being the most technically qualified. In the long run, it will be more profitable to take your money to Las Vegas than to spend B&P funds on efforts that lack a clear, well-defined bid strategy.

An effective bid strategy is one based on a careful evaluation of the customer, program requirements, potential competitors, and your team's capability. The outcome of this evaluation is a set of actions and plans that will enable you to capture the bid opportunity. Many organizations document their bid strategy in what is commonly referred to as a capture plan.

CUSTOMER ASSESSMENT

The customer is the procuring agency responsible for purchasing the goods or services that make up the bid opportunity. In addition, you may need to consider the ultimate user of those goods or services if they are part of the source selection process. The more information you have about the customer, the better. Consider the following information categories to focus your bid strategy on critical customer elements.

Customer Name/Organization

Identify the name of the procuring agency and the department or division responsible for the bid opportunity; list names and phone numbers for key customer personnel. Also, list users, if applicable, and identify key user contacts. For key players, identify any biases or concerns that could influence your bid approach. For example, are there any areas that the customer sees as high risk, or are there elements of a technical solution that would be viewed in a favorable light?

Customer Buying Pattern

On what basis does the customer award contracts? Does low cost always win? Or, are some procurements awarded based on best value? How close to the lowest bid do you have to be to win if you have a better technical solution? Does the customer have a favorite contractor? Over the last three years, who has won the most contracts from this customer? What is your success rate? Does the customer have a favorite or preferred technical solution, product, or manufacturer, or any other bias that could influence bid outcome?

If the customer always picks the low bidder, then an important bid strategy is set. Knowing biases toward competitors, suppliers, or technical solutions also provides important insights into bid strategy. Aligning your bid with the customer's biases and avoiding things they don't like will improve your win probability.

Customer Acquisition Strategy

Analyze the customer's acquisition plan. Does the customer normally publish a draft RFP, host pre-proposal conferences, ask for written responses to draft RFP material, conduct one-on-one discussions with bidders, require oral proposal presentations, require information about your past performance, conduct site visits, evaluate proposal and performance risk, issue evaluation notices, or ask for best and final offers? Knowing the typical acquisition process and the amount of time allotted for proposal preparation provides valuable information for proposal planning and strategizing. You also should be aware of the information required by a typical customer RFP. Some procurement agencies ask for a minimal amount of information. Others ask for everything but the kitchen sink. Does the agency typically request plans (quality, safety, software, systems engineering, configuration management, etc.) or résumés for key personnel? Does the agency limit the number of pages allotted for the proposal?

For planning purposes, determine the following:

- Procurement milestone and schedule (draft RFP, RFP, proposal due, contract award)
- Contract type and terms
- Period of contract performance and options
- Contract value
- Deliverables

- Any special requirements or certifications (security, quality, software, environmental, etc.).

Customer Documents

List available documents that define the customer's requirements, such as statements of work, specifications, statements of need, operational requirements documents, or draft RFP material. Include documents that define any pet processes the agency embraces or describe how they conduct source selection.

Past Performance with Customer

List every program you are currently performing, or have performed over the last five years, for this customer. For each program, identify any formal evaluation conducted by the government. List any problems such as cost or schedule overruns. Also, list any unique requirements and things you did well. Determine how you will overcome any negative image with the customer and how you will exploit instances of good performance or extraordinary achievements.

Having experienced a problem on a past program is not necessarily detrimental; it depends on how you handled the problem. At a minimum, you should be prepared to explain what measures you have taken to prevent comparable problems from occurring in the future. On the other hand, you can use good past performance to demonstrate your ability to perform successfully on future contracts.

Document the outcome of your customer assessment. This is an important component of developing a bid strategy.

PROGRAM REQUIREMENTS ASSESSMENT

Clearly defining program requirements is an important ingredient of making a bid decision and building a bid strategy. Requirements are defined by the technical effort required to perform the contract. This translates into requirements for technical disciplines, personnel, systems, processes, facilities, and any other specific need. Compare program information to the capability of your organization to identify strengths and weaknesses and to use as input into a bid strategy.

The following areas identify categories of information for defining program requirements. Document program requirements using these categories. A good summary of program requirements can easily be achieved within one or two pages. Keep it brief, but capture essential information.

Brief Description of Program Requirements

Provide a brief summary of program requirements. Differentiate between contracts that require you to develop a new product or modify an existing product and those that require you to provide services. For example:

> **Development contract:** *Design, develop, integrate, test, and install a new telecommunications system for the Alpha agency.*

> **Services contract:** *Provide sustaining engineering services and maintenance support of flight simulators at five U.S. locations for one base year and four one-year options.*

> Sometimes a contract may require both product development and services. For example: *Design, develop, integrate, test, and install a new telecommunications system for the Alpha agency and provide two years of operation and maintenance support after the system is installed.*

Contracts that require initial product development differ significantly from service-type contracts from a bid strategy perspective. Service contracts normally require you to provide people who perform services for your customer. Providing engineering services to a federal agency, performing aircraft maintenance for the U.S. Air Force, or providing instructors to teach audit procedures to IRS agents are all examples of service contracts. Normally, an incumbent contractor is currently performing those services. Hence, these competitions require you to unseat the incumbent. Or, they involve maintaining a contract you are currently performing. In many instances, you will be able to hire the incumbent workforce if you are the successful non-incumbent bidder.

Service contracts tend to be very cost-competitive, involve less risk, and generally offer a more restricted range of innovative solutions. Development contracts, on the other hand, often involve more risk and offer more opportunity to develop creative solutions.

Identify key program milestones as part of the program description. For development programs, these could include design reviews, system integration, customer acceptance testing, first article installation, and dates for completion of production units. For service contracts, milestones might include a transition period during which you assume responsibility for the contract, dates for the start of options, or any other significant program event.

Technical Disciplines Required

Identify the key technical disciplines required to perform the contract. Keep this general. You do not need to list every labor category required. Just note the key disciplines.

Personnel

Do you have the necessary personnel to perform the contract? If not, how will you overcome this shortcoming—subcontractors, contract labor, etc.? If there is an incumbent contractor, will you be able to hire the existing workforce? If not, how will you staff the program after contract award?

Sometimes the customer sets minimum qualifications or certification standards for technical personnel. Likewise, some customers set minimum experience and qualifications for key personnel. Make sure you are aware of such requirements and are prepared to meet them.

Processes and Systems

Does the program require any special or unique processes or systems? For example, a customer may require bidders to have an automated inventory control or maintenance data collection system. Other examples might include a specific computer-aided design (CAD) system, a video post-production studio, or numerically controlled manufacturing equipment. Such requirements can be important. They may give you or one of your competitors an advantage.

Does the customer require any specific certifications? Typical examples include a requirement for a quality assurance program certified to ISO 9000-series standards or software development processes that have been certified against the standards set by the Systems Engineering Institute (SEI) Computer Maturity Model (CMM®). Again, any required certification can become a source of competitive advantage. In some cases, companies try to get such certifications included in the solicitation to give them an advantage.

Location and Facilities

Does the procuring agency require any special facility requirements, or does it specify where work is to be performed? Sometimes it is an advantage to be located close to the customer. Occasionally the customer may require you to have an office within a specified distance from their office. In other cases, specialized facilities may be required. Just be sure you are aware of such requirements and have the ability to meet them.

Penalties and Other Special Requirements

Identify any contract penalties or special contract clauses. Penalties most often involve contracts where you operate or maintain a system for your customer. In these cases, the customer may withhold part of your regular payment if you fail to achieve a specified equipment availability rate or fail to restore a downed system within the allotted amount of time. Contract penalties create risk. They impact your overall program plan and bid strategy because they potentially affect profit.

Note any special contract requirements. They may define when and how contract options will be exercised, require that you obtain certain data to support product development, or require that you establish a working relationship with other contractors. They are important because they can impact your bid cost or technical approach or involve program risk.

COMPETITIVE ASSESSMENT

No one would climb into the ring for a title boxing bout without knowing his or her opponent. Likewise, no one shows up for the Super Bowl without having assessed the strengths and weaknesses of the team they are going to face. Nor would a general send troops into battle without information about the enemy. What works for sports teams and military encounters also applies to proposals. To state the obvious: You cannot expect to win if you do not know who you are competing against.

You should always know who your competition is and what they are likely to offer. Competitor analysis is a critical component of preparing a winning proposal. Collecting and organizing this information is an ongoing task. It is during the pre-proposal phase that competitor information is used to develop a bid strategy. In performing a competitor assessment, consider the following questions:

Who is your principal competition? List those companies you expect to bid.

What experience do they have with the customer? For each company, list current contracts with the customer. Assess the quality of performance for each contract as perceived by the customer. Do you have a copy of each contract? If not, get one. As indicated previously, keeping a copy of your competitors' contracts is a rich source of information about competitors, especially pricing information.

What is your past experience competing against each company? If you have competed against this company in the past, did you win? If so, what strategy did you use? If you lost, what strategy did the winner use? What could you have done to win?

What are the primary strengths of each competitor for this procurement? Strengths must be evaluated against the specific requirements of the procurement and the criteria that will be used to evaluate each bidder. This information is contained in RFP Section M. However, it is still fruitful to list potential strengths apart from RFP evaluation criteria. Moreover, you will want to develop a preliminary bid strategy before the RFP is released.

Evaluating Competitor Strengths and Weaknesses

Some typical categories to consider in evaluating competitor strengths include:

- *Experience*—length, extent, and relevance of company experience performing tasks comparable to those required by the procurement.
- *Personnel*—number and qualifications of personnel available to work on the contract and their experience performing comparable tasks. This can be a real strength if the customer knows and "likes" your key personnel.
- *Specific technical competency*—technical areas where the company has acquired a reputation for excellence: systems engineering, logistics, software development, system integration, component repair, instruction, manufacturing, maintenance, etc.
- *Facilities/location*—may be required for some procurements. If your competitor has specialized facilities and you do not, then that becomes strength for your competitor. Being located close to the customer may be seen as a positive, or it could be a contract requirement. Again, this could be a strength for one or more of your competitors.
- *Cost*—always a key component of a winning proposal. You must be knowledgeable about the cost strategies used by each competitor and how you compare with each in terms of cost competitiveness.
- *Other*—any unique areas where a competitor can demonstrate a strength. Do not overlook any area where a competitor can potentially gain advantage.

What are the primary weaknesses of each competitor for this procurement? Weaknesses, like strengths, must be assessed against the specific requirements of the procurement. Use the same areas listed above to evaluate potential competitor weaknesses.

How is each competitor likely to respond to the RFP? This question requires you to estimate how each competitor will approach the competition. In essence, it means that you must discern their bid strategy.

Performing the Assessment

Once you have compiled information about the customer, the procurement, and competitors, you are ready to perform a competitive assessment. This is where you compare your company against known competitors using all the available information. Two levels of comparison are required: one general and the other specific to the procurement at hand. For the general comparison, score yourself and each competitor using the bid decision criteria contained in Chapter 6 (Figure 6-1). This will provide a numerical score for each competitor and help highlight general areas of competitor strengths and weaknesses.

The specific assessment requires you to use the evaluation criteria contained in Section M of the RFP. These are the criteria the customer will use to score each proposal and select a winner. I recommend that you develop a matrix that lists probable competitors and evaluation criteria, as illustrated in Figure 7-1.

As shown, this example includes three competitors. It also shows evaluation criteria for three technical factors (T1, T2, and T3), two management factors (M1 and M2), and cost. For each evaluation criterion, compare the competitor with your company and determine if the competitor has a greater capability (+), an equivalent capability (=), or less capability (–) than your company. If evaluation criteria are not available, use your best estimate of those criteria, or use specific program requirements.

Once the RFP is released, you can verify and update your original estimates. Be sure to note any differences in the relative importance of evaluation criteria. A competitor strength in a highly weighted evaluation area is more significant than a strength in a less important area.

The competitive assessment should be performed by the group responsible for capturing the program. Have each person complete the competitive assessment individually. Then compare the results as a group. The ensuing discussion of differences in individual competitor assessments can provide the ingredients for a good brainstorming session. Disagreements in assessments may indicate the need for additional marketing information. Also, be honest. A common mistake is to underestimate competitors and overestimate your own capability. When in doubt, give the advantage to your competitor. The consequences of overestimating a competitor are less serious than the consequences of underestimating.

Figure 7-1. Sample Competitive Assessment

Company	Evaluation Criteria					
	T1	T2	T3	M1	M2	Cost
Competitor A	=	=	–	=	–	+
Competitor B	+	–	=	–	+	=
Competitor C	–	–	=	–	–	+

From the information gained from both the general and specific competitive assessments, develop a list of strengths and weaknesses for each competitor. Include your best estimate of the bid strategy each competitor will adopt for this competition. For each competitor strength, identify some potential ways you could counteract or overcome this strength. Likewise, for each competitor weakness, identify how you could exploit this weakness in your proposal.

DEVELOPING A BID STRATEGY

There is no easy way to explain how to develop a bid strategy—there are simply too many variables. Individual procurements vary too much to establish a standard. The best starting point is to assemble all the information you have gained about the customer, the program, and competitors. Look for any conceivable area where you can gain competitive advantage. What can you do to satisfy the customer's need better, fulfill a desire, avoid a risk, reduce cost, improve reliability, be more responsive, reduce customer workload, standardize systems or processes, offer more performance, enhance efficiency, or cater to a customer bias? What aspects of the program—technical requirements, people, processes, systems, facilities, personnel, schedule, etc.—offer potential opportunities to capture the upper hand? Is there any way you can leverage your capability? Are there trade studies or analyses you can perform to "ghost" the competition or enhance the perception of your approach? (Ghosting is a tactic whereby a competitor's weakness is highlighted by emphasizing your strength or by creating the impression that the competitor's approach is more risky or less desirable than what you are proposing.)

Review contract terms and conditions, contract type, period of performance, and special contract clauses to identify things you might do that are more clever than your competitors. Leave no stone unturned. Consider everything, no matter how trivial it may appear at first. From this dizzying array of information and possibilities, you must craft a bid strategy that will enable you to better the competition.

There are two levels of bid strategy. The first is general. It is an overall approach to the procurement that yields an overarching strategy. Most often general strategies revolve around cost. The second strategy is actually a series of strategies. Each is focused on a specific aspect of the procurement or a particular competitor strength or weakness.

General Strategy

The best way to illustrate an overarching bid strategy is by example.

Example 1: Marginally Compliant, Low Cost

Many years ago, I was recruited to start a new subsidiary for a major aerospace company. We planned to launch the new company by winning a major procurement. Unfortunately, we did not have any existing contracts. Nor did we have any specific technical capability apart from that of our parent company. All of the major competitors were firmly entrenched. Clearly, we were not going to win this competition by convincing the customer that we were technically superior.

Instead, we adopted an approach where our goal was to be technically compliant while offering a price that would be too attractive for the customer to refuse. We reviewed every element and aspect of the program to identify areas where we could reduce cost. We also focused on the major cost drivers, paying particular attention to ways we could minimize those costs. Personnel cost accounted for about 70 percent of our bid cost, so we did everything possible to reduce personnel.

Our strategy was a low-priced, marginally compliant approach. Our proposed solution was technically compliant, but just barely. We also took some risks. Every action and decision was based on providing the lowest-cost solution that met program requirements. In the end, we won a $150 million dollar contract with a bid significantly below the next higher bidder. In case you are wondering, yes, we bid profit, although at a relatively low rate.

Example 2: Best Value

In another case, I was working for a company whose cost structure made it unlikely they would be the low bidder. So, we adopted a best-value bid strategy. Best value means you will be able to convince the customer that the value of your solution is worth the higher cost. We attacked every program element with a view toward convincing our customer that we had the best approach—best performance, lowest risk, lowest lifecycle cost, easy maintenance, long-term supportability, etc. We emphasized value to the customer at every turn and "ghosted" less expensive approaches as being inadequate or risky. When the smoke had cleared, we won a $400M program with a bid more than 15 percent higher than the rest of the competition.

Example 3: Low-Risk Systems Integrator

The third example of an overarching strategy does not involve cost. In this case, the customer was an aircraft manufacturer who had just won a major contract to provide an integrated aircrew training system, including aircraft. They were required by the government to compete the ground-based training system.

Our analysis of customer and program requirements revealed the following: First, as the aircraft prime contractor, our customer was more interested in selling airplanes than worrying about the rest of the training system. Second, this was to be a completely integrated system. Finally, although the customer was a major aerospace company, the performing division was a recent acquisition, with a culture and operating style more akin to a small company.

From this information, we built a three-fold strategy. First, we emphasized a low-risk, technically compliant solution. Our intent was to ensure our customer that they would not have to worry about our approach—it was low risk and would not require them to divert energy or attention away from their primary focus of building airplanes. Second, every aspect of our approach and technical proposal emphasized a system engineering approach and the ease with which we would integrate our technical efforts with those of our customer. Finally, our organization was about a tenth the size of the other competitors. We went out of our way to stress that being a smaller company would be an advantage. We emphasized that we would be easy to work with, knew how to be a good subcontractor, and would follow the lead of our customer. This strategy, along with other specific strategies, enabled us to win the contract, which was one of the largest ever for this type of work.

Most often, general strategies involve only one focus. Occasionally, as in this example, the general strategy contained a multiple focus. Regardless, a general strategy covers your entire approach. It is the basis for making program decisions, and it must completely permeate your entire proposal.

Specific Strategies

Develop a specific bid strategy for every element of the procurement. These bid strategies should key off your competitive assessment. They are intended to offset a competitor advantage, exploit a weakness, or gain competitive advantage in a specific area.

Specific bid strategies do not need to be glamorous or earthshaking. Your goal is to achieve a better score than your competitors for each proposal area. You do not have to be great, just better. Home runs are nice, but most games are won by consecutive base hits. Moreover, you really do not have to be better than the competition. Instead, you only need to *convince* the customer that you are better. In the world of proposals, perception becomes the reality upon which source selection decisions are made. How you present your case is just as important as what you have to offer. Often, it is more important.

You must understand the customer thoroughly and search every single aspect of the procurement to identify areas where you can gain competitive advantage. Remember, you are just looking for an edge, a little something to nose ahead of the competitors.

If the customer requires an equipment availability rate of 95 percent, can you offer 97 or 98 percent without incurring any additional cost? Can you respond to customer service requests faster than the contract requires? If the contract requires a computer speed of 1GHz, can you offer something faster? If the customer asks you to walk a mile, can you go a mile and a quarter? Of equal importance, can you convince the customer that what you offer is better—that it offers a benefit?

What actions can you take to offset a competitor's strength? Can you add a subcontractor with equivalent or better capability? Is there any action you can take, or area you can emphasize, that will counteract this strength? For example, is there anything about your competitor's software development approach you can ghost? Go back and remind yourself of the problem the customer is trying to solve. What is important? Is it schedule, cost, reliability, supportability, portability to other applications, interface with legacy systems, software development environment, future ability to upgrade, or proprietary data rights? If you think hard enough, I bet you will come up with something tangible.

Consider performing some tradeoff studies or analyses that will enhance the perception of your approach or detract from that of your competitor. For example, imagine your competitor is going to host his new product on computer platform X. You plan to use platform Y. During the pre-proposal phase, you perform a tradeoff study that compares platforms X, Y, and Z. Amazingly, the results of your study show that platform Y is clearly superior to X and Z. In your proposal, explain how you performed the tradeoff study and share the results in a way that will cause the customer to question why anyone in their right mind would ever choose anything but platform Y. Document the study and offer in your proposal to provide a copy to your customer.

Here is another twist. Historically, your customer has had problems with contractors keeping track of requirements or with their ability to manage software configuration baselines. Highlight these as program risks and then explain how you will avoid them.

Developing specific bid strategies for competitor weaknesses uses the same process as for strengths. Only here you need to emphasize your capability (strength) and highlight the risk or shortcoming of a particular weakness. Be sure to demonstrate the customer benefit derived from your "strength."

There is rarely a situation where competitor strength cannot be neutralized. If you can counter competitor strengths, exploit their weaknesses, and highlight your own strengths, then you will win more than your share of contracts. Almost any issue, viewed in the proper perspective, can become a strength.

If you select a subcontractor, then highlight the advantage of the specialized skill, capability, or experience they offer and how this is going to benefit the customer. If practical, solicit information from multiple potential subcontractors and perform an analysis to select one. Use this information in your proposal to convince the customer that you have the best choice and to ghost a competitor who may have selected someone you rejected. Alternatively, if you do not have any subcontractors, explain how your approach avoids the risk of subcontractor management. This could be especially advantageous if one of your competitors is proposing subcontractors.

We have discussed cost as a general bid strategy. However, cost also can be a specific strategy. Look for cost strategies at each program element. Is there anything you can do to reduce cost that still fits within your overall bid strategy? Make sure that actions to reduce cost do not become a weakness in the eyes of the customer. Long-term contracts and those that include options may offer rich opportunities.

Review the RFP to fully understand how cost will be evaluated, again being vigilant to detect potential strategic advantages. For example, in a recent procurement, bidders were asked to propose as contract options a series of fairly expensive equipment relocations. Because the customer did not know in which year the relocations would be required, bidders were asked to include prices for each of nine option years following award of the basic contract. To determine total bid cost, the customer planned to add together the costs for *all* the options for each year of the contract. Although the relocation option might never be exercised, or at most, would be exercised once or twice, the price for all nine years was added together.

A possible bid strategy for this situation would be to first estimate the likely cost of probable relocations. Let's assume that our estimated relocation cost was $45,000. We would include this cost once in the first (base) year of the contract and bid "not separately priced" (NSP) for all of the relocation options. If we bid $45,000 for each of the nine option years, the evaluated cost would be $405,000. Bidding it for just the first year yields a $360,000 reduction in evaluated cost ($405,000–$45,000). It also increases profit by $45,000 if the option is never exercised because the cost is contained in the basic contract. Alternatively, this strategy involves risk. You could lose money if the customer exercises the option more than once. Therefore, every bid strategy decision must evaluate the corresponding risk-reward consequences. In this case, is a reduction of $360,000 in evaluated cost worth the risk?

Service Contracts

Building bid strategies for service contracts involves some special considerations. Most service contracts already are being performed by an incumbent contractor. If you are not the incumbent, then you must be clever enough to unseat the existing contractor. This can be difficult if the customer is reasonably satisfied with the incumbent's performance. To be successful, you must be innovative. To complicate matters further, service contracts tend to be brutally cost-competitive. Often, labor accounts for the vast majority of direct cost. Moreover, the Service Contract Act (SCA) covers many of these contracts. SCA contracts dictate, by geographical area, the minimum wage and benefits for specified labor categories. In such cases, the number of personnel proposed and your company's indirect costs and bid profit account for practically all the available cost variables.

In short, to win these contracts, you must bid fewer people, propose a cheaper skill mix, or have lower bid rates (overhead and G&A costs). Reducing head count to cut your bid cost may incur performance risk. At some point, it could result in your being eliminated from the competition. Reducing cost and remaining technically compliant can be a difficult balancing act. Yet, it may represent your best chance of securing a win.

If the customer truly considers value, then you can strategize about ways to increase the value—that is, benefit to the customer—or to reduce program risk as ways to gain competitive advantage. This assumes that you can do so without significantly increasing your cost. Otherwise, you must figure out how to cut cost. As described, you will need to evaluate every aspect of the program to identify potential areas for cost savings. I hate this terminology, but you must be able to "think outside the box." Here are two real-world examples.

Example 1. An existing contract required the contractor to provide instructors to teach flight simulator sessions and academics to Air Force pilots at multiple sites. Historically, this contract had been awarded to the lowest qualified bidder. Contract wages were governed by SCA. Under SCA, pay raises are determined by labor surveys performed by the Department of Labor. Delays in these surveys and generally inadequate wages were causing a high personnel turnover rate, which had been impacting contract performance. As contract recompetition approached, bidders were faced with a dilemma. Low cost seemed to be the winning formula. Yet it was clear that SCA wages would be insufficient to retain the necessary personnel.

This time the customer indicated that they would not just award to the low bidder, but would consider measures taken to retain the existing workforce. Working with the incumbent, we hired an outside personnel company to survey workers and determine what they valued in terms of salary and benefits. Although we bid SCA wages, we built a bonus, benefits, and work schedule program that matched the survey results. Our proposal received high marks, and we won the contract even though we were not the low bidder. In this case, we solved the customer's problem and mitigated program risk at an affordable price.

Example 2. In another case, an incumbent contractor was providing contractor logistics support for F-16 flight simulators and maintaining the simulator product baselines through sustaining engineering services. The simulators were driven by aging computer systems that were difficult and expensive to maintain. Moreover, multiple simulator software baselines had evolved over many years. This made software updates time-consuming and expensive. This was a fixed-price contract covered by the Service Contract Act.

As contract recompetition approached, the incumbent was concerned that another bidder would be able to undercut its cost significantly. To offset this potential, we developed a strategy focused on providing a best-value solution without increasing current contract cost. We determined that we could replace the old computers with a PC-based solution and pay for the upgrade with subsequent savings in support costs. This would give the customer all new computers, which improved performance and reduced both the time and expense of future software changes. In essence, the customer was getting a computer upgrade for free. This strategy proved successful, and the incumbent won a ten-year contract.

Again, this bid strategy incurred risk. First, the contract was for one base year and nine one-year options. It would take about six years to recover the expense of replacing the computers. If for some reason the contract was terminated early, then the company would lose money. Second, there was no guarantee that the customer would accept our offer to replace the computers. Knowing the program and the customer enabled us to mitigate these risks to an acceptable level.

Bidding As the Incumbent

Here are some strategic tips if you are the incumbent contractor. Start preparing for recompetition about twelve months ahead of time. Use this period to resolve any performance problems and go out of your way to please the customer, even if it cuts into your profit margin. Customers are more likely to remember your last year of performance than the preceding years. So, you have the opportunity to make up for past sins with good recent performance. Identify areas where the customer would like to see improvements, problems the customer is facing, or areas that could involve risk. Develop plans and strategies to attack these areas under the new contract. Review your staffing levels and look for ways to improve efficiency.

A common incumbent mistake is to bid the status quo. Do not rest on your laurels. There are plenty of innovative, hungry contractors just waiting to snatch away the contract. Bring in someone from outside the incumbent team to give you an independent assessment of your approach and bid strategy. Sometimes the incumbent team is too close to the contract to see possible areas of improvement.

Unless your performance has been abysmal, you have an inherent competitive advantage. Protect this advantage. Look for processes and systems to improve performance or efficiency that you can develop and implement at company expense before the contract is recompeted. This can make it doubly difficult for someone to unseat you because the benefits of such systems and processes do not remain with the contract. They belong to you. The customer may not want to lose them. Moreover, competing contractors may be hard-pressed to replace entrenched systems that are already in place and have a proven track record.

If you are not the incumbent, then you must convince the customer that it is worthwhile to replace the existing contractor. The customer must have a reason to switch. Start looking for valid reasons six to twelve months before the competition. Apart from poor performance, you must soundly beat the incumbent by a margin that justifies the risk of changing contractors. Ties go to the incumbent. To win, you will have to propose something that improves performance, reduces cost, mitigates risk, or otherwise satisfies a customer want, need, or desire. These are the basic ingredients from which a successful bid strategy is fashioned.

RISK/OPPORTUNITY COMPONENTS OF BID STRATEGY

Every bid carries with it a corresponding set of potential risks and opportunities. Both should be integrated into bid strategies. Risks arise from two interrelated sources. One involves the risks associated with performing the contract and its attendant terms and conditions. The other is generated by bid strategies themselves. Bidding a program with a payment penalty for failing to achieve equipment availability goals involves risk. So does bidding NSP for relocation options rather than fully pricing each one, or bidding a computer upgrade with a six-year payback period.

Risks must be balanced by the expected gain or advantage they offer. Take the availability penalty as an example. Assume that availability is a function of the number of maintenance personnel and the depth of spare parts. Decreasing either people or material reduces bid cost but decreases availability in this simplified example. The advantage of a lower price must be weighed against the risk of incurring a payment penalty and the size of that penalty, forgetting momentarily the potential impact on your relationship with the customer. The amount of risk your company is willing to accept may represent a significant part of a winning bid strategy. Sometimes, the winning contractor is the one who accepts the greatest amount of risk or is able to develop a unique or innovative way to mitigate risk.

The flip side of risk is opportunity. Every bid carries with it some opportunities beyond those represented by winning the contract. Potential opportunities include future additions to contract value via engineering change proposals, the chance for follow-on work, growing market share, maintaining dominance in a particular area, protecting an area or contract from assault by competitors, or as the gateway to future procurements.

Occasionally, customers procure programs in phases. You must win one of the initial contracts to remain in the competition. A current procurement trend within DoD is the use of indefinite delivery/indefinite quantity (ID/IQ) contracts. These contracts serve as "gateways" for future contracts. That is, you must win one of them to either receive or compete for future business.

Clearly, future potential opportunities, or the strategic value afforded by a contract, must be considered in developing bid strategies. Risks and opportunities must be weighed and balanced to arrive at a bid approach acceptable to your organization. You may be willing to accept a higher level of risk on a contract because of the opportunities it represents. Note that risk always translates into money. So, accepting a higher level of risk means that you are willing to risk some of your profit.

In other cases, you may simply bid a lower profit margin as a way to gain access to future business or in hope of increasing contract value. You may be willing to accept a 3 percent profit (versus 7 percent) on the initial contract if you believe that there is a good chance to add future work at a profit margin of 12 percent. Bidding lower increases the probability that you will win. Future work at a higher margin will enable you to realize a reasonable profit over the life of the contract, but perhaps lower than if you won the program at the higher (7 percent) initial rate.

There are always tradeoffs. The key is to assess thoroughly the risks and opportunities associated with a bid and integrate this information into your bid strategies. In Chapter 4, we discussed how to perform a strength–weakness–opportunity–threat analysis for each unique line of business being pursued by your organization. This same general approach can be applied to a specific bid opportunity. (See Figure 4-2 for a sample form.)

THE WHEN AND WHO OF DEVELOPING BID STRATEGIES

Bid strategies are not developed in a single sitting. They evolve over time as you accumulate information about the bid opportunity, the customer, and competitors. You should start as soon as you have enough information to begin formulating strategies. As new information becomes available, continue developing and refining your strategies. You should plan to have a general set of strategies in place before the RFP is released. However, strategizing often continues throughout much of the proposal development phase. It may extend up until just before the proposal is submitted. You are not finished until you are satisfied that no further improvements are possible.

It is amazing how much a new piece of information or fresh insight can alter a given bid strategy. Be prepared to turn those insights into strategies if it will improve your win probability. Nonetheless, you must remain mindful of the fact that it takes time to integrate a new or altered strategy into your proposal. So, there are some limitations.

Bid strategy development is a team activity. The person responsible for capturing the bid opportunity should lead the team. You may want to include representation from marketing, proposal and program management, plus technical and cost personnel, as appropriate. Of greater importance is the ability of team members to integrate a lot of information into bid strategies that are capable of helping you gain competitive advantage. At least one member should be a seasoned veteran in the art of bid strategy development. Such individuals tend to be quite rare. If you do not have someone with these credentials, then consider hiring a consultant to help with this part of the bid process, at least for strategically important bid or "must win" situations.

The best strategies come out of intense brainstorming sessions. Do not discard seemingly preposterous ideas. Great strategies occasionally find their origin in what may initially appear to be sheer craziness. Also, create an environment where vehement disagreement among team members is allowed to occur. Some of the best strategies emerge from intense disagreement, sometimes highlighted by shouting and bordering on fisticuffs. Conflict is often the handmaiden of creativity. Just be sure you have team members who can disagree to the point of strangulation, go away and lick their wounds, and then return to work as effective members of the team.

CAPTURE PLAN

Many organizations document the outcome of their bid strategy development in what is commonly referred to as a capture plan (see Appendix A for a sample). As the name implies, this plan contains the actions and strategies that will be implemented to capture the target business opportunity.

Building a capture plan has several advantages. First, it formalizes the strategy development process and creates a legitimate end product. The danger of informal processes is that they may never produce a tangible product. For bid strategies, this amounts to a lot of talk but no action. Second, a documented plan can be distributed easily to proposal team members. This will greatly enhance their ability to integrate elements of the plan into the proposal or to offer critical recommendations concerning the plan itself.

Of all the actions you can take to gain competitive advantage, developing and implementing a bid strategy should be near the top of your list. Few activities pay as rich a dividend. Rigorously collect, document, and analyze information about the customer, program requirements, and competitors. Use this information to develop general and specific bid strategies. Seize every opportunity to gain advantage over competitors regardless of how minor an advantage may appear. Added together, many small or even trivial advantages equal a noticeable difference, which may be enough to win the competition.

Exploit the talents of your capture team by creating a working environment that fosters creativity. Refine bid strategies over time. Remain flexible and be willing to adjust a strategy based on new information or perspective. Take measured steps to ensure that bid strategies are reflected in your proposal. Otherwise, their development will only amount to an academic exercise.

Chapter 8

Building and Organizing the Capture Team

Acquiring new business is a team activity. A frequently used approach is to establish a "capture team" and give it responsibility for securing a piece of new business. Capture teams consist of a leader and a core group of managers to oversee proposal and program development.

Ultimately, the effectiveness of the capture team is a key determinant of whether you win or lose. The team members develop and implement your bid strategy and lead the proposal development effort. Here is an all-too-typical scenario that illustrates this point.

An organization has properly positioned itself with the customer. They have good past performance, a superior technical solution, and an affordable price. Yet, at the end of the day, they lose the contract. The culprit? A poorly prepared proposal—one that failed to clearly articulate the technical solution, failed to show its benefits to the customer, and generally failed to effectively communicate the right message. This mistake happens every day. Its genesis is a failure to recognize the key ingredients of team effectiveness and the unique skills required of capture team members.

A host of factors contribute to team effectiveness. Clearly, the skill and relevant experience of individual capture team leaders is a significant factor. So is the way they are organized and managed. Yet an often-overlooked ingredient of team success depends upon team members knowing and executing their team assignments.

A basketball play known as the "pick and roll" provides an example. The team that has the ball executes this play near the defender's goal. One player sets a "pick" by placing himself between the defender and his teammate who is dribbling the ball toward the basket. When the defender goes around the pick to cover the ball handler, the player setting the pick "rolls" away from the defender and heads toward the basket. As the defender approaches the ball handler, he lobs the ball over the defender's head to the other player, who is now temporarily unguarded. With a clear path to the basket, the player who had set the pick now completes a lay-up and scores two points.

As this play unfolds, the other team members draw their defenders away from the action to clear the path to the goal. The pick and roll works when everyone knows the play and faithfully executes their assigned role and responsibilities.

Answering the question "who gets involved and when?" is an important part of your new business planning activities. Having the role, responsibility, and authority of each participant defined is a vital part of team success. The absence of defined roles for business and proposal development personnel during the new business development process can undermine the effectiveness of your bid pursuit efforts. This is especially true as a bid opportunity transitions from a pure marketing activity to one that requires the participation of other capture team members.

Organizations that have a well-defined plan to direct new business activities and assigned roles and responsibilities for each development phase gain competitive advantage. Those who do not implement such plans often suffer the consequences of disjointed and uncoordinated new business development efforts. Key long-range positioning and pre-proposal activities under these circumstances fail to adequately support downstream proposal development efforts—with regrettable consequences.

Select, organize, and manage your capture team to maximize the effectiveness of new business development activities. Implementing a well-structured and well-defined capture team environment will prove to be a worthwhile effort that will enable you to capture competitive advantage at the same time.

CAPTURE TEAM MEMBERS

Plan to appoint a capture manager as soon as an opportunity appears legitimate, but no later than once a preliminary bid decision is made (see Chapter 7). The capture manager remains in place from the time the opportunity is recognized until a contract is awarded or the opportunity is abandoned. Other key members of the capture team should include the following:

- Proposal manager
- Program manager
- Production manager/proposal administrator
- Technical volume manager
- Cost volume manager
- Contracts manager
- Marketing manager.

Regardless of proposal size, each position must be filled. Except for marketing, these positions typically require only part-time participation during the early stages of the new business lifecycle. Depending upon the size and scope of the proposal, some positions may remain staffed at the part-time level throughout the proposal development phase. For example, few business opportunities require a full-time contracts manager.

Apart from the largest proposals, the role of capture manager can be filled by either the proposal manager or the program manager. The choice depends upon the qualifications of available personnel. The best combination is when the same person fills the role of capture manager and proposal manager. This enhances the integration of bid strategies into the proposal. Nonetheless, in some cases the program manager is the better choice.

CAPTURE TEAM ORGANIZATION

Organizationally, the capture manager is responsible for the entire bid effort. Figure 8-1 shows a typical capture team organization. The program and proposal managers report directly to the capture manager. They work closely together, yet each has a different set of roles and responsibilities.

The proposal manager is responsible for the proposal. The program manager is responsible for efforts related to defining the program and building a program plan. Everyone else works for and reports to the proposal manager.

Figure 8-1. Sample Capture Team Organization

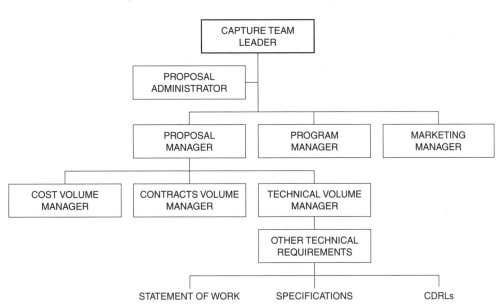

People assigned to prepare the technical proposal work for and are supervised by the technical volume manager. Likewise, additional cost personnel assigned to the proposal work for the cost manager. These roles, responsibilities, and reporting relationships apply only to the proposal. They are different from those normally in effect outside the proposal.

For small proposals, or for small organizations, one person may fulfill multiple proposal roles. However, I strongly advise against having the same person serve as both proposal and program manager. A common tendency is to pick people with excellent technical experience but little proposal experience to manage proposals. With few exceptions, this is a mistake. Managing proposals requires unique skills and knowledge that cannot be acquired from the normal work environment. Your proposal win probability will be higher if you use a proposal manager with demonstrated expertise and extensive experience in proposal development.

CAPTURE TEAM ROLES AND RESPONSIBILITIES

To avoid confusion among individual proposal members, develop a matrix of roles, responsibilities, and authority for key members of the capture team. Get management to approve this matrix and implement it on individual proposals. Make sure you communicate this information to relevant managers in your organization and members of the capture team.

Capture Manager Role

The role of the capture manager is to organize and coordinate all of the activities required to pursue the opportunity and prepare a proposal. He or she calls the plays. The capture manager is responsible for developing the bid strategy, briefing senior management about the opportunity and keeping them apprised of bid progress, and overseeing proposal planning and development. The capture manager coordinates pre-proposal and proposal activities with other elements of the organization, plus any major subcontractor or consultant efforts.

The capture manager should lead meetings with the customer and approve any customer communications such as those prepared in response to a draft RFP. Marketing still plays a full role in the business development process, but now falls under the authority of the capture manager. The capture manager bridges the gap between marketing and proposal development and provides a focal point totally responsible for capturing a piece of new business.

Capture managers must have the authority to carry out their assigned duties. Otherwise the effectiveness of their role is eroded to the point of destroying the value of the position. Under normal circumstances, this means that the capture manager should control the B&P budget and report to senior management. Most likely this will be the head of new business development (marketing) or program management.

Proposal Manager Role

The proposal manager works for the capture manager or holds both positions. He or she is completely responsible for planning and preparing the entire proposal. The simplest proposals require a technical volume and separate volumes or sections for cost and contracts. Many proposals require additional material. Typical examples include an executive summary, a statement of work, or a past performance volume.

The proposal manager builds the proposal schedule, prepares proposal outlines and writing guides for authors, verifies proposal assignments, prepares the proposal directive, conducts the proposal kickoff meeting, and manages day-to-day proposal activities. He or she ensures that the proposal complies with all RFP requirements, integrates bid strategies into the proposal, works with authors and technical personnel to identify features and benefits to include in the proposal, plans and coordinates proposal reviews, and makes the final decisions concerning every aspect of the proposal. The proposal manager also manages the preparation of responses to government questions after the proposal is submitted and leads the preparation of any required oral presentations or site surveys.

Program Manager Role

The program manager also works for the capture manager or holds both positions. The program manager is responsible for executing the program at contract award. He or she should be assigned as soon as a favorable bid decision is made. His or her role is to participate in the development of bid strategies and to approve decisions that will impact subsequent program planning and execution. Typical areas include the selection of subcontractors, technical solutions proposed, program schedules, staffing levels, and pricing inputs.

Important decisions that affect the potential success of the program are made during the pre-proposal and proposal development stages. It only makes good sense that the person ultimately responsible for the outcome of those decisions be involved. Being responsible for executing the plan contained in the proposal forces some accountability into this part of the bid process. It also helps ensure continuity between proposal development and program execution. Trying to manage a program where you did not participate in the technical solution, staffing, cost, and contractual commitments contained in the proposal truly defines the term "pig in a poke."

Production Manager/Proposal Administrator Role

Reporting to the proposal manager, the proposal production manager (sometimes called the proposal administrator) is responsible for formatting and producing the final proposal and packaging it for delivery to the customer. This person ensures that the proposal follows all RFP format requirements, conforms to all proposal directives, and conforms to any company publication standards. He or she handles all of the administrative tasks required to produce both review and final copies of the proposal. This includes things like making tabs and dividers, ordering binders, preparing the proposal cover, building spines for binders, coordinating and integrating proposal graphics, building tables of contents for each proposal volume, making copies to meet proposal delivery requirements, and producing electronic copies of the proposal if required. The proposal administrator also coordinates proposal editing, creates regular backups of proposal material, and manages proposal configuration to maintain the most current version of draft and final proposal material.

Technical Volume Manager Role

The technical volume manager is responsible for preparing the technical volume of the proposal, plus any attachments that address technical content. For smaller proposals, the program manager may fulfill this responsibility. For major proposals, individual volume managers may be assigned to oversee separate portions or volumes of the technical proposal. The technical volume manager often is a participating author as well as manager. He or she also reads draft proposal sections to ensure that they comply with the proposal outline and checks content for technical accuracy and compliance with program decisions.

Cost Volume Manager Role

The cost volume manager is responsible for preparing the cost volume of the proposal. This involves more than just "plugging in numbers." Many proposals require cost volume narratives that describe your basis of estimate—how you arrived at your cost—plus information about your company's indirect rates, escalation factors, forward-pricing rates, cost of money, and myriad other factors that contribute to your overall proposed price.

Based on RFP instructions, the cost manager must determine how the effort will be priced and presented in the cost volume. Some factors include whether or not pricing is in calendar or fiscal year; whether labor will be reflected in person hours, months, or years; and whether costs will be shown by month, quarter, or year. The cost manager also must work with the technical team to get costing input and with the persons in your company responsible for obtaining material and any other costs besides labor.

Working with the program manager, the cost manager also develops a list of labor categories to be used in the bid and obtains direct labor rates for each. The cost manager develops (or helps the program manager develop) the work breakdown structure (WBS) to gather cost information. In some cases, customers require cost information in special forms or formats. If so, the cost manager must prepare and include them in the cost volume.

Some RFPs require that cost information be entered only for CLINs listed in Section B. For these cases, you are not required to submit any additional cost information with your proposal. This may appear to simplify the costing exercise. However, cost build-ups, bases of estimates, and time-phased costs for each element of the WBS (separated by labor category and material) are still required to support subsequent program management.

Contracts Manager Role

The role of the contracts manager is to read the draft and final RFPs to determine if the applicable terms and conditions are acceptable to the company, and to identify any special RFP clauses that require management attention. The contracts manager completes representations and certifications required by the RFP and prepares any additional information that needs to be included in the contracts section of the proposal.

Occasionally, the RFP includes a model contract or list of attachments that must be completed and returned with the proposal. Typical attachments include statements of work, product or system specifications, small business subcontracting plans, or any other information that will become part of the final contract. The contracts manager normally does not prepare these documents but is responsible for including them in the final proposal.

The contracts manager also is the primary interface between your company and the government contracting officer. Once a final RFP is released, all correspondence between your company and the customer should flow through the contracts manager.

Marketing Manager Role

The role of the marketing manager is to position the company strategically with the customer for the forthcoming bid. The marketing manager collects information about the customer, program requirements, and competitors to support bid decisions and the development of bid strategies. He or she also coordinates information exchange between the capture team and the customer and coordinates customer visits.

Generally, marketing is most heavily involved and assumes a lead role during long-range positioning and the pre-proposal phases. For activities related to the bid being pursued, the marketing manager reports directly to the capture manager once a capture team is established.

Marketing has a tendency to disappear once an RFP is received. However, you lose a valuable resource if the marketing manager is not available or fails to participate during proposal development. Marketing does not need to write the proposal, but their customer insight and knowledge of competitors should be readily available to the capture team. If practical, have the marketing manager participate in proposal reviews as well as any other key proposal decision-making meetings.

Other Proposal Functions

These proposal roles represent the minimum. Additional assignments may be necessary to prepare other documents required by the RFP. If the RFP requires a past performance volume, for example, then you may need to assign another manager to oversee its preparation. Requirements for additional technical documents should be organized under the technical volume manager.

The term "manager" in this context is not meant to convey someone who only oversees the work of others. Instead, it refers to the person responsible for ensuring that the work gets done.

Most B&P budgets will not stand the burden of pure managers. So, everyone should have a proposal assignment in addition to his or her role as manager. The cost manager, for example, is clearly a working-level assignment. To the maximum extent practical, have people serve multiple proposal roles. B&P resources are precious and need to be preserved. At the same time, do not scrimp and do not overburden people with too many proposal assignments. The key here is balance.

REQUIRED QUALIFICATIONS FOR CAPTURE TEAM LEADERS

Theoretically, organizations assign their most talented and experienced personnel to work on proposals. After all, proposals are the lifeblood of future business and the prerequisite for survival in the world of competitive contracts. In reality, the more likely scenario is that the best available people will be assigned to the proposal. Hence, in most cases, you will have a mix of talent and experience.

People assigned to the proposal effort generally have other jobs. They may be unwilling participants in a process they do not fully understand, and they may be unaccustomed to the hectic work requirements dictated by proposals. These shortcomings can be overcome with a seasoned proposal manager and a core team of experienced capture-team leaders. A short training course on proposal basics is always a good idea and can be used to familiarize the proposal team with essential skills (as highlighted in Chapter 6).

The output of your capture team will be no better than the quality and experience of the people assigned to it. People who hold leadership positions on the capture team, therefore, must have significant proposal experience. This is especially true for the capture team manager and proposal manager—and doubly true whenever the proposal team includes inexperienced members. As a benchmark, expect key capture and proposal managers to receive pay and status comparable to or better than senior engineers and technical personnel in your organization. Otherwise, you may surrender competitive advantage to companies willing to adequately compensate people with skills crucial to their future business success.

The following are some recommended requirements for capture team managers.

Capture Manager

Specific knowledge required for capture managers includes: (1) a broad understanding of your company's organization, strategic plan, products, services, personnel, technical capability, and costing policies; (2) familiarity with the customer and its technical requirements, acquisition policies, and methods for evaluating proposals; (3) keen awareness of potential competitors; (4) experience in developing and implementing bid strategies; and (5) solid knowledge and experience in proposal development.

Proposal Manager

Ideally, the proposal manager will have similar fundamental knowledge as the capture manager. Additional knowledge areas required of proposal managers include: (1) thorough and detailed understanding of the acquisition and source selection process; (2) ability to translate bid strategies into proposal narrative; (3) complete knowledge of all facets of proposal development—RFP analysis, development of proposal outlines, storyboards, themes, features/benefits, author guides, proposal reviews, etc.; (4) understanding of desktop publishing concepts; (5) ability to develop a detailed plan and manage all proposal activities to achieve that plan; (6) knowledge of the proposal review process; and (7) ability to manage and effectively interact with a wide diversity of people and technical disciplines in a high-pressure work environment. Although not a critical prerequisite, a good general technical background is a real asset for proposal managers, as are good writing and editing skills.

On the personal side, proposal managers must be able to lead and motivate the proposal team. This often requires the combined grace of a saint and the heartless perseverance of Attila the Hun. At times, proposals require a tough taskmaster to maintain a rigorous development schedule. At other times, they require a sympathetic ear. An effective proposal manager knows when and how to exhibit either behavior.

Proposal Administrator

The proposal production manager, or proposal administrator, must have experience formatting and preparing proposals for federal procurement agencies. Additional skills and knowledge include: (1) expertise in desktop publishing and whatever software products—word processing, graphics development, etc.—your company uses to prepare proposals; (2) ability to extract proposal format and packaging instructions from an RFP and turn them into proposal production instructions; (3) ability to coordinate and integrate graphics into the proposal; (4) ability to manage the configuration of proposal sections to ensure that proposal personnel are using the most current version; and (5) capability to coordinate all the production activities necessary to produce, package, and deliver the proposal to the customer.

The proposal administrator works closely with the proposal manager. Attention to detail and the ability to maintain discipline of production activities are attributes of effective proposal administrators.

Technical Volume Manager

The technical volume manager must have previous experience preparing and overseeing technical proposals. This person should have sufficient technical expertise to verify the accuracy of technical information contained in the proposal. He or she also must have the ability to determine if the proposal narrative complies with RFP requirements. This is a more difficult task than it first appears.

RFP compliance covers two areas. One is the technical requirements defined by the RFP. The second is compliance with RFP requirements for narrative content: Does the proposal section clearly and completely provide all the information requested by the RFP?

If practical, the program manager also can serve as the technical volume manager. However, the program manager must have sufficient proposal experience and skills to meet the qualifications of a technical volume manager. Otherwise, it is better to have two separate people fill these proposal positions.

Cost Volume Manager

The cost volume manager must be thoroughly familiar with your company's pricing policies and systems. This includes all of the factors required to prepare a cost proposal for the government. The cost manager must be capable of extracting costing requirements from the RFP and possess an understanding of how the customer will evaluate the submitted cost proposal. This person also should be able to contribute to the development and integration of pricing strategies. The ability to develop a program WBS, help other proposal team members prepare a basis of estimate to support the cost proposal, and prepare any required cost proposal narrative are additional requirements for the cost volume manager.

Contracts Manager

The contracts manager must be well versed in the Federal Acquisition Regulation (FAR), plus any supplemental regulations your customer uses. He or she must be able to identify any RFP terms, conditions, or special contract clauses that involve risk or require special attention by the proposal team or management. Likewise, this person should be capable of spotting terms or conditions that might give you an advantage in developing a bid strategy.

USING CONSULTANTS

Properly employed, consultants can provide an excellent, cost-effective way to supplement your capture team. Consultants also can help fill voids whenever qualified people from your organization are unavailable to support proposal activities. Consultants can contribute in three general areas: capture/proposal management, technical expertise, and subject matter expertise.

Proposal consultants potentially provide a level of experience and expertise that may not be readily available in your organization. They can be especially valuable in developing and implementing bid strategies and in performing the myriad tasks required to prepare a winning proposal. Many consultants will manage the entire proposal effort and help write the proposal. Alternatively, you may want to use a consultant only to perform selected proposal tasks, like helping develop the bid strategy or conducting a review of your proposal before it is delivered to the customer.

Technical consultants provide assistance in cases where you need specialized expertise that is not available within your organization, or when you want to use the credentials of the technical expert in your proposal. Many years ago I bid a program where we were required to purchase two wide-body aircraft. No one in our organization had ever done that before. Therefore, we hired a person who had 25 years' experience purchasing commercial aircraft. He helped us write our proposal and then worked with us after we won the contract.

Technical consultants also can be used to supplement your proposal team whenever you have a staffing shortfall. In busy organizations, it often is difficult to get the level of technical expertise you would like to have assigned to the proposal. If so, a consultant may provide a cost-effective solution.

The third group of consultants is generally referred to as subject-matter-experts (SMEs). These are people who have specialized knowledge that can be applied to improve the quality of your proposal. They may possess information necessary to demonstrate that you understand the problem being addressed by your proposal.

SMEs may be representatives of the people who will use your proposed product or service. For example, a company bidding to provide aircrew-training services to F-15 pilots may want to hire a retired F-15 pilot. In this case, they could draw upon the SME's knowledge to gain insight into current training operations or to better understand the operational environment where training will be conducted.

SMEs can be used in any area where you need knowledge or insight that is not available from your own organization. Often these are people who previously worked for the government or one of your competitors.

Companies that use proposal consultants effectively gain competitive advantage over those who do everything themselves. Test this logic. Some proposal consultants have a demonstrated win record of 90 percent. If they work for you, you have statistically a 9 in 10 chance of winning, everything else being even. If they work against you, and you do not have someone of equal capability, you have statistically a 9 in 10 chance of losing. You be the judge of where the competitive advantage lies.

Assessing Your Need for Consultants

There is a general misperception that small companies have a greater need for consultants than their larger counterparts. Indeed, small companies may have limited personnel available to work on proposals. Yet, my experience suggests that this is a misperception. Proposal consultants can be used cost-effectively regardless of company size.

Of greater concern than organization size is the value of the bid opportunity, the complexity of the proposal required, the level of competition, and expected profit margins for the type of business being pursued. The proper comparison is the cost of preparing a proposal with and without the consultant, the corresponding win probability, and the amount of profit to be realized if you win the program. An effective proposal management consultant should be able to reduce your bid costs, increase win probability, or both. Otherwise, you are better off using in-house talent.

For companies that bid many small procurements, it may be more efficient to use a consultant for selected portions of the bid cycle. Alternatively, you might consider having the consultant review your proposal process and make recommendations for improvements, or work with you on several proposals in a mentoring role to train your own staff.

Selecting Consultants

Properly selected and used, consultants can significantly improve your proposal win probability and help reduce your B&P costs. The key is selecting people who can positively contribute to the success of your organization. Picking technical consultants or SMEs generally is fairly straightforward. You simply select someone who has the required technical credentials or experience. However, if you expect them to write a proposal section, then look for someone with at least three to five years of significant proposal experience.

Picking effective proposal management consultants is more difficult, perhaps because good proposal skills are hard to define and identify. Here are some recommendations for selecting and using a proposal consultant to serve as capture team leader or proposal manager.

Pick a consultant with at least ten years of proposal management experience and someone who has been working as a proposal consultant for at least three years. Do not use someone who just got started, regardless of their past experience. Ask for and verify client references. Obtain a list of the consultant's proposal activity for the last five years, including a list of winning proposals. Look for someone who has worked for multiple clients and across multiple procuring agencies. Avoid consultants who have gained all of their experience at one company. He or she may be an excellent consultant, but there is no way to tell given such a narrow track record.

Finally, select a consultant with a demonstrated record of winning proposals. At a minimum, choose a consultant with a consistent win record above 70 percent. Over the last 15 years, I have maintained a win rate between 85 and 93 percent. Other proposal consultants have comparable or better records. However, be fair in your assessment. Sometimes companies lose for reasons well beyond the proposal consultant's control.

Once you have identified a consultant who meets these criteria, ask for a statement of work that clearly identifies the scope of work to be performed by the consultant and the period of performance. Some consultants provide advice and assistance. Others provide hands-on management. A few will even write selected proposal sections or edit the proposal for you in addition to managing the proposal. Make certain you know what you are paying for.

The consultant's statement of work should identify how he or she will charge their time (daily or hourly), how and when they will submit invoices, and any other direct expenses, such as travel. Some proposal management consultants will prepare your proposal for a fixed price, and others will discount their billing rate contingent upon a bonus if you win. Tailor the payment structure to what you need. Also make sure you have the consultant sign a nondisclosure statement that legally prevents them from disclosing proprietary or company-confidential material.

PROPOSAL MANAGEMENT

Managing a proposal to the government is among life's most demanding challenges. It is not for the weak of heart. Nor is it something sane people do for very long. Yet there is no doubt that the proposal manager plays a crucial role. His or her ability to effectively orchestrate the seemingly infinite number of tasks required to prepare a proposal has a direct impact on the success of your bid efforts. There is no substitute for talent and experience or the demonstrated ability to lead teams. Having an established proposal process in place, along with the necessary proposal development tools, is another essential ingredient of proposal management success.

The majority of this book addresses procedures, guidelines, tips, and recommendations that can be applied effectively to manage proposals. Part 3 is devoted solely to the process of proposal development. It provides techniques and instructions on how to analyze customer requirements and prepare a winning proposal. Implementing and monitoring the success of these processes is the responsibility of the proposal manager, assisted by capture team managers.

The proposal manager, in addition to orchestrating the seemingly unending number of tasks required to prepare a proposal, must decide in advance how to manage the proposal team and create an effective work environment. Within this context, he or she will continuously battle issues like maintaining proposal schedule, keeping the team on track to prepare a completely responsive proposal, and maintaining a system of effective communications.

The proposal manager must be prepared to deal with a host of management issues. For example, how will you handle a situation where a proposal member is not capable of performing the assigned proposal task? What will be your policy for missed deadlines? How will you deal with interpersonal conflict on the team? Decide in advance. Determine your proposal policy, set a work schedule, and develop the groundrules that define the type of working environment you plan to establish. Communicate this information to the proposal team so everyone is reading from the same page.

Effective proposal management is yet another brick in the house of competitive advantage. Do it well and you will succeed more often than not. Stumble and the entire team falls with you.

Management Style

Apart from the roles and responsibilities previously discussed in this chapter, proposal managers play three separate roles: coach, cheerleader, and commandant.

As coach, their job is to ensure that each player is properly prepared and equipped to perform his or her assigned proposal tasks. This includes providing proposal team training, developing tools to help proposal authors (see Chapter 10), and giving authors timely feedback about their performance.

As cheerleader, the proposal manager must encourage the proposal team. This is especially important when things are not going well, like after a devastating red team review, a long succession of long workdays, or the demoralization of an RFP amendment that requires a major change to the proposal.

As commandant, the proposal manager often must make difficult and unpopular decisions. He or she also must occasionally push the team beyond its natural endurance level or confront an author who is not meeting the schedule. In other instances, the proposal manager must impersonate Attila the Hun to get timely support from other parts of the organization.

Work Environment

Proposals are not developed in a democratic environment. Everyone does not get an equal vote. Things move too fast, and many of the keys to winning appear illogical or even nonsensical to the uninitiated. Informed decisions need to be made quickly by the proposal manager and followed to the letter by the proposal team. Everyone should be allowed an input, but the proposal manager makes the final decision.

This probably sounds harsh. It may be an alien concept for many. Nonetheless, this type of dictatorial work setting typically is necessary to conserve time and prepare a proposal that complies with all RFP requirements. Therefore, it is critical that proposal members trust the ability and leadership of the proposal manager. Otherwise, they will have a difficult time following his or her leadership.

Effective proposal managers quickly instill this type of trust in their proposal team. How they achieve this trick varies according to the basic management style of each individual.

Proposal Work Schedule

Everything else being even, the amount of time devoted to preparing your proposal is directly related to win probability. Generally, the more time you spend, the higher the probability—unless, of course, you waste time or have an ineffective process. Hence, maximizing time available for proposal preparation is yet another component of gaining competitive advantage.

Consider the following comparison. If you work a five-day week while your competitor works a seven-day week, you spend about 29 percent (2/7) less time on your proposal. If you work a six-day week, the differential drops to about 14 percent. Either way, you give your competition a time advantage. Alternatively, you cannot expect to work the proposal team continuously without losing productivity. The key is to maximize the time available to work on the proposal without killing the proposal team.

For proposals of 45 days or less, plan to work a six- or seven-day week, but give each person at least a half-day off per week to attend to their personal affairs. Let people select their own half-day. This work pace is easily sustainable for six weeks. Furthermore, many non-key personnel assigned to the proposal can be released from the normal proposal work schedule during the final phase of proposal editing and refinement or after they completely and satisfactorily fulfill all their proposal assignments.

For longer proposals, consider working a six-day week, or start off with a seven-day week and then cut back on the work schedule once you are comfortable with the team's progress.

Long workweeks are unpopular, and they can be difficult on proposal teams. If you use the same group of people on every proposal, then you cannot repeatedly enforce a long workweek.

Team Communications

Maintaining timely, effective communications is essential to proposal success. Proposals are dynamic, and things change quickly. Moreover, a single change in one proposal area can impact multiple other areas. A change in your technical approach or product design, for example, will likely affect costing and any required logistical support. Even simple changes can have a profound impact on your proposal. If such changes are not communicated quickly, then other efforts suffer. Time and effort are wasted as proposal teams continue working with out-of-date information. You cannot afford to waste time if you hope to submit the winning proposal.

The difficulty of maintaining communications grows exponentially with the size of the proposal team. Special efforts are required for larger proposal teams. Yet, under the best of circumstances, good proposal communications pose a challenge, especially if your team is spread among multiple locations.

Actions you can take to enhance team communications include the following:

- Host a proposal kickoff meeting
- Conduct daily proposal status meetings

- Provide all proposal team members ready access to proposal information
- Co-locate the proposal team.

Proposal Kickoff Meeting

Plan to host a kickoff meeting shortly after you receive a draft or final RFP. Invite the entire proposal team, major subcontractors, and any functional managers whose support will be required during the proposal. The following topics should be covered at each meeting:

- Description of the technical and programmatic requirements of the contract
- Strategic value of the contract to your organization
- Overview of the bid strategy
- Proposal schedule
- Proposal outline (if available)
- Proposal assignments (including functional managers and subcontractors)
- What is expected of proposal team members
- Communications tools to be used
- Proposal security
- An overview of your management style and your expectations of the team.

The kickoff meeting sets the groundwork for subsequent proposal development activities. It provides a good opportunity to explain the importance of the bid to the entire proposal team, including functional managers who may not directly participate in proposal preparation. This also is the time to give the team an overview of the entire proposal development process and to explain how progress will be monitored and reported.

Daily Proposal Status Meetings

The purpose of proposal status meetings is twofold. First, they permit daily monitoring of proposal progress. Second, they create a setting and forum to foster daily communication among proposal team members.

The proposal manager should conduct a daily proposal status meeting at the same time each day, preferably late in the day. Most people are more productive in the morning. Save this time for work on the proposal. Normally these meetings should last no longer than 15 to 20 minutes.

Each meeting begins by having each person report progress toward his or her individual proposal assignment. Every proposal team member will have a scheduled due date for each individual assignment. Have each person report the status (percent complete) of each incomplete proposal assignment and either verify that they are on track to meet their individual schedule or state the reason why not.

Everyone is responsible for meeting schedules and must identify immediately any potential schedule slippage. This is the time to highlight any resource shortfalls or issues that could jeopardize proposal schedule or quality. Record each issue as an action item. Assign responsibility for each action item to a capture team manager and set a date when the action is to be completed. Review the status of open action items at each meeting. Actions that require coordination or authority beyond the capability of individual capture team managers should be assigned to the proposal manager or capture team leader.

By monitoring proposal status daily, you can identify potential problems early and implement corrective action before they turn into a disaster. This also affords an opportunity to identify individual team members who may be struggling with their proposal assignment or a situation where available resources are inadequate. In either case, implement actions to remedy the problem.

Daily proposal meetings also enable timely team communication. Use them to discuss any issues that affect the entire team, including any changes in technical approach, proposal formatting, or customer requirements. If an issue requires a detailed discussion that involves only a subset of the proposal team, schedule a separate meeting so you do not take up the time of the entire team.

Ready Access to Proposal Information

Every member of the team needs ready access to proposal information. This includes customer information such as a complete RFP, answers to bidders' questions, and any customer information that needs to be integrated into the proposal. Additional information includes the bid strategy and proposal development documents: a proposal outline, responsibility matrix, proposal directive, proposal schedule, and any other document used to guide proposal preparation (described in Chapter 10). Not only do team members need quick access to proposal information, but they need access to the latest configuration. So, plan to develop and implement a system to manage the configuration of all proposal information (see Chapter 14 for some recommendations).

A simple solution to information access is to create an on-line proposal directory and provide each proposal member access via an intranet. Nearly all organizations have intranet capability to provide employee access to e-mail and company computer directories. A notice of any change to the proposal or supporting documentation also should be sent to every proposal team member via e-mail and followed up at the daily status meeting.

Many customers use an Internet-accessible website to post contract information such as answers to questions, clarifications, and amendments to the solicitation. In these cases, have at least three people, including the proposal manager, check the website three times each day: early morning, noon, and evening. Immediately disseminate any customer changes to the proposal team and then review the changes during the daily status meeting.

Co-location of the Proposal Team

Co-locating the proposal team is one of the most effective ways to foster team communication. People are more likely to walk to the next office or cubicle to talk to another team member than they are to phone or e-mail, especially if the issue does not appear to be particularly important. Moreover, phoning often is inefficient because people are away from their offices. The same applies to e-mail.

Communicating with off-site subcontractors or other organizations required to provide proposal input is always problematic. If possible, require them to be on-site with your proposal team. This will save you a mountain of headaches. If this is not possible, here are some tips for managing off-site proposal team members:

1. Make sure they have a copy of all proposal development documents and schedules.
2. Provide them access to your on-line proposal directory (if possible). For major proposals, consider creating a proposal website with limited access and post proposal documents and information to the website.
3. Have off-site team members participate in daily status meetings via teleconference.
4. Require team members to submit e-mail deliveries of all their proposal assignments according to the proposal schedule.
5. Require team members to be on-site at regular intervals, or ask that they place a representative at your facility to serve as a conduit back to their organization to expedite communications.

If possible, require the entire proposal team to be on-site at least for the last two weeks of proposal preparation. This tends to be a frantic time. Delays due to long-distance communications can seriously undermine your ability to produce a quality proposal.

Successful Proposal Managers

Each proposal manager will develop his or her management style based on personality and what has worked in the past. Within that context, some basic attributes consistently define successful proposal managers.

Successful proposal managers generally possess a keen ability to communicate effectively with people at all levels of the organization, from company presidents to technical proposal writers to publications staff to financial and administrative personnel. They command and instill confidence in others by their technical knowledge, business development savvy, command of proposal development principles, understanding of government source selection, and self-confidence.

Successful proposal managers also know when to push their proposal team, when to empathize, when to encourage, when to be flexible, and when to relax. Most have a well-developed sense of humor. Finally, successful proposal managers are inherent problem-solvers. They are quick to seek work-arounds. If one approach does not produce the desired result, they try another and another until the barrier is removed or the problem is resolved. Fundamentally, they are leaders, facilitators, communicators, and listeners.

How you staff, organize, and manage the capture team offers a rich opportunity to either gain or surrender competitive advantage. Select highly qualified and experienced capture team managers, especially the capture team leader and proposal manager. The quality and capability of the capture team is among the greatest contributors to preparing a winning proposal.

Supplement your proposal team with qualified consultants to fill personnel shortfalls, or use them to enhance the expertise applied to your proposals. Pre-qualify consultants so that they are available when you need them.

Recruit and retain seasoned proposal managers. Create a proposal work environment that fosters success and teamwork. Implement procedures to promote the rapid exchange of information among proposal team members. Monitor proposal progress daily and quickly identify and solve potential problems that could adversely affect the quality of your proposal.

Develop and implement well-defined roles, responsibilities, and levels of authority for capture team managers. Team members equipped with the knowledge of what to do and when to do it, along with the necessary authority, will significantly enhance team effectiveness and lead you down the road to victory.

Part 3

The Proposal Development Phase

Chapter 9

Analyzing Customer Requirements

The proposal development phase begins once you receive a draft or final RFP. During this phase, you integrate your bid strategy with customer requirements and transform the product into a winning proposal.

A clear understanding of customer requirements is a prerequisite to winning. Customer requirements come in two flavors: informal and formal. Informal requirements are the needs, desires, and fears of your customer bounded by the specific need being solved. They are determined through marketing efforts and pre-proposal contact with the customer. Formal requirements are those defined by the RFP. They take precedence over informal requirements. Nonetheless, both should be combined and used to develop your proposal.

Oftentimes, formal RFP requirements can be interpreted only in light of informal customer knowledge. However, be careful about how you use knowledge about informal customer requirements. Adding requirements to those contained in the RFP, or significantly expanding the scope of RFP requirements, will increase your cost, which could undermine your chances of winning.

Formal customer requirements are determined through an exhaustive analysis of the RFP. What might appear to be a straightforward process frequently becomes an arduous and confusing undertaking. Under the best circumstances, analyzing the customer's RFP to define program and proposal requirements poses a challenge. Many government RFPs are disjointed, inconsistent, inaccurate, or fraught with ambiguities. Some RFPs are so disorganized that they require considerable translation and interpretation before they make sense. (In fairness to government procurement agencies, assembling an RFP that effectively and consistently communicates the government's requirements is a major challenge. Moreover, RFPs occasionally are clear, concise, and reasonably well-organized.)

Preparing a coherent proposal response amidst inconsistent, contradictory, and confusing RFP requirements is just a part of the job. Those who learn to decipher RFP requirements and meet customer requirements gain competitive advantage. Those who do not suffer the consequences.

Having a good understanding of customer requirements before the RFP is released is a big advantage. You can use this knowledge to fill in the "gaps" and interpret vague and inconsistent RFP requirements. In other cases, poor quality RFPs may offer opportunities for creative interpretation that can be integrated into a bid strategy.

Chapter 7 describes how to review a draft RFP and respond to inconsistent or missing RFP information. This process can be used for both draft and final RFP documents. In either case, the capture team must decide how to handle such problems.

GETTING STARTED

Assemble the proposal team and make RFP reading assignments. Make sure everyone understands his or her assigned RFP analysis tasks. For small procurements, have the whole team read the entire RFP. Otherwise, the core capture team should read the entire proposal. Other members of the technical proposal team can limit their reading to Sections B, C, L, and M, plus any technical attachments such as a statement of work, statement of objectives, specification, etc. Your contract manager should thoroughly review Sections B through K and any contracts-related portions of Section L.

Do not permit proposal team members to read just the section of the RFP pertaining to their technical specialty. Everyone on the proposal team should be familiar with the overall technical requirement. This will make it easier to coordinate different technical disciplines and to integrate individual proposal sections.

Plan to make three passes through the RFP to accomplish your initial RFP analysis. During the first reading, skim the information without taking notes or stopping to analyze requirements. This will provide you with a general sense of overall RFP requirements. On the second reading, take notes and highlight significant RFP sections, especially those that require additional analysis. Finally, read the RFP the third time to confirm or adjust your initial findings.

Everyone should make a list of questions, concerns, ambiguities, or inconsistencies resulting from their RFP review. The capture team can then review those lists to determine the action required. You will need to resolve any apparent RFP inconsistencies to ensure that everyone understands the customer requirements your proposal is supposed to solve.

RFP ambiguities can be handled in several ways. First, you can ask the customer a question to clarify the problem. If you choose to ask a question, use the guidelines presented in Chapter 7. Remember, bidders' questions and the government's responses normally are provided to all bidders. Second, you may use your knowledge of the customer to resolve an inconsistency or ambiguity. Finally, you can decide to leave an inconsistent or ambiguous RFP requirement unaddressed and interpret the requirement in your favor. If so, list this assumption in the contract section or basis-of-estimate portion of your cost proposal.

When interpreting ambiguous RFP issues, *never* make an interpretation detrimental to your approach. If something is ambiguous, it can be interpreted either way realistically. Given a choice, always interpret things to your advantage.

Using RFP Ambiguity As a Competitive Advantage

To illustrate how you can use ambiguity to your advantage, consider the following example. Our proposal team was bidding a contract that included development and production phases. Development costs were bid on a cost-plus basis, but production was bid as a firm fixed price. (Chapter 13 explains different contract types.) Part of the contract required us to design and install a series of complex computer networks and interconnect networks at a variety of locations. Unfortunately, many of the building drawings were not available. Therefore, we were faced with the prospect of bidding expensive T-1 lines without knowing the layout of individual buildings or what it would take to install the networks.

The RFP was unclear about whether installation was a development or a production task. Different proposal team members argued ardently for each interpretation. Bidding installation as a production task with a firm fixed price represented enormous cost risk. To offset this risk, we would be forced to increase our bid price significantly, which potentially would have made us less competitive. Alternatively, if we bid installation as a development task, we could limit our risk by defining the task. If the actual task turned out to be more extensive, we would be able to increase our cost under the cost-plus terms of the development contract.

Our choice in this case was either to ask a question or to interpret the RFP ambiguity in a way that would allow us to mitigate a significant cost risk. By asking a question, we risked getting an answer we could not stand. In addition, by asking the question, we would alert the competition and hence lose the opportunity to use this area to our advantage.

Eventually, we decided to treat the network installation as a development task. We included installation as a development task in our WBS dictionary, listed it in our assumptions, and made it a part of our cost basis-of-estimate. We won the contract, but not without worrying about whether or not the government would view our approach as unresponsive to RFP requirements.

Reading the RFP

There are many approaches to reading and reviewing RFPs. Here is an approach I like.

Start with RFP Section B. It defines what the government is buying and what you must deliver. It typically is where you enter your proposed price, or it references a pricing form or matrix to be used for your pricing. Next read Section C. It provides a description of the technical requirements of the contract. If the RFP includes a statement of work or specification, it will be contained in or referenced by Section C. Briefly read these documents. Do not stop to take notes or highlight points. Just get an overview of the requirements.

Now, read Section L, sometimes titled, "Instructions to Offerors (ITO)" or "Proposal Instructions to Offerors (PIO)." Note basic proposal format instructions, the number and type of proposal volumes, and specific instructions on how to prepare each volume or section, along with the specific technical questions to be addressed. Then read Section M. This section lists and describes the evaluation criteria that will be used to select the winner. Sections L and M together tell you what must be included in the proposal and how your response will be scored.

Next, skim Sections D and E. They identify things like marking, packaging, shipping, and inspection. Then review Section F. It lets you know when items must be delivered to the government—this is the foundation for your program schedule. Finish the RFP by briefly reading any additional RFP attachments, and conclude by skimming Sections G through K. Pay a little more attention to Section H, which contains special contract clauses. Sometimes special requirements contained in this section have a significant technical impact.

Most of the information in Sections G, J, and K will be of interest only to the contract manager assigned to the proposal. Once you have a general feel for what is required, begin the RFP analysis in earnest. Before submitting your final proposal, expect to read the RFP about a dozen times. Each reading will likely produce a fresh insight into RFP requirements.

KEY PROPOSAL PLANNING AND PREPARATION DOCUMENTS

Formal customer requirements provide the foundation for your program approach and the ingredients of your proposal. Three documents should be prepared to support proposal planning and preparation: (1) program requirements document, (2) proposal requirements directive, and (3) evaluation criteria document. Chapter 9 describes a further refinement of customer requirements to develop a detailed proposal roadmap.

Program Requirements Document

Prepared by the program manager, the program requirements document summarizes contract deliverables and schedule, plus any other relevant contract requirements. Read RFP Sections B and F and build a list of deliverables. If the contract includes separate lots or options, make sure to note these. Develop a high-level program schedule based on this information. If possible, create the schedule with a commercially available software package, like Microsoft Project. If the contract includes options, then you must include start and delivery dates for each. Sometimes, RFPs only provide a not-later-than date for option exercise. If this is the case, then use those dates as the start dates for initial schedule development.

Attach a copy of the program WBS to the program requirements document. Some RFPs include a WBS. If so, you may need to expand it to accommodate your costing efforts. If not, then develop one. The WBS provides the foundation for collecting cost estimates.

Review RFP Sections D and E. Note any special test or inspection requirements and incorporate test dates in the program schedule. Also, list any special test locations or provisions and any special packing or handling requirements. Finally, list any key, special, or critical performance requirements from the statement of work, specifications, Section H, or any of the attachments. Special requirements include things like quality assurance requirements (e.g., ISO certification), software certification level, minimum requirements for key personnel, equipment reliability or availability, associate contractor agreements, or anything required to perform the contract.

If the RFP includes a list of contract data requirements list (CDRL) items, then summarize CDRL deliveries on the program schedule. If you are required to build your own CDRLs, you may need to add these to the program requirements document after you have developed your program planning.

The program requirements document provides a concise summary of contract requirements and schedule, plus any peculiar or specific requirements. Everyone on the proposal team should review the requirements document and have a copy handy for reference.

Proposal Requirements Directive

Prepared by the proposal manager, the proposal requirements directive summarizes the proposal preparation requirements. Information for the proposal directive is obtained from Section L. It lists the required proposal volumes, the number of copies required by the government, page limitations, how the proposal should be bound (e.g., three-ring binder), and whether or not an electronic copy of your proposal is required. It also includes basic instructions for proposal organization and format (e.g., required type and font, line spacing, page margins). If the RFP does not specify format, then use whatever standard format your organization normally uses for technical documents or ask the customer if they have a preference.

Include any additional plans or documents required as part of the proposal submittal. Some RFPs require bidders to prepare their own statement of work and CDRLs. Others require preliminary plans, such as a configuration management plan or a transition plan. The proposal directive should include all plans and attachments required by the RFP, organized under the volume in which they will be submitted.

The proposal directive should contain proposal milestone dates for key events, like when the first draft is due, proposal review dates, final editing and quality assurance, and delivery to the customer. A more detailed proposal preparation schedule will be developed and distributed to the proposal team; milestone dates are key events everyone should keep in mind to coordinate organizational-level efforts.

Include basic proposal conventions, standards, or any style requirements in the proposal directive. This will help minimize confusion among proposal authors. It also will minimize subsequent efforts to correct or standardize this type of information. An example is how you will refer to your company in the proposal. If you are the American Standard Telecommunications Company, will you refer to yourself with the entire name, use an acronym (ASTC), or use a shortened name (American Telecom)? Issues like this may seem trivial, but experience suggests that they can consume an enormous amount of time and effort to resolve. This is time better spent on more important matters.

As a rule of thumb, do not use acronyms or abbreviations for company names, unless you are IBM or AT&T, which are recognizable to everyone. Instead, use a shortened version of the company name. Evaluators are more likely to remember this name than an unfamiliar acronym.

Include in the proposal directive things like how you will refer to your proposed program "team" if it includes major subcontractors, the use of personal pronouns like "we" in place of your company name or program team, whether you will capitalize the title of program personnel such as "Program Manager," how you will handle acronyms, how you will refer to your customer, and whether you will express units of measures as metric, U.S., or both. Every proposal will be different. It is not possible to list everything that needs to be included in the proposal directive. When it doubt, put it in the directive. Doing so will save you much wasted time later on when time is an especially precious commodity. Once you build a proposal requirements directive, you can use it on subsequent proposals by tailoring it to meet the specific requirements of each proposal.

Evaluation Criteria Document

If you want to win, you must write to the evaluation criteria used to score your proposal. A careful analysis of evaluation criteria is a prerequisite to preparing a winning proposal. Section M contains the evaluation criteria that will be used to evaluate your proposal. Everyone on the proposal team needs to be familiar with these criteria. Individual authors must be intimately familiar with the criteria that correspond to their assigned portion of the proposal.

Prepared by the proposal manager, the evaluation criteria document summarizes evaluation criteria, determines the weight of area and factor criteria, lists any general evaluation considerations, and breaks out potential evaluation standards. It also contains government procedures for evaluating past performance and proposal risk if the government plans to assess risk for these areas.

Area and factor weights can be used to determine preliminary page count limits for proposal sections. This is especially valuable for page-limited proposals. You want to put your emphasis where it will do the most good. The relative importance of evaluation areas and factors also can provide guidelines on how to allocate your proposal resources. Again, the greatest emphasis is placed on those factors that are more heavily weighted.

However, a caution is warranted here. There are no *unimportant* proposal sections. In your zeal to maximize your score for heavily weighted factors, do not neglect factors that are relatively less important. This is a common mistake with significant consequences. All factors and subfactors are added to arrive at a composite score. One poor score can drag down the entire score for that factor and area.

Dissecting Evaluation Criteria

The first step is to identify the evaluation areas or items that will be used to evaluate your proposal. Every proposal is evaluated in at least two areas: technical and cost. In addition, contract information will be checked to ensure that you comply with RFP requirements. Some agencies evaluate past performance and assign it a point score. Other agencies, like DoD, assign past performance a risk rating and combine it with the technical evaluation. All of this information is contained in RFP Section M.

Here is a Section M example where the evaluation factors are not equally weighted:

> *Proposals will be evaluated using the four factors, which are listed below. Technical is equal in importance to Past Performance and each is more important than the Cost/Price factor which is significantly more important than the Small Business and Small Disadvantaged Business Subcontracting Plan factor.*
> *A. Technical*
> *B. Past Performance*
> *C. Cost/Price*
> *D. Small Business and Small Disadvantaged Business Subcontracting Plan*

The relative importance of these evaluation factors can be expressed as follows:

Technical = Past Performance > Cost > Small Business Plan

Even though you do not know the exact relative importance of these factors, you can estimate them fairly accurately. Start by assigning each factor the same weight. Then adjust the weighting of each factor based on the information contained in Section M. If each factor in the above example is weighted equally, it would account for 25 percent of the total evaluation.

A general rule for adjusting factor weights is: Adjust each factor by 5 percent when a factor is greater/lesser in importance and 10 percent when it is significantly greater or less than another factor. Applying this rule produces the following relative weights for the example above:

Technical (30%) = Past Performance (30%) > Cost (25%) > Small Business Plan (15%)

You can vary relative weights forever. But you will quickly discover that there is not a lot of variability in how you assign weights and still remain consistent with the language of Section M. It depends on how you judge terms like "more important" and "significantly more important." You can make finer adjustments based on your experience and knowledge of the customer. You also can use the relative emphasis given to corresponding topics in Section L to make additional adjustments.

Some agencies use a point-scoring system where areas and factors are assigned a set number of points. For these cases, no further analysis is required to determine the relative weight of areas and factors.

Some RFPs further divide factors into subfactors and provide their relative importance. From the example above:

The following Technical subfactors are in descending order of importance:
T.1 Systems Engineering and Design
T.2 System Development
T.3 Logistics
T.4 Management

If the subfactors were of equal importance, they would each be worth 25 percent of the total score for the technical area. Arranging the four factors in descending order of importance with a 5 percent gap between each produces the following weighting:

T.1 = 32.5%
T.2 = 27.5%
T.3 = 22.5%
T.4 = 17.5%

If one factor or subfactor is significantly more important than another, the government typically will state it in Section M. The difference in relative weights may be less than 5 percent, but if it is very small, then the government is more likely to say they are of equal importance. Alternatively, the relative difference may be greater than 5 percent. Again, if the relative difference is much greater, Section M would likely use terminology to make this point.

The important point here is that you can derive a reasonable estimate of the relative weights given to areas, factors, and subfactors using the information contained in Section M. However, remember that this is an estimate. It should only be used as a guideline or a point of reference for making preliminary decisions about things like page count allocation. At the same time, it does provide the proposal team with a view of the relative importance of those areas and factors that must be addressed in the proposal. Figure 9-1 summarizes the information for the above example.

Sometimes evaluation criteria for cost are divided into factors or subfactors. If so, Section M will identify the factors and define their relative importance. In those cases, use the technique illustrated above to estimate the relative weight of each cost factor. Cost also may be evaluated for its realism, reasonableness, and consistency with the technical proposal. These all are important determinants of how you approach pricing.

Figure 9-1. Estimate of Relative Evaluation Factor Weights

Factors	Subfactors	Percent of Factor	Percent of Total
Technical			**30%**
	T.1 Systems Engineering and Design	32.5%	
	T.2 System Development	27.5%	
	T.3 Logistics	22.5%	
	T.4 Management	17.5%	
	Total of All Technical Subfactors:	100%	
Past Performance			**30%**
Cost			**25%**
Small Business Plan			**15%**
TOTAL OF ALL FACTORS			**100%**

Evaluating Past Performance

In DoD procurements, past performance is assigned a risk rating (high, moderate, or low). Other agencies may score past performance information and include it as part of the overall technical evaluation. Again, Section M describes how past performance will be evaluated and may identify the specific evaluation areas. Here is a typical Section M example that identifies past performance evaluation factors:

> *Demonstrated satisfactory or better performance during the last three years on contracts and/or subcontracts, which are similar in scope, size, type, and complexity to that which is anticipated in this solicitation. Factors for consideration include quality of technical work products, quality of service, timeliness of performance, cost control, compliance with subcontracting plan goals for small disadvantaged business concerns, and customer satisfaction.*

In most instances, factors used to evaluate past performance will be the same factors used to evaluate the technical proposal. If Section M lists the factors, then you know for sure what they are. If Section M does not provide that level of detail, assume that past performance will be evaluated for each of the areas and factors listed as evaluation criteria.

Identifying Evaluation Standards

Recall from Chapter 3 that evaluators score your proposal by comparing it to a set of evaluation standards. These standards are keyed to the areas, factors, and subfactors contained in Section M. Normally, we do not know what they are, but we can anticipate which specific topics they address. In some cases, we can estimate the standards themselves.

Apparent evaluation standards can be determined from analyzing and comparing RFP Sections L and M. This information can then be refined by a thorough analysis of the statement of work, specifications, and Section H, plus any relevant RFP attachments.

It is difficult to specify a formula for determining evaluation standards. RFPs vary enormously in the level of detail provided and how well different RFP sections correlate. Some RFPs provide a lot of detail in describing evaluation factors. Others are quite brief. Nonetheless, a preliminary determination can be made from the information contained in Section M. In addition, other RFP information (e.g., Section L) can be used to refine the apparent standards found in Section M.

Listed below are some typical evaluation factor descriptions. The selected samples come from different procuring agencies and vary in the level of detail provided.

> **Factor T.1.1 <u>Remaining Technical and Logistic Requirements</u>** - *The offeror's proposal will be evaluated to determine the offeror's ability to meet remaining technical and logistic requirements, such as specialty engineering, computer resources, logistics, land-based operations, and system improvements.*

__Factor T.1.3. Management__. Demonstrated effectiveness of proposed plan for managing work assignments, including the strategy for managing work assignments with quick turn-around "rapid response" deadlines and providing for smooth, efficient coordination of efforts, and expected responsibilities of all prime contractor and any subcontractor and consultant personnel on individual work assignment teams, including the offerors plan to provide field work and laboratory analysis included in Section 3.1 of the RFP statement of work. Adequacy of communication and control mechanisms to ensure effective coordination and timely management of activities to be conducted under the contract.

__Factor T.2.1 Logistics.__ The degree to which the proposed approach provides for logistics support will be evaluated, including meeting the availability, maintenance planning, supportability and warranty requirements. The approach to contractor field services, the material support package, and data and documentation will be evaluated as well as the configuration management approach. The proposed training program will also be evaluated.

By dissecting and analyzing these Section M statements, we can identify potential evaluation standards. Using Factor T.2.1 from the example above, let's identify every topic, area, or item in each sentence as a candidate evaluation standard. The factor description contains three sentences, which can be broken down topically as follows:

1. *Approach to logistics support:*
   - *Availability*
   - *Maintenance planning*
   - *Supportability*
   - *Warranty requirements.*
2. *Approach to:*
   - *Contractor field services*
   - *Material support package*
   - *Data and documentation*
   - *Configuration management approach.*
3. *Proposed:*
   - *Training program.*

Each bulleted item represents a potential evaluation standard. You will need to evaluate other RFP areas (Section L, SOW, specifications), along with your knowledge of the customer, to refine likely evaluation standards more precisely. For example, your proposal will need to address the "availability" requirements referenced in the evaluation criteria statement and convince evaluators that your proposed logistics approach will easily meet or exceed those requirements.

The specific requirements usually will be located somewhere else in the RFP, such as the statement of work or performance specification. For example, you might find that 95 percent equipment availability is required with an operational schedule of 16 hours per day, seven days per week.

Identifying likely evaluation standards enables you to focus proposal topics and issues directly aligned with evaluation criteria and standards. This is part of the basic ingredients of gaining competitive advantage and producing a winning proposal.

Figure 9-2 shows a way of summarizing areas and topics for probable evaluation standards. This information is combined with the relative weighting information derived earlier (Figure 9-1). This collective document makes up the proposal evaluation document.

Figure 9-2. Sample Evaluation Criteria Information for Proposal Evaluation Document

AREA	FACTOR	SUBFACTOR	STANDARDS*
TECHNICAL	System Engineering and Design	• System Analysis and Definition	
		• Design Approach	
	System Development	• Software Process	
		• Production Capability	
		• System Verification	
	Logistics		• Availability • Maintenance planning • Supportability • Warranty requirements • Contractor field services • Material support package • Data and documentation • Configuration management approach • Training program
	Management	• Program Management	
		• Management Tools	
COST	Acquisition Costs		
	Lifecycle Costs		Based on 10 years from time of deployment

*Standards are only shown for the Logistics factor

DOCUMENT CONFIGURATION MANAGEMENT

Following a review of the requirements document, proposal directive, and evaluation criteria document, and any necessary revisions, they are placed under configuration control. That is, no one is permitted to change them without permission from both the program manager and the proposal manager. If one of these documents is changed, then a new copy is provided to each proposal member, along with a summary of the change. In addition, ask each member to confirm that they have received and reviewed the change.

Translating RFP requirements into a set of proposal management documents may not appear to offer much in the way of gaining competitive advantage. Admittedly, this part of the process is not rocket science. Nonetheless, a thorough and effective RFP analysis, and the preparation of a set of documents to guide proposal development, may produce a higher return on investment than you imagine.

Create the proposal development documents described here to set the boundaries within which you will prepare your proposal. Use this information to structure your proposal, set the foundation of your technical approach, and understand how the government will evaluate your response. Make these documents readily available to the proposal team and ensure that they are kept up-to-date so everyone is reading from the same page. This alone will enhance team effectiveness and efficiency.

The first step of a long journey often is the most important. Head in the wrong direction at the outset and you may never arrive at your intended destination. Use this phase of the proposal development process to take that initial first step toward preparing a winning proposal. Gain advantage over those who slight this phase and rush unprepared down the path to defeat.

Chapter 10

Developing a Proposal Preparation Plan

Once you have completed a thorough review of the RFP and prepared the documents described in Chapter 9, it is time to develop a detailed proposal preparation plan. Planning is a pivotal junction in the proposal development process. Like most of life's endeavors, the quality of the output is directly related to the effort invested in planning. For proposals, poor or inadequate planning is a sure formula for failure.

The small amount of time available to prepare a proposal makes it especially difficult to recover from a false start. Hence, one of the greatest opportunities to capture competitive advantage is through effective proposal planning. Alternatively, inattention to proposal planning, or the lack of good planning tools, practically guarantees that you will prepare a losing proposal. The only hope in this case is that you will be competing with companies equally inept in the planning process.

Five documents represent the weapons in an effective proposal planning arsenal. The first three define the content to be included in the proposal:

- **Proposal outline:** A complete outline of the proposal, consisting of paragraph numbers and headings
- **Proposal requirements matrix:** A list of Section M evaluation criteria and other RFP requirements for each proposal paragraph contained in the proposal outline
- **Author guide:** A storyboard process that specifies what is to be contained in each proposal section.

The other two documents support proposal management. They establish responsibility for every proposal task and define completion dates for each:

- **Proposal responsibility matrix:** Lists the person responsible for each entry in the proposal outline
- **Detailed proposal schedule:** Specifies duration and completion dates for each proposal activity.

Collectively these documents define the who, what, and when of proposal development. The preparation of each is described below. The order in which they are addressed is based on continuity of topic and not the order in which they would normally be developed. The proposal outline, responsibility matrix, and schedule are developed concurrently. The proposal requirements matrix and author guides are developed sequentially after the proposal outline is complete.

PROPOSAL OUTLINE

Government evaluation standards used to score your proposal are organized according to the instructions provided in Section L. Therefore, unless the RFP expressly directs otherwise, you must organize your proposal in the exact same order as information is requested by Section L. This is one of few absolutes in preparing government proposals. Failure to follow this simple instruction may cause your proposal to be completely noncompliant.

A few years ago, a client of mine lost an important program. They were shocked. They had far more relevant experience and were better qualified technically than the company that won. They also felt that they were slightly favored by the procuring agency, and their bid cost was lower. I was hired to analyze their proposal to determine why they lost.

The answer was simple. They had organized their technical proposal according to the evaluation criteria contained in Section M of the RFP instead of the instructions of Section L. Technical proposal material was not located where the evaluators expected to find it. Moreover, much of the information requested by Section L was not provided because there were no corresponding evaluation criteria contained in Section M. This tragic mistake cost my client an important program and wasted valuable B&P resources in the process.

It may seem intuitive to organize your proposal according to the criteria the government will use to evaluate your proposal. There is just one small problem. This tactic almost guarantees a losing proposal. *Do not deviate from the order of instructions provided in Section L unless the RFP specifically directs it.* This does occur occasionally. Sometimes customers ask bidders to organize their proposals according to a statement of work or a technical specification, but these are exceptions.

Authors often complain about following the order of Section L. They claim that the government-requested order of information is illogical. This normally is a valid criticism. Many times, the requested order of information makes writing difficult. Unfortunately, deviating from Section L to make writing assignments easy for authors has dire consequences.

Gain competitive advantage by presenting proposal information so that it occurs where evaluators expect to find it and by making it easy to identify.

Creating an Overall Proposal Outline

The first step is to read the proposal preparation instructions contained in Section L carefully. These are variously referred to as "Instructions to Offerors," "Proposal Preparation Instructions," or "Proposal Instructions to Offerors." Build an overall proposal outline based on the division of volumes and sections requested by Section L. Use the same volume and section numbering scheme contained in Section L. Figure 10-1 shows a sample Section L breakout of proposal volumes, which yields the following overall proposal outline:

VOLUME I: EXECUTIVE SUMMARY AND TECHNICAL TASK ORDER

1.0 Executive Summary

2.0 Technical Task Order

3.0 Transition Plan

VOLUME II: COST/PRICE AND CONTRACT DOCUMENTATION VOLUME

1.0 Cost/Price

2.0 Contract Documentation

To fill in the next level of detail, examine Section L to see if sections are broken out further. Figure 10-2 shows a sample breakout for Section 2 of Volume 1. In this case, specific RFP paragraphs are not numbered. Therefore, we will use the overall organization suggested by the RFP. The technical proposal

---

Figure 10-1. Sample RFP Section L Breakout of Required Proposal Volume

VOLUME	VOLUME TITLE	COPIES	PAGE LIMIT
I	Volume I - Executive Summary and C-141 TTS Technical Task Order	3 Paper 2 CD-ROM	
I	Section I - Executive Summary		3
I	Section II - Technical Task Order		40
I	Section III - Transition Plan		10 Plus Schedule
II	Volume II - Cost/Price and Contract Documentation Volume	3 Paper 2 CD-ROM	
II	Section I - Cost/Price		No Limit
II	Section II - Contract Documentation		No Limit

Figure 10-2. RFP Paragraph Headings for Section 2 of Volume I

Section 2 Program Technical Task Order

Program Aircrew Training System (ATS)
Training System Support Center (TSSC)
Training Management System (TMS)

---

is Section 2 of Volume 1. It consists of three subsections. Our proposal outline will follow the same order of topics numbered accordingly:

Section 2: Program Technical Task Order
2.1 Program Aircrew Training System (ATS)
2.2 Training System Support Center (TSSC)
2.3 Training Management System (TMS)

The next step is to develop a detailed outline for each section. Section L instructions for the Training System Support Center (TSSC) are shown in Figure 10-3. To build the outline, follow the order of subjects and use the customer's language to build paragraph titles. This will help evaluators find what they are looking for. Every Section L "should" or "shall" statement specifies a separate requirement. Keep this in mind to determine paragraph breaks in your outline.

Figure 10-4 provides the proposal outline for the TSSC derived from the Section L instructions listed in Figure 10-3. To illustrate the process, the first few sentences from Section L are as follows:

> *The offeror should describe their approach and proposed resources to operate and maintain the PROGRAM ATS TSSC. Provide an overview of routine/preventive recurring maintenance, emergency service calls, and any other maintenance to meet the 95% availability on each device at each site. Identify the methods at the site and system level used to maintain the Logistic Support Package (LSP), Inventory Control System (ICS), and Maintenance Data Collection (MDC):*

The proposal outline for these sentences becomes:

> *2.2.1 XYZ's Approach and Proposed Resources To Operate and Maintain The TSSC*
> *2.2.2 Overview Of XYZ's Maintenance Approach To Meet The 95% Availability Requirement*
> *2.2.3 XYZ's Methods to Maintain LSP, ICS, MDC at the Site and System Level*

This process is continued until you have a proposal outline for each section of the entire technical proposal and other proposal volumes where an

Figure 10-3. Section L Instructions for Section 2: Training System Support Center

__2.2 Training System Support Center (TSSC)__ The offeror should describe their approach and proposed resources to operate and maintain the PROGRAM ATS TSSC. Provide an overview of routine/preventive recurring maintenance, emergency service calls, and any other maintenance to meet the 95% availability on each device at each site. Identify the methods at the site and system level used to maintain the Logistic Support Package (LSP), Inventory Control System (ICS), and Maintenance Data Collection (MDC): Address the LSP's ability to manage, inspect, calibrate, test and distribute as required hardware, and spares to include package, handling, storage and transportation. Indicate ICS's access capability and status display capability to include furnishing current up to date reports upon request of assets. Indicate MDC approach to track the status of maintenance actions, spares/repair parts consumption, and labor hours for the ATS. Identify approach to replenish parts and support equipment for the aging ATS system, indicate the approach to obtain supplies (government and commercial sources should be identified), identify in-house or contracted-out repair and fabrication capabilities of aging parts. Describe the methods for integration and maintenance of the multiple baselines of hardware, software, firmware, technical data, and courseware for the PROGRAM ATS. Identify the approach to hardware, software, firmware, technical data, and courseware development and maintenance and the commitment of resources required to maintain the ATS configuration. Define how you will ensure a first time quality delivery of courseware of both content and format covering syllabi, lesson plans, seminar facilitator guides, instructor guides, student guides, CBT lessons, workbooks, tests, and evaluation forms. Provide an overview of a routine and emergency ATS courseware update.

outline is appropriate. Note that paragraph headings closely correspond with the Section L language.

Include your company's name, shown as "XYZ" in the example, in paragraph headings. This helps evaluators associate the proposed approach with your company. This may sound trivial, and it probably is. However, evaluators tasked with scoring multiple proposals may get confused over who is proposing what.

Sometimes it is difficult to decide when a new paragraph level is required. For example, the Section L instructions for section 2.2.3 address multiple topics. I elected to include them as paragraphs under section 2.2.3. Another approach would to create separate sections for each (e.g., 2.2.4, 2.2.5, 2.2.6). The key in this case is traceability between Section L and your proposal. Sometimes, a review of the Section M evaluation criteria will provide a clue for determining the proper level of organization.

Figure 10-4. Proposal Outline for Section 2.2 Based on Section L Instructions

Section 2.2 Training System Support Center (TSSC)
Section introduction

2.2.1 XYZ's Approach and Proposed Resources to Operate and Maintain the TSSC *The offeror should describe their approach and proposed resources to operate and maintain the TSSC.*

2.2.2 Overview of XYZ's Maintenance Approach to Meet 95% Availability Requirement *Provide an overview handling of routine/preventive recurring maintenance, emergency service calls, and any other maintenance to meet the 95% availability on each device at each site.*

2.2.3 XYZ's Methods to Maintain LSP, ICS, MDC at the Site and System Level *Identify the methods at the site and system level used to maintain the Logistic Support Package (LSP), Inventory Control System (ICS), and Maintenance Data Collection (MDC):*

2.2.3.1 Ability of XYZ's LSP to Support Logistics Functions *Address the LSP's ability to manage, inspect, calibrate, test and distribute as required hardware, and spares to include package, handling, storage and transportation.*

2.2.3.2 Capability of XYZ's Inventory Control System (ICS) *Indicate ICS's access capability and status display capability to include furnishing current up to date reports upon request of assets.*

2.2.3.3 XYZ's Approach to Maintenance Data Collection *Indicate MDC approach to track the status of maintenance actions, spares/repair parts consumption, and labor hours for the ATS.*

2.2.4 XYZ Approach and Capability to Support Equipment for the Aging ATS System *Identify approach to replenish parts and support equipment for the aging ATS system, indicate the approach to obtain supplies (government and commercial sources should be identified), identify in-house or contracted-out repair and fabrication capabilities of aging parts.*

2.2.5 XYZ Approach to Integrate and Maintain Multiple Baselines *Describe the methods for integration and maintenance of the multiple baselines of hardware, software, firmware, technical data, and courseware for the PROGRAM.*

2.2.6 XYZ Approach and Resources to Maintain ATS Configuration *Identify the approach to hardware, software, firmware, technical data, and courseware development and maintenance and the commitment of resources required to maintain the ATS configuration.*

2.2.7 XYZ Approach to Ensure a First Time Quality Delivery of Courseware *Define how you will ensure a first time quality delivery of courseware of both content and format covering syllabi, lesson plans, seminar facilitator guides, instructor guides, student guides, CBT lessons, workbooks, tests, and evaluation forms.*

(Text in italics is the Section L requirement)

In most cases, each sentence from Section L includes more than one topic or requirement. To illustrate, consider the Section L requirement of section 2.2.1:

2.2.1 The offeror should describe their approach and proposed resources to operate and maintain the TSSC.

At least two topics are requested:

1. *your <u>approach</u> to operate and maintain the TSSC, and*
2. *your <u>proposed resources</u> to operate and maintain the TSSC.*

If "operating and maintaining" the TSSC are separate processes, and each deserves a separate write-up, then your proposal must address four topics: two for your approach and two for your proposed resources. Whether or not you allocate separate subsections for each is a judgment call. If the proposal section is short, say one page or less, then a separate breakout may not be necessary.

The most important point is for your proposal to address every topic and item contained in the Section L sentence. Otherwise, this portion of your proposal may suffer a lower score or be judged as nonresponsive. Incidentally, the order of your proposal for this section is "approach" first and "proposed resources" second. This follows the order of topics provided by Section L.

Note from the sample proposal outline shown in Figure 10-4 that the Section L language is retained and shown in italics. I recommend that you retain this information in the proposal outline and in the first draft of proposal material. You will find that this helps authors focus on the primary topic to be addressed by each proposal section, which will enhance its responsive to the RFP requirements.

PROPOSAL REQUIREMENTS MATRIX

The completed proposal outline, based on Section L, provides the foundation for your proposal. However, you are not finished yet. Section L only provides the topics to be addressed by your proposal. Section M evaluation criteria must be integrated into your proposal. So must other RFP requirements to be addressed in each proposal section.

The proposal requirements matrix is just an extension of the proposal outline. It provides the author with all the RFP information necessary to write a responsive first draft. This matrix lists and correlates the information from Sections L, M, and others that should be addressed by each proposal section. Other RFP information may include segments of the statement of work, special contract clauses, or specifications. If the RFP requires you to write your own statement of work, then it should be correlated with the proposal.

Prepared by the proposal manager, this document provides a simple, convenient form to display the RFP requirements that need to be addressed by each proposal section. It saves the author the time and effort of looking up and organizing all the relevant RFP sections he or she needs to prepare assigned proposal sections. It also can be used to support subsequent proposal reviews (see Chapter 14). Using a common reference to prepare and then evaluate proposal sections provides continuity between the different phases of proposal development.

Creating the Proposal Requirements Matrix

The starting point to develop the requirements matrix is the proposal outline. The next step is to analyze the evaluation criteria contained in Section M and in the evaluation criteria document previously prepared (see Chapter 9). Evaluation criteria must be correlated with their corresponding Section L instructions contained in the proposal outline. Figure 10-5 shows the evaluation criteria for the Training System Support Center (section 2.2 of the proposal outline).

Figure 10-6 shows the proposal requirements matrix after evaluation criteria have been integrated into the proposal outline. Note that the matrix includes a column for "Other RFP Requirements." These are RFP requirements, other than those in Sections L and M, that further define the content and focus of the proposal section. Other requirements can be derived from the statement of work, specifications, CDRLs, or Section H special contract clauses. Note in Figure 10-6 that a statement of work entry concerning equipment availability occurs for proposal section 2.2.2, *"Overview Of XYZ's Maintenance Approach To Meet 95% Availability Requirement."*

Several points need to be made about Section M evaluation criteria. First, the detail and specificity of evaluation criteria differ enormously across RFPs. Some provide sufficient detail. Others appear to be little more than a paraphrase of Section L. Second, the order in which evaluation criteria occur in Section M often does not follow the same ordering of topics contained in Section L. Therefore, you will have to analyze evaluation criteria to determine their corresponding Section L instructions and where they need to be addressed in your proposal.

Finally, in some cases, evaluation criteria contained in Section M will not appear to correlate in any meaningful way with Section L. This is especially problematic. You may need to integrate other RFP requirements, such as the statement of work, into your proposal outline to see the correspondence between the contents to be provided in your proposal and the corresponding evaluation criteria. Or, you may need to apply your knowledge of the customer and the problem being solved to fully interpret evaluation criteria. If every effort fails to discern the relationship between the re-

Figure 10-5. Section M Evaluation Criteria with Breakout of Criteria for Subfactor 2

Award will be made to the offeror proposing the combination most advantageous to the Government based upon an integrated assessment of the evaluation factors and subfactors described below. The evaluation factors are listed below in equal order of importance. Within the Technical Task Order factor, the subfactors are listed in descending order of importance.

Factor 1 – Technical Task Order
  Subfactor 1 – Aircrew Training System (ATS)
  Subfactor 2 – Training System Support Center (TSSC)
  Subfactor 3 – Training Management System (TMS)
Factor 2 – Proposal Risk
Factor 3 – Cost/Price Evaluation

Subfactor 2 Training System Support Center (TSSC)

This subfactor is met when the offeror's proposal demonstrates a comprehensive TSSC approach to fully address the requirements of the RFP.

Items of Special Interest:

1) Offeror's overall approach to operate and maintain the TSSC.

2) Offeror's approach to maintain the Logistic Support Package (LSP), Inventory Control System (ICS), Maintenance Data Collection (MDC), hardware, spares (to include Package, Handling, Storage and Transportation). Approach to supply, repair, fabricate, and replenish parts and support equipment.

3) Offeror's approach to integrating and maintaining the multiple baselines for hardware, software, firmware, technical data, and courseware for the ATS.

4) Indicated capability to maintain the 95% availability requirement of the ATS devices.

5) Indicated capability and commitment of resources to develop and maintain the quality of software, firmware, technical data, and courseware for the ATS.

6) Offerors proposed maintenance plan for the ABC System.

quested proposal content and the evaluation criteria, then consider submitting a written question of clarification to the government.

Regardless, it is up to you to determine the proper correlation. Lacking a clear understanding of the evaluation criteria and their relationship to your proposal increases significantly the risk that your proposal will be nonresponsive to RFP requirements. This can be disastrous if one of your competitors has the key.

Sometimes, RFPs contain evaluation criteria that are not included as topics in Section L instructions. Notice that Subfactor 6 from Figure 10-5 is not contained in the Section L instructions (compare with Figure 10-3). When this occurs, you must integrate the evaluation criteria into the proposal outline even though there is no corresponding Section L requirement. Otherwise, you will fail to address an entire subfactor. This alone could cost you the competition. For the present example, we would add a para-

Figure 10-6. Proposal Requirements Matrix for a Portion of Section 2.2

Proposal Outline Based on Section L Instructions	Section M Evaluation Criteria	Other RFP Requirements
Section 2.2 Training System Support Center (TSSC) *Section introduction*		
2.2.1 XYZ's Approach and Proposed Resources to Operate and Maintain the TSSC *The offeror should describe their approach and proposed resources to operate and maintain the TSSC.*	*Offeror's overall approach to operate and maintain the TSSC.*	
2.2.2 Overview of XYZ's Maintenance Approach to Meet 95% Availability Requirement *Provide an overview handling of routine/preventive recurring maintenance, emergency service calls, and any other maintenance to meet the 95% availability on each device at each site.*	*Indicated capability to maintain the 95% availability requirement of the ATS devices.*	**SOW 1.2.3 Equipment Availability** *All ATS equipment shall meet a scheduled availability rate of 95% or greater. Equipment shall be available 16-hours per day, seven days per week.*
2.2.3 XYZ's Methods to Maintain LSP, ICS, MDC at the Site and System Level *Identify the methods at the site and system level used to maintain the Logistic Support Package (LSP), Inventory Control System (ICS), and Maintenance Data Collection (MDC):* **2.2.3.1 Ability of XYZ's LSP to Support Logistics Functions** *Address the LSP's ability to manage, inspect, calibrate, test, and distribute as required hardware, and spares to include package, handling, storage, and transportation.* **2.2.3.2 Capability of XYZ's Inventory Control System (ICS)** *Indicate ICS's access capability and status display capability to include furnishing current up-to-date reports upon request of assets.* **2.2.3.3 XYZ's Approach to Maintenance Data Collection** *Indicate MDC's approach to track the status of maintenance actions, spares/repair parts consumption, and labor hours for the ATS.*	*Offeror's approach to maintain the Logistic Support Package (LSP), Inventory Control System (ICS), Maintenance Data Collection (MDC), hardware, spares (to include Package, Handling, Storage and Transportation). Approach to supply, repair, fabricate, and replenish parts and support equipment.*	

graph, 2.2.8 "XYX's Proposal Maintenance Plan for the ABC System," to the proposal outline and the Proposal Requirements Matrix.

AUTHOR GUIDE

The proposal outline provides a topical outline for the entire proposal. The proposal requirements matrix expands this outline by integrating evaluation criteria and other RFP requirements into the outline.

The next step in the planning process is to determine the specific content of each proposal section. The importance of this step cannot be overemphasized. It is the foundation upon which your proposal is built. If the foundation is faulty, then the entire proposal will suffer. The magnitude of such an error is placed in context when you consider that failing to submit a responsive, compliant technical proposal is the single greatest contributor to losing proposals.

A host of techniques exist to support this stage of proposal development: annotated outlines, writing scenarios, storyboards, writing guides, etc. Each has its own set of proponents. Many proposal books and seminars claim that their approach is superior to all others. Some even guarantee success if you just follow their recommended approach. In reality, all approaches have the same goal: prepare compliant and responsive proposal sections that produce high marks from government evaluators.

My preference is to build what I call an author guide. As the name implies, it is a tool intended to help authors plan what they are going to include in each proposal section. It consists of two sheets and is prepared by the responsible author. Sheet 1 replicates the information from the proposal requirements matrix and leaves space for the author to develop a more detailed outline of the proposal section, including key points to be made. It also provides space to list any recommended graphics to support the proposal section narrative. Sheet 2 provides space to include things like section themes, bid strategies, and features/benefits, and a section to identify potential areas of proposal risk and the actions you have taken (or will take) to mitigate those risks.

Initially I have authors complete only the first sheet of the author guide. Once they have completed a draft that is responsive to all RFP requirements, they can turn to the task of integrating themes, bid strategies, discriminators, features/benefits, and other elements that will enhance the proposal.

Sheet 1 of the Author Guide

Sheet 1 of the author guide is shown in Figure 10-7. The top portion of the guide restates the RFP requirement, which is derived from the proposal

Figure 10-7. Sheet 1 of the Author Guide with Sample Information Shown in Italics

AUTHOR GUIDE (Sheet 1 of 2)	
Volume/Section:	
Proposal Heading And Title: *2.2.5 XYZ's Approach to Integrate and Maintain Multiple Baselines*	
Author: *Smith*	**Phone/Email:**
Section L Statement	**Other RFP Requirements to be Addressed**
Describe the methods for integration and maintenance of the multiple baselines of hardware, software, firmware, technical data, and courseware for the ATS.	
Evaluation Criteria: *Offeror's approach to integrating and maintaining the multiple baselines for hardware, software, firmware, technical data, and courseware for the ATS.*	
Detailed Outline and Points to Be Made:	
Recommended Graphics to Support Section:	

requirements matrix. The remainder of the sheet provides space for the author to prepare a detailed section outline and to define any supporting graphics.

The first task in developing a detailed outline is to analyze the Section L instructions carefully. What information is the customer asking for? What are the important components of a responsive reply? Translating the Section L instructions into an outline and then into proposal narrative may appear to be a simple, straightforward undertaking. It is not. Getting proposal authors to write proposal sections responsive to RFP requirements is among a proposal manager's greatest challenges. It also is among the most important.

Two exercises to help authors complete Sheet 1 of the author guide follow. They are especially beneficial when your team includes relatively inexperienced proposal authors.

Dissecting Section L Requirements

Have authors break each Section L sentence into its component parts: subject, verb, object, and topic. For example:

The offeror shall describe their approach to data management.
Subject: Offeror *(that's you)*
Verb: *shall describe*
Object: *approach* to data management
Topic: data management

The subject is the offeror. The verb is "describe," the object is "your approach," and the topic is "data management." So, the author needs to focus on the proposed "approach" to "data management." Some of the value of this exercise is the attention required by the author to break up the requirement into its component parts. This focus alone can be beneficial.

Now the author needs to decide what information to include in each subparagraph. A useful technique is to have authors analyze the verbs used in the Section L instructions.

Analyzing Verbs Used in Section L Instructions

Verbs used frequently in government RFPs include:

- *Describe*
- *Discuss*
- *Explain*
- *Identify*

- *Provide*
- *List*
- *Submit*

Each verb suggests a slightly different set of information. For example, "describe" normally requests more extensive information than "list." Figure 10-8 lists typical verbs and suggests the connotation of each. Ask authors to analyze the verb used in the Section L statement as a way of helping determine what information to include. The most important part of this exercise is to force a detailed analysis of the RFP requirement and the information being requested by the customer.

I do not imagine that customers spend a lot of time selecting the right verbs to include in Section L instructions. Nonetheless, paying attention to verbs can help focus your response.

When the RFP asks you to "describe" something, you should create a word picture that communicates the essential elements of what is being described. To describe an object, we might state its purpose or function and then list its key attributes or features. Here is a simple example to illustrate this point:

Describe your automobile.

Its primary purpose is transportation. Key attributes include make, model, year, and perhaps color. If we wanted to add additional informa-

Figure 10-8. Typical Section L Verbs and Their Implied Connotations

VERB	CONNOTATION OR MEANING
Describe	Picture, illustrate, specify, characterize
Discuss	Talk about, explain, review
Identify	Name, classify, catalogue
Include	Address also, attach
Explain	Discuss, talk about
List	Catalogue, inventory
Provide	Furnish, give
Submit	Provide, attach, submit with proposal
Summarize	Overview, concise, brief, short, condensed

tion, we might include things like automatic transmission, air conditioning, six-disc CD player, automatic windows and locks, cruise control, etc.

To apply this principle to your proposal, start by listing the object's purpose or function and its key attributes. Organize them from general to specific, and then decide what level of detail you want to include in your response.

Describing a process or system is slightly different. Unlike objects, processes lack physical features. To describe a process, consider listing the person or organization responsible for the process, identify its purpose, list key inputs and outputs, and identify major phases, components, or steps. Use this information to organize your response.

Yet another approach is to identify the "who, what, where, when, why, and how" of the process. Consider another simple example:

Describe the process you use to change the oil in your car.

Who: *You*

What: *Change the oil and oil filter*

Where: *In your garage*

When: *Every 200 miles*

Why: *To maintain clear engine oil and prevent costly repairs*

How: *List the steps, required tools, and any special considerations required to change the oil.*

> ### Steps
> *1. Park car in garage*
> *2. Place oil pan under car and remove oil-drain plug*
> *3. Remove old oil filter*
> *4. Let oil drain and replace oil drain plug*
> *5. Install new oil filter*

6. Remove oil filler cap and pour in oil
7. Replace oil filler cap and dispose of old oil
<u>Parts:</u> *5 quarts 10-30W oil and new oil filter*
<u>Tools:</u> *5/8-inch wrench, oil filter wrench, 10-quart oil pan*
<u>Considerations:</u> *Let engine cool before draining oil to prevent burns*
Catch oil spilled from removing oil filter

This becomes the basis for your detailed outline. You then would use this information to prepare your response. Here is an example of what such a response might look like:

> *I change the oil and oil filter in my car every 2,000 miles to maintain clean engine oil. This prevents expensive engine repairs and increases the life of the car. Using my home garage, I drain the old oil and replace it with five quarts of superior brand 10-30W oil and a new brand XL-30 oil filter, each of which can be purchased at any auto parts store. An oil change takes about 15 minutes. It requires an oil filter wrench, a 5/8-inch wrench or one that is adjustable, and an oil pan with at least a seven-quart capacity to catch the old oil.*
>
> *First, I park the car in the garage and let the engine cool. Then I position the oil pan under the car to catch the old oil and loosen the drain nut on the oil pan of the car. I remove the old oil filter, taking care to ensure that any spilled oil is caught in the oil pan. I allow about five minutes for the old oil to drain, install the new oil filter, and replace the oil-drain nut on the oil pan. Next, I remove the oil filler cap on the top of the engine and carefully pour each can of oil into the oil receptacle. The oil change is complete once the oil cap is replaced and the old oil removed and properly disposed.*

RFP questions normally are far more complex, but the basic principles still apply. Keep in mind that these exercises are just tools that help identify and organize information to include in your response.

The "who, what, where, when, why, and how" exercise also can be used to develop the framework for responses to RFP questions that ask you to "explain" or "discuss" an object, process, or system. A different strategy is required for verbs like "identify," "list," or "submit."

When the RFP asks you to "identify" something, it usually means they want you to name, classify, or catalogue the object of the question. The basic response to "identify" is to provide the information requested and then decide how much embellishment you need to add. For example:

Section L: Identify the quality standards that will be used for the Delta program.
<u>Response:</u> We plan to use ISO 9001 quality standards on the Delta program.

This is the simplest response possible. In most instances, more information would need to be added to fully satisfy the evaluator reading this section of your proposal. If you are asked to identify an approach, process, or method, then you will need to expand the scope of your response.

Verbs like "list" and "submit" typically require even less information. For example:

Section L: Offerors shall list the application software to be used on this program.

Response: We plan to use three software application programs on this program: [list of software applications goes here. If the list is long, put it in a table and reference the table.]

Section L: Offerors shall submit a copy of their Software Development Plan with the proposal.

Response: Our Software Development Plan is included with our proposal response as Attachment B to the Technical Volume.

Completing Sheet 1

Once authors have a general understanding of the information being requested by the RFP, they can then use their technical or subject matter knowledge to further expand the outline and identify important points to be included in the proposal response. The detailed outline also must integrate requirements contained in the evaluation criteria and other relevant RFP requirements. If a graphic or illustration is going to be used within the proposal section, it should be so noted on the author guide.

The detailed outline should be captured on Sheet 1 of the author guide and reviewed by either the proposal manager or the technical volume manager. Ideally, this will occur before the author starts writing. However, this is not always practical. In such cases, review the outline as soon as possible and make any necessary corrections. When authors have more than one assignment, consider reviewing each outline as it is completed rather than waiting for the author to complete all the outlines.

A practice that can be helpful to other authors is to post completed author guides on a wall in the proposal area. This permits other authors to see the information being provided in other sections that might impact the content or focus of their section. This also provides proposal and technical volume managers the ability to see a complete summary of the technical proposal content.

Sheet 2 of the Author Guide

I recommend completing a first draft proposal section before you attempt to integrate themes and bid strategies. You can cram all the themes, discriminators, and "grabbers" you want into a proposal, but it will likely be a loser if you fail to respond completely to all RFP requirements.

Experience suggests that most people assigned to work on proposals have a hard enough time just writing a responsive proposal section. Asking them to develop convincing themes and identify discriminators, in addition to addressing all RFP requirements, generally is too much. The result of such an approach typically is a proposal section that includes a lot of hype and very little substance.

Section themes, discriminators, and information that integrate your bid strategy into the proposal are indeed important attributes of a winning proposal, but first things first. Start with a compliant, responsive section and then add all the "bells and whistles." A responsive, well-written proposal without all the extras is capable of winning. A nonresponsive proposal with all the extras will rarely produce a winner.

Once a proposal section is responsive to RFP requirements, begin integrating information that will enable you to gain competitive advantage. There are three general sources for this information. The first source is your bid strategy developed during the pre-proposal phase and refined to reflect specific RFP requirements. The second source is your specific approach to satisfying the customer's requirements, which is embedded in your proposed response to RFP requirements. The final source of information is your understanding of customer needs, desires, fears, and biases, the need being solved by the contract, and what is important to include in the proposal.

The starting point is to complete Sheet 2 of the author guide, shown in Figure 10-9, for each proposal section. Some of this information is derived directly from your bid strategy and assessment of competitors. The remainder is generated by integrating what you know about the customer and performing a feature-benefit analysis of what your are offering.

Developing Proposal Themes

A theme is a message you want to communicate to the customer. It can be a special point, an emphasis, a unique or superior benefit to the customer, a supported claim, or a way of highlighting a strength or a competitor's weakness. Focus on developing themes that either provide you a competitive advantage or neutralize a competitor's strength.

A good theme is direct, addresses a program issue or customer concern, and can be supported by concrete evidence. Themes are integrated throughout the proposal. They often occur in volume, section, and subsection introductions, but not exclusively.

Themes can be divided into two general categories: common and unique. Common themes are statements that one or more of your competitors can make. They are important, but they may not yield much of a competitive advantage. For example, the benefit of an automated software requirements tool may be "common" if competitors use a comparable tool. It would still be an integral part of a discussion on requirements traceability, but it may not give you an edge on the competition, unless they forget to include it.

Unique themes, or discriminators, are statements unique to your company or proposed approach. They are based upon particular advantages your company can offer or upon distinct disadvantages of your competitors. They include key features of your proposed approach and the attendant benefits gained by your customer. Discriminators are vital, credible

Figure 10-9. Sheet 2 of the Author Guide

AUTHOR GUIDE (Sheet 2 of 2)	
Section Theme: *Key message of section*	
Bid Strategy: *Strategy to be integrated/way to exploit competitor weakness/way to offset competitor strength*	
Competitor Strengths	**Competitor Weaknesses**
Themes to counter or neutralize competitor strengths	*Themes to exploit competitor weaknesses*
Feature/Benefit Analysis	
Features	**Benefits to Customer**
Ways to Reduce Proposal Risk	
Risk Areas	**Actions to Reduce Perceived Risk**

points meaningful to your customer. They provide the ammunition required to convince the customer that your organization is the best source for the contract.

Finally, themes can be categorized according to whether they are overarching themes or specific themes. Overarching or general themes implement program-wide bid strategies (as illustrated in Chapter 7). They carry a general message or emphasis that applies to every area of the proposal. Alternatively, specific themes apply to a selected portion of the proposal or a specific section or subsection. They most often apply to a specific aspect of your proposed approach. Features and their corresponding benefits, for example, typically are specific themes.

To develop specific themes, review your assessment of competitor strengths and weaknesses, plus your own strengths, with respect to the technical content of each proposal section and subsection. Combine this information with your knowledge of the customer and any peculiar or special RFP requirements. Your organization's past and current experience and success performing comparable work is a great source of themes. In-place processes and systems, shown to be effective on similar programs, also provide rich ingredients for specific themes. Likewise, the relevant experience of people you are bidding to perform the contract can be used to fashion an important theme.

There is a remarkable sameness in competing proposals. Talk to anyone who has served on a government source selection team. What you will likely hear is that frequently there is no real difference between competing proposals. When that occurs, the award usually is made solely on the basis of cost. Lacking a compelling reason otherwise, the government will always pick the low bidder. Well-developed and strategically positioned themes help separate you from the rest the pack.

Themes are sales tools. Use them to convince the customer your organization should be awarded the contract. They should differentiate you from the competition in a positive way, or at least help neutralize the competition. Themes have value only to the extent that they are meaningful in some way to the customer and to the need being solved by the solicitation. Keep this important point in mind as you develop your proposal themes.

Identifying Features and Benefits

A primary source of specific themes comes from analyzing the features of what you are proposing. Every part of your design, every system, every process, literally every aspect of what you are proposing, has a set of features. Figure 10-10 lists some general characteristics from which features can be derived.

Features are the attributes, characteristics, elements, or components that further describe the object or process being discussed. You can describe your car by listing its make, model, and year of manufacture. Its features are all the accessories that fully define the car. A sports car enthusiast might tell you about the size of her car's engine, its horsepower, or the six-speed transmission and the rack-and-pinion steering. These are all features. The owner of a mini-van, however, might be more likely to tell you about its seating capacity, its removable rear seats, and maybe its cargo-hauling capacity. Again, these are features. The features we talk about are those that have value or meaning to us. The features you communicate to your customer are the ones he considers important.

Figure 10-10. Potential Categories to Identify Features and Benefits

• Improve performance • Increase efficiency • Reduce cost (acquisition/lifecycle) • Improve reliability • Make it easier to repair or maintain • Make it easier to use or reduce workload • Reduce errors • Reduce lifecycle cost • Improve supportability • Hardware/software upgradeability/portability • Certified processes or systems	• Make it easier to manage or control • Improve communications • Enhance customer visibility into program activities • Improve safety • Enhances documentation • Anything the customer/user values or thinks is important • Anything that reduce risk • Proven systems or processes with demonstrated track record • Improves security

Features are important, but people generally do not *buy* features. They buy benefits. Therefore, to sell, you must not only highlight features, but also demonstrate how those features will benefit the customer. People do not buy cars. They buy transportation. They do not buy a 250 horsepower engine, but the ability to accelerate from 0 to 60 miles per hour in under five seconds or the ability to enter the freeway without risking their lives. Similarly, you do not buy an air conditioner, but the ability to maintain air temperature at a comfortable level when it is hot outside.

To transform a feature into a useable theme, you must link it to a benefit. In addition, the benefit must be of value to the customer. Or, you must persuade the customer that it is a benefit. Do not leave it up to the evaluator to guess or intuitively link a benefit to a proposed feature. Express it clearly. If possible, quantify the benefit.

To develop features and their corresponding benefits, review the content of each proposal section. Identify the features of any proposed hardware, software, system, interface, approach, or process being discussed. Sometimes it is more difficult to identify features for processes than it is for tangible objects. Yet, processes have features too. Ask yourself why you use this particular process rather than some other process or approach. Why did you select it? How are process results used? If you did not use this process, how would you accomplish the task? Have you used this process successfully on comparable programs? There are always aspects of a process that make it effective, efficient, more reliable, etc. These are candidate proposal features.

Developing themes from features is a three-step process:

1. List all features for product/process/plan/approach
2. Identify the value/benefit of the feature
3. State how the feature specifically benefits the customer or user

For example:

- Feature: *Electronic Ignition System*
- Benefit: *Ten percent less expensive than traditional ignition system and increases time between engine tune-ups from every 5,000 miles to every 15,000 miles.*
- Benefit to Customer: *Reduces total acquisition and support costs by 15% and requires equipment to be removed from service less frequently for maintenance.*

Proposing a 5-gigahertz microprocessor may be a phenomenal feature, but it counts for naught unless it produces a meaningful benefit to the customer. Things that benefit you may not be of value to the customer. For each feature and benefit, ask yourself, "So what?" Answering this question may help you express the benefit of a feature to the customer. After you have completed the list of features and benefits, decide which ones to include in your proposal.

Reducing Proposal Risk

You can write a great proposal section, cram it full of compelling themes, and still lose if you receive a high-risk rating. Hence, one of the keys to writing the winning proposal is to convince the customer you offer a low-risk approach. (Section M specifies whether a formal proposal risk evaluation will be performed and outlines the risk evaluation procedure.)

Risk is an important consideration even in cases where it is not formally evaluated. Regardless of formal evaluation criteria, it is always a good idea to convince the customer that you have considered and mitigated any potential risks that could jeopardize program success.

To conduct a formal risk assessment, government evaluators assign a risk rating based on your proposed approach and probable success of accomplishing RFP requirements. Risk is assessed according to three risk ratings—low, moderate, and high—and it typically considers technical performance, schedule, and cost (see Chapter 3 for details).

Receiving a proposal risk rating of moderate or high can spell disaster for your technical proposal. Customers universally avoid risk unless there is a persuasive reason otherwise. Most often, winning proposals receive low risk ratings across all evaluation factors. There are exceptions, however.

Customers are generally more risk-tolerant for development programs, especially those involving new technology, than they are for service-type contracts. Furthermore, recall that proposal evaluation is always relative to what competitors bid. Everything else being even, you can win with a risky approach if it is less risky than that proposed by your competitors, or perhaps if the risk is offset with comparable customer benefit.

Proposal risk is not "real" risk, but the perceived risk as assessed by source selection evaluators. Your proposal task is to convince them that you have taken the necessary steps to mitigate potential risks. Competitive advantage most often goes to the bidder with a low proposal risk rating. It may be acceptable to carry several areas with a moderate risk rating, but only if you can show clearly the benefits of such an approach.

Sheet 2 of the author guide has a space to record potential proposal risks and the actions you have taken to mitigate each risk. Read over your proposal section. Identify real or perceived risk areas related to your proposed approach and the RFP requirements. Try to put yourself in the role of the customer as you review your proposed approach. It is customer perception that counts here.

Once you have a list of potential risks, review them to determine which will be significant and meaningful to your customer. Do not list every conceivable risk. Otherwise, you may frighten evaluators by suggesting that everything you are proposing is risky. After you have culled the list to those that merit being addressed in your proposal, state what actions you have taken, or will take, to mitigate them to an acceptable level. Then integrate risk reduction actions into the outline and technical proposal.

Through your pre-proposal interactions with the customer, you should already have a good idea of those areas the customer perceives as risky. Some typical sources of risk are listed in Figure 10-11.

Some RFPs specifically require you to address risk management, including providing a list of potential program risks and the steps you have taken to mitigate those risks. In such cases, bidders usually include a risk table in their proposal (see Figure 10-12 for an example). This satisfies the risk management requirement, but it alone does not eliminate the importance of integrating risk mitigation strategies throughout your proposal.

Include clear statements about how you will mitigate potential proposal risks. Mitigation strategies must be tailored to the specific risk, program requirements, and customer. Some factors that help mitigate assessed risk are listed in Figure 10-13.

Ghosting Competitors' Approaches

Ghosting is a strategy to exploit a competitor weakness or counter a strength. Ghosting can cause the customer to view a competitor's approach as less desirable or more risky than what you are proposing. Proposal risk offers an area to develop a potential ghosting strategy.

If you suspect that a competitor is going to use a subcontractor to perform an important part of the contract, then highlight the point that you are avoiding the risks involved with using subcontractors. This can be espe-

Figure 10-11. Common Sources of Perceived Proposal Risk

- Significant software development efforts
- Lack of experience performing comparable contracts under similar conditions or requirements
- Proposing new or unproven technology, systems, or equipment
- Designs that require long lead-time equipment
- Integration of hardware/software with legacy systems
- Areas on past programs that have caused problems for the customer
- Programs where equipment obsolescence over the life of the contract is an issue
- Experience of personnel assigned to program, especially key personnel
- Subcontractors proposed to perform significant or critical portion of program
- Perceived understanding of technical requirements/problem to be solved
- Maturity level of proposed process/plans/systems
- Perceived ability of offeror to monitor, manage, and control program
- Perception of poor or inadequate planning
- Schedules that appear overly optimistic
- Unrealistic level of effort proposed for particular task or area
- Perception that offeror may be difficult to work with or manage
- Staffing new programs that require a significant number of engineering or technical personnel
- Transitioning an existing program from an incumbent
- Long-term supportability of systems and equipment, especially those that involve technology
- Anything that even hints of a "trust me" attitude

Figure 10-12. Sample Risk Management Table Entry

1. Risk Area: Initial Staffing	Risk prior to Mitigation: Moderate	Risk after Mitigation: Low
Risk Description/Rationale: Staffing is the most critical element for a successful transition to a new contractor. Incumbent staff must be retained on the program for legacy knowledge, and additional staffing sources must be readily available to supplement any shortfall from the incumbent workforce.		
Impact on Cost/Schedule/Performance: Lack of sufficient staffing could delay normal operational schedules and cause system degradation due to poor maintenance practices.		
Risk Mitigation: As described in the Transition Plan, Alpha's staffing plan is focused on capturing all key incumbent personnel and provides extensive back-up resources to supplement any shortfalls in staffing from existing Alpha operations.		
Impact of Mitigation on Other Program Elements: None		

Figure 10-13. Ways to Mitigate Perceived Proposal Risk

• Successful experience performing similar requirements under comparable conditions • Experience with similar contract types • Demonstrated maturity of proposed process/plan/approach/system • Experience of assigned personnel • Don't expect customer to "trust you"	• Trade studies to select equipment or approach • Demonstrated understanding of technical requirements or problem to be solved • Documented make/buy studies and competitive selection of vendors or subcontractors

cially effective if the customer has experienced problems in the past where subcontractor performance has negatively impacted program success. Highlighting a risk and presenting your mitigation strategy also can ghost a competitor who fails to identify the same risk, if that risk applies to the competitor's approach.

Trade studies represent another way to ghost a competitor's approach as being inferior to what you are proposing. Let's say you are proposing computer "X" and a competitor is proposing computer "Y." You conduct a trade study to evaluate candidate computers, including "X," "Y," and "Z." The results show clearly that computer X represents the best choice. List the reasons you selected computer X and the reasons you rejected computer Y.

Because you control the study, you can set trade study evaluation criteria and weights to give the results you want. Besides, there should be some valid reasons why you chose computer X. Include them in your proposal. By presenting trade study results, you can lead the customer to the same conclusion: Computer X is the right choice. Incidentally, conducting trade studies to validate your proposed approach also is an excellent risk mitigation strategy.

Ghosting can be used to highlight a competitor weakness. First, you can emphasize your strength, experience, or competence in a particular area and show how this is important to program success. Or, you can point out how lacking this "strength" could jeopardize or undermine program success. Yet another way of ghosting is to point out why you are not proposing an approach that you suspect one of your competitors is proposing. For example:

- *"We considered using chemical X in our process, but abandoned it when we discovered it had led to the death of half the population of Pakistan."*

- *"We use a reflected optics aim point system to avoid the safety hazards of a laser eye point system."*
- *"Our system uses a collimated display, which avoids the inherent shortcomings of an uncollimated display, including safety of flight and degraded training effectiveness."*

Ghosting is about manipulating customer perceptions. It is a way of stacking the deck against your competitors. Manipulation does not mean being underhanded. Nor does it suggest being dishonest. Honesty is an absolute in proposals. It is acceptable to exaggerate the truth, but not to invent it. Never lie in a proposal or claim something that is clearly false. Nonetheless, it is acceptable to present information that shows your organization and your proposed approach in the best possible light, much in the same way you would in a personal résumé. Within the boundaries of honesty, it is okay to present information in a manner that casts doubt on the approach or capability of competitors.

PROPOSAL RESPONSIBILITY MATRIX

The proposal responsibility matrix shows the person responsible for every proposal preparation requirement. The easiest way to develop a responsibility matrix is to paste the proposal outline into a table. Then assign a person to every single section or subsection of the proposal outline.

The core capture team will fill the roles of proposal manager, technical volume manager, contracts manager, and cost volume manager. Individual author responsibility is then assigned to cover every remaining proposal requirement. Also plan to include page count allocations in the responsibility matrix. For page-limited proposals, use the relative weights of evaluation criteria to calculate a page estimate. Then factor this by the amount of information being requested by Section L for each section. Remember to allocate pages for section and volume introductions.

Figure 10-14 provides a sample responsibility matrix using the proposal outline for Section 2.2—*Training System Support Center.* The completed matrix should cover all proposal volumes and sections, including any required attachments, such as statements of work, specifications, etc. A responsible person must be assigned to every item of the proposal outline. Whenever two or more people collaborate on a section, assign primary responsibility to one of them.

The responsibility matrix provides a good tool to monitor individual proposal progress at daily proposal status meetings. Expand the left-hand side of Figure 10-14 to include schedule completion dates for each proposal require-

Figure 10-14. Sample Responsibility Matrix for Section 2.2 of the Proposal Outline

Proposal Requirement	Person Responsible	Page Count
VOLUME I:	Proposal Manager	
Section 1.0 Executive Summary	Green	3
Section 2.0 Technical	Technical Volume Manager	40
2.2 Training System Support Center (TSSC)		**27.0**
Introduction		1
2.2.1 XYZ Approach and Proposed Resources to Operate and Maintain the TSSC	Martin	4
2.2.2 Overview of XYZ Maintenance Approach to Meet the 95% Availability Requirement	Jones	4
2.2.3 XYZ Methods to Maintain LSP, ICS, MDC at the Site and System Level	Jones	3
2.2.3.1 Ability of XYZ's LSP to Support Logistics Functions	Jones	1
2.2.3.2 Capability of XYZ's Inventory Control System (ICS)	Jones	1
2.2.3.3 XYZ's Approach to Maintenance Data Collection	Jones	1
2.2.4 XYZ Approach and Capability to Support Equipment for the Aging ATS	Jones	2
2.2.5 XYZ Approach to Integrate and Maintain Multiple Baselines	Smith	2
2.2.6 XYZ Approach to Develop and Maintain All Aspects of C-141 ATS Configuration	Smith	2
2.2.7 XYZ Approach to ensure a first-time quality delivery of courseware	Gonzales	2
2.2.8 XYZ's Maintenance Plan for the ABC System	Woods	4

ment contained in the matrix. During the status meeting, have each person report progress toward their next scheduled proposal requirement.

DETAILED PROPOSAL SCHEDULE

Proposal schedules have three levels or tiers. The first tier is a schedule for the overall proposal. The second tier is a separate schedule for each proposal volume or major section. The final tier is a detailed schedule that includes every item contained in your proposal outline.

Tier 1 Proposal Schedule

Tier 1, or the overall proposal schedule, is first developed during the pre-proposal phase. It is then adjusted to reflect any subsequent changes in the draft or final RFP. Tier 1 schedules include only major proposal activities and milestones. They are used to coordinate the overall proposal effort. However, all lower tier schedules are keyed to the Tier 1 schedule.

Key variables used to build an overall proposal schedule include:

- Amount of time allotted by the government to prepare your proposal
- Number of proposal drafts you plan to write in addition to the final version
- Number and type of proposal reviews
- Any required management reviews
- Time to prepare and deliver the proposal to the government.

Be realistic in estimating the amount of time required to complete proposal tasks. Leave a little slack in your schedule to accommodate unforeseen contingencies. Things always end up taking longer than you planned.

Some common mistakes to avoid include:

1. Scheduling a proposal review before authors have had adequate time to prepare responsive proposal sections
2. Expecting authors to include everything—themes, strategy, features/benefits, etc.—in first draft proposal material
3. Trying to squeeze in more proposal iterations than time will allow
4. Failing to recognize the dependency between the technical and cost proposals and that many technical authors also are responsible for preparing staffing and cost estimates
5. Failing to allow enough time after the final proposal review for final editing and quality assurance.

Generally, I prefer three proposal iterations: two drafts and a final. Ideally, the first draft proposal is prepared in response to a draft RFP and before the final RFP is released. Otherwise, you may be hard-pressed to complete two drafts after the final RFP arrives and still allow enough time for reviews and final proposal preparation.

Today, most government agencies allow between 30 and 60 days to respond to a RFP. Some task-order RFPs allow less than 30 days, and some major programs give bidders more than 60 days. Figure 10-15 provides sample overall proposal schedules based on a 45-day and a 30-day response time (numbers in parentheses are for a 30-day response). The sample includes a draft proposal, an internal review, and revisions prior to the first formal review (red team). Time is allotted to make corrections based on the red team review and then a final edit before production and delivery.

For the 45-day schedule, 5 days are devoted to preparation, 14 days for the first draft, and then 7 days to revise the draft before the red team review. This includes time for a quick internal check for responsiveness to RFP requirements and then a revision before the red team review. Three days are allotted to prepare for and conduct the red team review. Thirteen days are given to correct deficiencies detected by the red team and to complete a final edit. Finally, 3 days are dedicated to perform final production and deliver the proposal to the customer. This gives a total of 34 of the 45 days to prepare the proposal, with the remaining 11 days allocated to preparation, reviews, production, and delivery.

For the 30-day schedule, activities are more compressed. Only a single pass is made for the first draft proposal, with no revisions performed before the red team review. For this schedule, 20 days are devoted to preparing, correcting, and editing the proposal, and 10 days are allotted for preparation, review, and final production.

Figure 10-15. Sample Proposal Schedule for 45- and 30-Day Response Times

	PROPOSAL PREPARATION SCHEDULE		
Event No.	Event/Activity	Days Allotted	Days Elapsed
1	**RFP Released**	0	0
2	RFP Distributed and Reviewed	1	1
3	Proposal Roadmap Complete	2	3
4	Authors Complete Outlnes/Storyboards	2	5
5	Authors Complete 1st Draft	14 (12)	19 (17)*
7	Authors Revised 1st Draft	7 (0)	26 (17)
8	Prepare Red Team Review Materials	1 (0)	27 (17)
9	Conduct Red Team Review	2	29 (19)
10	Revise Final Proposal	8 (5)	37 (24)
11	Final Editing and Quality Check	5 93)	42 (27)
12	Proposal Production and Final Quality Check	2 (2)	44 (29)
13	**Proposal Packaged and Delivered**	1	45 (30)
*Numbers in parentheses indicate the schedule for a 30-day response time.			

It should be clear from either schedule that precious little time is available to prepare your proposal. Therefore, the more work you can accomplish before the RFP is released, the better.

Tier 2 Proposal Schedule

The Tier 2 schedule is keyed to the milestone events of the overall schedule. It provides a separate schedule for each proposal volume and includes a finer level of detail for proposal activities. Proposal activities for the technical volume, for example, differ from those required for the cost and contracts volume. Each requires its own detailed schedule.

A Tier 2 schedule for the technical proposal requires a breakout of major technical volumes, sections, attachments, or additional technical requirements like the preparation of a statement of work. Some technical proposals consist of multiple volumes, such as management, engineering, and logistics, or the development of plans, schedules, or specifications that are included as part of the technical proposal. Each major technical requirement must be scheduled separately to allow easy monitoring of proposal progress and to help ensure a coordinated technical effort. This is especially important when there is a sequential dependency between two or more sections of the technical proposal. For example, if you must finish preparing a product specification before completing a section of the technical proposal, then this must be accounted for in your Tier 2 proposal schedule.

Your schedule for the cost and contracts volume will be determined by the specific cost volume requirements dictated by the RFP, the type of procurement, and your own internal cost estimating process. Some RFPs require only a completed Section B. Others require considerable cost volume narrative, including a basis of estimate for each area of your proposed cost. These individual cost activities must be scheduled. In addition, the cost estimate is directly dependent upon your proposed technical solution.

The same people writing the technical proposal may be required to provide input into the cost estimating process. The Tier 2 schedule is the place to schedule individual costing activities and to show their relationship, if any, to the technical proposal schedule. A common mistake that proposal teams make is to allow the final technical solution to remain in flux until the last minute. With insufficient time remaining, the cost volume team then is unable to develop and document an adequate cost estimate. This may cause government evaluators to downgrade your proposal due to perceived cost risk or a lack of traceability between your proposed technical solution and your bid cost. If this happens, you are surrendering competitive advantage to the competition.

Another factor in building a Tier 2 cost volume schedule is the type of internal cost reviews to be conducted, especially those given to senior management. If you work in an organization that is part of a larger corporate structure, then you probably will need to schedule time for corporate review and approval.

Tier 3 Proposal Schedule

The third tier proposal schedule is a detailed day-by-day schedule. It is derived by scheduling each activity contained in the proposal responsibility matrix. For example, Jones has several proposal assignments, as shown in Figure 10-12. Each needs to be scheduled. Moreover, the schedule due dates should not all occur at the end of the total allotted schedule. If 14 days are allotted for a first draft proposal with a scheduled due date of October 1, then the individual schedule for Jones might look like this:

Section 2.2 Due: September 21
Section 2.3 Due: September 26
Section 2.4 Due: October 1

Tier 3 schedules focus on the next proposal milestone to be achieved. For example, completion dates would be entered for the first draft proposal only until that milestone was achieved. Thereafter, completion dates would be entered for the next proposal milestone. This enables individual daily schedules to be based on the amount of work to be accomplished within the boundaries of milestone and Tier 2 schedules.

My preference for establishing Tier 3 schedules is to ask individual proposal authors to schedule each of their assigned proposal sections within the boundaries of the milestone date. This gives authors the freedom to assess schedules and manage their own workload. The only caveat is that not everything can be scheduled to be due on the last day before the milestone. Authors who have more than one assignment must spread them over the available timeframe.

Having a day-by-day proposal schedule may seem to be an unnecessary level of detail. It is not. Time is precious. Therefore, it is critical to identify problems early enough to solve them before they negatively affect the proposal. A Tier 3 schedule also enables individual proposal sections to be reviewed as they are completed versus waiting until the milestone date. Authors receive timely feedback both to correct completed material and to guide preparation of future proposal sections. Finally, building a daily proposal schedule often reveals shortfalls in proposal resources that are not evident otherwise. An author may not notice the magnitude of his or her assigned tasks until they start building a daily schedule. Again, this enables the early identification of potential problems while sufficient time remains to solve them.

Enormous competitive advantage is the spoils of the bidder who successfully plans to prepare a completely compliant, responsive proposal that highlights themes and discriminators to sell the proposed solution. Seize this advantage through effective planning. Develop a proposal outline that perfectly reflects the Section L instructions. Integrate evaluation criteria and other RFP requirements into an easy-to-use matrix. Then prepare author guides to establish a proposal preparation blueprint based on this information. Integrate your bid strategy and key characteristics of your proposed approach into the author guide.

Ensure that every proposal requirement is covered by assigning it to a responsible person. Develop a detailed, day-by-day schedule for each proposal requirement and each person assigned to the proposal. Monitor individual performance against schedule during daily proposal status meetings. Identify potential problems early and take immediate corrective action.

No aspect of the proposal development process is less forgiving than the planning phase. Fail here, and the prospects of winning are dim indeed. All too often proposal teams feel pressured to start writing. So they launch into a first draft response without a plan. Resist this temptation. Time spent planning will pay huge dividends when it comes to writing proposal narrative. Rarely will you hear anyone claim that the reason they lost a competitive bid was because their planning was too good.

Chapter 11

Writing the Winning Proposal

The material contained in your proposal is the only information that source selection evaluators have to evaluate your technical proposal. In fact, they are expressly forbidden to include other information. An exception is when oral presentations or site surveys are included as part of the technical evaluation. Even then, this information normally is supplemental to what you submitted in your written proposal.

Your customer may know you and may be familiar with your experience and capability. Even so, do not count on a favorable customer bias or their knowledge of your organization when you prepare your proposal. Such reliance is ill-advised and very risky.

To write the winning proposal, you must clearly respond to all RFP requirements and structure your response so that it appears where evaluators expect to see it. An evaluator will sit down with your proposal along with a list of evaluation criteria and standards organized according to the Section L instructions. He or she will read your proposal to determine the extent to which your written response meets those standards. Because evaluation criteria are tied to Section L, it is critical to present material in the same order as it is requested in this section. In addition, you must address the evaluation criteria and incorporate any other relevant RFP requirements.

The order of priority for addressing RFP requirements is:

- Section L instructions
- Section M evaluation criteria
- Statement of work
- Specifications or CDRLs
- Special contract clauses.

You also must provide sufficient information to convince the customer that you are the best choice for the contract.

WRITING TO EVALUATORS

The customers for your proposal are government evaluators who make up the source selection team. They read your proposal, compare it to evaluation standards, and assign it a score or rating. Although they do not make the source selection decision, their evaluation results are the foundation upon which the source selection decision is made. Toward that end, they are not only the final voice, but also the only voice that matters, in determining the merit of your proposal. You must convince individual evaluators that your proposal offers the best solution to meet their requirement. In simple terms: Satisfy your customer and you win; fail to satisfy your customer and you lose.

Who are source selection evaluators? Mostly, they are people like you and me. They generally want to do a good job and care about conducting a fair and effective source selection. However, keep in mind that evaluating proposals is a very difficult and often thankless job. Evaluators may enjoy their task even less than you enjoy reading RFPs and writing proposals. They may be inexperienced. Rarely do they have enough time to perform their tasks properly. They often are not experts in the subject matter they are asked to review. Frequently they have very little experience evaluating proposals. They have biases, likes, and dislikes. They are influenced by the same things as other people. Furthermore, more than one government evaluator may be suspicious or distrustful of government contractors.

How you view the people who will evaluate your proposal can have a significant impact on how you prepare your proposal response. This in turn impacts the score your proposal receives and ultimately the probability that you will win the competition.

Have you ever reviewed a large stack of résumés, trying to decide which ones to retain for further review and which ones to discard? It is a difficult challenge. Faced with this task, people tend to unconsciously look for reasons to eliminate résumés from further consideration to simplify the review process. I think government evaluators sometimes use a similar approach to evaluating proposals, especially if there are many bidders.

Make the evaluators' job as easy as possible. Do not give them a reason to "set your proposal aside" or assign it a low score. Instead, give them all the information they need to complete their task and equip them with enough reasons to select you as the winner. This is easier said than done, but the following tips will help keep you on the right path:

- Present proposal information where evaluators expect to find it. Organize your proposal in the *exact* same order that Section L information is requested. If possible, use the same paragraph numbering scheme, paragraph headings, and key words as Section L to make it clear what information is being provided.

- Clearly and effectively answer the Section L questions. Evaluators read your proposal looking for the information they need to compare with the evaluation standard. If they have difficulty finding this information or determining whether or not your proposal fully addresses the standard, then they may assign a low score to this section. If the evaluator is tired, having a bad day, or happens to be lazy, you may receive an "unacceptable" or "unsatisfactory" rating. Recall that one poor rating can negatively affect the rating for an entire factor. It is impossible to overemphasize the importance of providing a clear, concise proposal answer to the information requested by Section L and placing it where the evaluator expects to find it.
- Write to the evaluators, not your technical peers. Do not presume that the evaluator possesses any technical expertise. Many do not. Your response must be understandable to the layperson. In addition, it must contain sufficient detail and information to satisfy the technical expert.
- Use simple, straightforward language to communicate your ideas. Avoid technical jargon and use acronyms sparingly, taking time to spell them out the first time they appear. Do not try to impress anyone with your extensive vocabulary or bury readers with your technical sophistication. Even relatively inexperienced evaluators recognize a verbal snowstorm when they see it.
- Do not omit requested information because you think the customer already knows it. As indicated above, evaluators are allowed to evaluate only what you submit in your proposal.
- Do not use language or style that even hints of arrogance. This tends to be a problem with very large companies and those who have especially strong technical expertise. No one likes arrogance, including evaluators. Arrogant language often does not appear arrogant to the author, because an arrogant statement may be true. "We are the best gismo manufacturer on the planet and no one else even comes close" may be true. Yet it probably will not be well received by evaluators. There are more graceful ways to boast about your company's strengths. A better rendering might be, "We have produced two million gismos over the last five years, more than twice as many as any other supplier. Moreover, our gismos have a 99 percent reliability rate, which leads the industry."
- Substantiate your claims. Unsupported claims tend to be viewed as little more than idle boasting or arrogance. In fact, no claims are better than unsubstantiated claims.
- Do not let your frustration or displeasure with the RFP or the way the customer is asking for information seep into your proposal. What the customer is asking for and the way it is being requested may be inane. That does not matter. It is, after all, the customer's RFP.

- Do not attack competitors directly or by name. Instead, "ghost" their approach, highlighting a competitor's weakness by emphasizing your strength or by creating the impression that the competitor's approach is more risky or less desirable than what you are proposing.
- Use the same language and terms used in the RFP. This applies not only to paragraph headings, but also to how you refer to objects or processes in your proposal narrative. If the RFP refers to a process as the "XYZ system," then you should also refer to this process as the XYZ system in your proposal, regardless of whether or not that is the term you normally use. Using the RFP language may help evaluators find information they are looking for.
- Do not assume that the evaluator scoring one section of your proposal has read the other sections. Proposals often are divided among evaluators. Some evaluators read only a single proposal section, or only those sections related to their area of responsibility. If a point made in another part of your proposal is relevant or important, then summarize its relevance or importance to the current section. If the other material is contained in the same proposal volume or section, then summarize the point and refer the evaluator to the other section for more detail. Of course, if you send the evaluator to another part of the proposal, be sure that the reference is correct and relevant. If an evaluator looks for a cross-reference and fails to find it, you may receive a lower score than if you had omitted the reference.

WRITING THE FIRST DRAFT

The proposal method I advocate focuses on responding to RFP requirements. For the first draft, do not worry about themes, discriminators, or features and benefits. Integrate them on the next pass. The danger lies in authors focusing on themes and discriminators at the expense of responding to RFP requirements. Even the most experienced proposal writers struggle with trying to integrate too much into a first draft.

This approach is based on two presumptions. First, it presumes that the first draft proposal is being written to a draft RFP. Therefore, ample time will be available to integrate things like bid strategies and themes. Second, this approach is based on working with a relatively inexperienced proposal team. If you have a team of seasoned veterans who routinely prepare proposals, then you may elect a different approach.

If you do not start your first draft until after the final RFP is released, and you have a relatively short response time, then you face a dilemma. Can you afford to wait until late in the proposal preparation cycle to integrate your bid strategy and to highlight reasons why the customer should pick you? All the themes, discriminators, features and benefits, and good words in the world will seldom produce a winner if you fail to respond adequately to RFP requirements. Consider the following analogy to illustrate this point.

Imagine you are asked to bake a cake that will be evaluated at the annual state fair. No judge will respond favorably to a plate of icing, candles, and glitter without a cake underneath. You must bake the cake first. Responding to RFP requirements is "baking the cake." Themes, discriminators, features, and benefits are the "glitter." They enhance, but do not replace, the basic cake.

Getting authors to write clear proposal narrative that responds to RFP requirements is among the most difficult aspects of preparing a winning proposal. It also is perhaps the single most important component. Unfortunately, many proposal team members struggle with their writing assignments. Here are a few tips for authors getting started on the first draft:

- Find a place to write that is free of distractions. Working in your office is probably a bad idea. Ideally, your organization will have a separate location for proposal preparation. Otherwise, find a place where you will not be interrupted by phone calls and your normal work routine.
- Start with the detailed outline contained in the author guide. This is your primary planning document. It provides the basic structure and content to get you started.
- Do not try to write the perfect first draft. This is perhaps the single greatest reason for writer's block. We call it a "first" draft because we know that it will require revision.
- Do not worry about grammar, spelling, typing errors, or anything else that will distract you from your primary assignment. These corrections can be made later. Just keep writing.
- Write the easiest parts of the proposal section first. If you get to a writing impasse, move on to another section.
- Do not worry about page allocations. My general rule is not to exceed three times the allocation. It is far easier to edit an oversized section than it is to generate it. Authors concerned about page allocation may not be a good judge of what to include and what to delete.
- If you get stuck or just cannot seem to get started, try "free writing." This is just writing whatever comes to mind: "Here I sit working on this stupid proposal. I don't know what to say or how to say it. I wish I were somewhere else. Maybe if I just let my mind wander, eventually I will be able to write something of value." Keep at it until you feel comfortable with writing, and then turn your attention back to the proposal. If this does not work, consider sitting with a friend or colleague and explaining to them what you are trying to say or explain in the proposal. Sometimes this will help organize or focus your thoughts to the point where you can capture them with words.

- Do not get frustrated or discouraged if you are having difficulty with your writing. Unless you are a member of the proposal staff, it is unlikely that you were hired for your writing ability. Even professional writers struggle with their writing and wrestle with periodic writer's block.

CLEAR AND EFFECTIVE COMMUNICATIONS

One of your primary objectives is to communicate your message clearly. If the evaluators cannot find the information where they expect to see it or do not understand what you are saying, then your competitors will likely gain competitive advantage.

Use paragraph headings from the proposal outline and author guide to organize content. The proposal headings and numbering contained in the author guide should not be altered, but you can use sub-paragraph headings to organize the topics within a section. This is especially important when a single Section L instruction includes multiple requirements and topics.

Focus your writing on the topic and do not stray. This is easier said than done. It is amazing how easy it is to write around a topic without ever addressing the Section L requirement. Consider the following lighthearted example:

> *SECTION L:* The offeror shall discuss his approach for making a peanut butter sandwich.
> *RESPONSE:* We are the best peanut butter sandwich makers in the industry. Our proven methods ensure our customers receive high-quality sandwiches at the lowest lifecycle cost. Our sandwich makers use state-of-the-art equipment and have extensive experience and significant expertise. In addition, our quality control department uses commercial "best practice" standards to ensure that our customers get what they want.

This is good example of how *not* to write. The text sounds okay, but it does not answer the Section L requirement. That makes it nonresponsive, which means it will receive a poor score. In addition, all the claims are vague and lack substantiation. This makes them meaningless. The same thing happens in real proposals, only the topics usually are more complicated than peanut butter sandwiches.

Write from general to specific and from simple to complex. If you are explaining a complicated process, provide a brief overview highlighting its key characteristics. Then fill in the details in subsequent sentences or paragraphs. Similarly, you can break a system or process into its major components, followed by a more detailed description of each component. For example:

> *Our systems engineering process consists of four interrelated and integrated steps: requirements analysis, functional allocation, synthesis, and systems analysis and control.*

Then describe each of these steps in the same order they were introduced.

Here is another example:

> *Our X-22 grenade launcher is among the most lethal and accurate weapons in the light infantry arsenal. Firing four different 40-mm projectiles, it consists of three parts to facilitate rapid cleaning and repair: a barrel assembly, trigger assembly, and stock assembly.*

Now, provide the details about each assembly, again in the order it was mentioned.

Starting with specific or complex information at the beginning of a section makes it difficult for the reader to understand. Avoid this pitfall. Moving from general to complex will help readers conceptualize the process or system you are describing. Moreover, it is a good way to organize proposal narrative logically.

REVISING THE FIRST DRAFT

After you have captured your first thoughts in writing, it is time to massage them into compelling narrative that fully and clearly satisfies all RFP requirements. The starting point is the author guide. Review the draft response against the requirements contained there and against your detailed outline. Have you addressed every RFP requirement? Have you made all the points you intended? Put yourself in the place of the evaluator. Does the section contain the information you would expect to see? Have you incorporated any customer biases, fears, or preferences into your write-up? Use the answers to these questions to help guide your next iteration.

As part of your revision efforts, you should start to correct spelling, grammar, and any other errors in the first draft. You also should use this version to begin organizing and polishing proposal narrative so that it communicates your message effectively.

Once you are convinced that your proposal section addresses each relevant RFP requirement effectively, it should be submitted for an internal or in-process review by either the proposal manager or the technical volume manager. The purpose of the internal review is to verify that the proposal section complies with and is responsive to all RFP requirements. This review also is used to provide feedback to the author that will help with the next draft.

PAGE-LIMITED PROPOSALS

Some RFPs limit the number of pages you are allowed to present in your proposal. Usually such limitations apply only to the technical proposal, but not always. In other cases, page limitations are levied only on particular sections of the proposal, excluding things like statement of work, specifications, plans, and detailed schedules. Exceeding page limitations has dire consequences. First, it suggests to the customer that you cannot follow directions. More importantly, pages beyond the limitation will not be evaluated. This alone could cause you to lose the bid.

Page-limited proposals are consistent with acquisition streamlining initiatives. Faced with the task of evaluating multiple proposals, the customer makes the evaluation task manageable by limiting the number of allowable pages. Without limitations, bidders tend to bury the customer in an avalanche of words, perhaps hoping that longer is better. In yesteryears I can recall loading our proposal onto an 18-wheeler with a forklift and driving it to the customer. Thank heavens those days are history.

RFPs that limit the number of allowable proposal pages also specify maximum allowable page sizes, margins, minimum font sizes, and line spacing to prevent bidders from nullifying the limitation. They normally specify what you may or may not include as appended material or exhibits, charts, videotapes, etc. These may be limited, completely barred, or admissible only under certain specified conditions. These RFPs also define pages that are not subject to the page count, such as cover sheets, tables of contents, and specific proposal sections. Page limitations and format are defined in Section L of the RFP and should be captured in your proposal directive.

Page-limited proposals discourage verbosity and affect how you structure your response. The challenge you face is addressing all RFP requirements and presenting a compelling sales message within the boundaries of the limitation. You may view page limitations as a barrier to presenting your case. Indeed, sometimes it appears to be an impossible task to fit all the requested information into the available pages. Yet, the resourceful proposal team can turn this into an advantage. Your competitors face the same challenge. Do a better job of fitting essential proposal information into your proposal, and you gain competitive advantage.

Read the wording of the page limitation instructions carefully. Note what is limited or restricted and what is not. The instructions may exclude certain items such as personnel résumés or schedules from the limitation. This will enable you to be as detailed as you like in these areas. Also, search to see if minimum font size is specified for tables or figures. If it is, then you must adhere to the limitation. If it is not, you may be able to use a slightly smaller font than what is specified for text. However, never go below about 8 points for graphics or tables. Otherwise, evaluators may not be able to read them. Some RFPs permit appended material.

Once you know what you can and cannot include, you can manage proposal content and location. Put "nice to have" but not essential information into proposal sections or attachments that are not page-limited. This will enable you to optimize proposal content and stay within the limits.

Here are some general tips for handling page-limited proposals:

- Do not attempt to write a proposal that will fit the page limitation. Instead, write a proposal that addresses all RFP requirements and presents the information necessary to capture the program. Then edit the proposal to fit page limitations.
- Consider using a two-column page format. This increases the amount of information per page. However, some RFPs specify single-column. In addition, two-column text is not a good idea if the proposal will be evaluated electronically. (It is too hard to read on a computer monitor.)
- Look for opportunities to present information in illustrations, graphs, and tables. Make illustrations only as large as they need to be. Illustrations often contain unnecessary detail. Use proposal space sparingly; crop and size illustrations accordingly.
- Do not sacrifice material that answers RFP requirements for sales propaganda. Themes are an integral part of your proposal, but they are not adequate substitutes for responsive, compliant proposal text.
- Do not repeatedly cross-reference material contained in other proposal sections to reduce page count. Some cross-referencing is acceptable, but only under specific conditions. Limit cross-references to the same general proposal section or volume. Remember that evaluators may not have immediate access to the referenced section. Summarize the point you want to make before making the cross-reference. Finally, for electronically evaluated proposals, you can hyperlink the cross-referenced section. Hyperlinking extends the limits of acceptable cross-referencing.

EDITING AND REVISION

Some proposal authors feel that the longer the narrative, the better the proposal. Yet more often, wordiness is due to a lack of writing experience.

Skillful editing is the single best tool available to manage page count. Eliminating excess verbiage from first drafts often is the only remedy. Unfortunately, the majority of those assigned to write proposal sections are not experienced or skilled proposal writers. They also generally lack the skills necessary to edit and refine the product to produce a terse, responsive proposal.

If you are blessed with an experienced proposal team that possesses good writing skills, then they can perform most of the editing. Otherwise, final editing will need to be performed by a technical editor assigned to the proposal team or another member of the proposal team with good editing ability. Ideally, your proposal administrator will have good editing skills.

Two types of editing, or trimming, are required. The first removes unnecessary and irrelevant verbiage and corrects simple spelling and grammatical errors. The second eliminates material of secondary importance and hones the final product to a razor's edge. Some specific tips for writing and editing are presented in Chapter 12.

GRAPHICS

Illustrations and tables can be an important part of your proposal. They help break up the monotony of endless lines of text. More importantly, they depict information that cannot be expressed properly with words alone. Well-designed graphics express complex information in an easily understood format. They also permit presentation of significant quantities of information in very limited space, which helps solve page-count problems.

Most proposals benefit from or require graphical presentations. Keep in mind the following criteria to determine when to use words and when to use tables and other illustrations to convey your proposal message. Charts, graphs, and pictures are effective when you need to:

- Describe complex technical processes, like systems engineering, or depict relationships. Typical applications include presentations of company or project organizations, customer–contractor interfaces, schedules, and activities or processes that lend themselves to flow charts.
- Describe something that requires the reader to form a mental image to understand what is being proposed, such as the production line in a manufacturing facility or a map with geographical locations marked.
- Show your company's facilities, engineering and manufacturing centers, and product or design features. (Photos are usually more suitable for these applications than pure graphics.)
- Present information in a form the evaluator will be able to recall easily. People tend to remember visual images over words. Graphics like system component diagrams provide a visual image that will help the reader comprehend the word description you provide with the proposal text.

Tables are useful when you need to present a lot of numerical data. Data like project staffing, or the number of employees in your company by labor category, are tailor-made for tables. So too is information that can be provided as a list or can be organized easily into categories. For page-limited proposals, tables offer the opportunity to save space, especially if the allowable font size for tables is smaller than for text.

Using Graphics Effectively

Well-designed and strategically placed graphics enhance your proposal presentation. Alternatively, poorly designed graphics that are confusing, hard to read, or not properly explained by proposal text can do more damage than good. Two general principles should be applied to graphics:

1. *The graphic or table should convey information essential to the point you are trying to make.* Do not put graphics in your proposal just for the sake of having graphics. Some proposal gurus insist that you need a set number of graphics per proposal page. That is plain nonsense. Graphics can indeed improve the general appearance of your proposal. Nonetheless, gratuitous graphics may detract from your message rather than add to it. Moreover, for page-limited proposals, you must weigh the advantage of using a graphic, rather than words, against the amount of space it consumes.
2. *The graphic or table must support and clarify the text, not replace it.* Do not assume that the evaluator will automatically understand the point you are trying to make with a graphic. You must interpret, summarize, or highlight key information and then explain its importance. Proposal text and graphics need not be totally redundant, but they must each be able to stand on their own. You can tease the reader with enough detail in the text to ensure that he or she will take the time to examine the graphic or table. Just inserting graphics into your proposal with a cursory reference, like "see Figure 1.2.3," is generally insufficient.

Only use graphics that emphasize a point, explain key facts in the text, or help the reader remember essential information.

Here are some additional tips to help guide the development of effective graphics and avoid common errors.

- *Design graphics and tables to the same scale.* Avoid broad discrepancies in size between graphics. Only use as much space as absolutely required for page-limited proposals.
- *Use the same terms in the graphic or table as you use in the text.* Otherwise, you may confuse the reader. For numeric data, ensure that the numbers in the text agree with those in the table.
- *Place the graphic or table as close as possible to the text that references it.* Ideally, the reference and graphic will appear on the same page.

- *Use a consistent format for graphics and tables.* Consistency enhances overall appearance and makes your data easier to follow or compare from one illustration or table to the next.
- *For complex illustrations, use highlighting, bold type, or thicker lines to draw attention to key points you want to convey.* Some experts apply what they call the five-second rule. If the reader does not get the main point within five seconds, then you need to redesign the graphic.
- *For tables crammed full of information, organize table content to draw attention to key data, or segregate different groups of data so they are easily distinguished by the reader.* If the table contains a long series of items, make it easier to read by arranging the data into groups, by highlighting every other line, or by inserting lines between groups of information.
- *Verify that the table or graphic number referenced in the text agrees with the number in the table or graphic caption.* Misreferenced graphics is a common mistake. Unfortunately, it suggests a lack of attention to detail, and it may confuse the evaluator.
- *If you must use abbreviations in an illustration, then identify them in the text or as a footnote or legend located adjacent to the illustration.*

Types of Illustrations

Illustrations take six basic forms: tables, pie or circle graphs, bar charts, line graphs, organization and flow charts, and pictures. The one you select depends on the type of information you have to display and the point you are trying to make:

- **Tables**—Tables permit data to be presented in row and column format. They are best used to present a significant amount of numerical data, lists, or categorical data.
- **Bar charts**—Bar or column charts depict relationships among groups or categories of information, or changes in data over time (e.g., employee turnover rates for the last five years).
- **Circle charts**—Use circle charts to show the relative sizes of groups compared to the whole. Circle charts show the proportion of each slice to each other slice and to the whole. For example, you might use a circle chart to show the percentage of your employees that are non-degreed, have a four-year degree, and possess an advanced degree.
- **Line charts**—Line charts allow readers to see trends in data over time. Line charts are very effective in showing a positive trend or improvement in some key parameter. For example, a line chart could be used to show a steady decrease in the number of software test discrepancies since you implemented a new process.

- **Pictorial graphics**—Pictorial graphics include organizational and flow charts, maps, photographs, and diagrams. Project organizational charts, flow charts, and system diagrams are common examples.

Action Captions

The use of action captions is a method intended to put a little pizzazz in the phrasing of table and graphics captions. Rather than dryly stating the content of a graphic, action captions reiterate a proposal theme or convey a message. Some examples follow:

Traditional Caption:	*Delta's project organization for the ABC program.*
Action Caption:	*Delta's project organization is staffed with key leadership personnel who have successfully demonstrated their ability on projects of comparable size and complexity.*
Traditional Caption:	*Alpha's risk management process for the ABC program.*
Action Caption:	*We applied our proven risk management process to produce a low-risk approach that ensures project success.*

The main advantage of action captions is that they allow you to reiterate or amplify a theme contained in the text of your proposal. Properly worded, they may be quite effective.

If you elect to use action captions, they must be applied consistently to every graphic in the proposal. Otherwise, you violate the consistency rule discussed above.

Developing hard-hitting action captions for every graphic and table is more difficult than it sounds. Forced action captions start to sound "cheesy" and may resemble sales hype more than compelling proposal themes. In such cases, you are better off with a boring but informative caption. If the action caption takes up two or more lines of space, and you are fighting page limitations, then you must decide which is more important: the action caption or an additional line of proposal text.

Proposals are fundamentally technical sales documents. If you can use action captions to communicate your proposal message more effectively, then by all means use them. However, if you find yourself struggling to develop action captions that don't sound like they came off the back of a cereal box, then you are better advised to use their less awe-inspiring counterparts.

Gain competitive advantage first by responding clearly and effectively to all RFP requirements. Place proposal material where evaluators expect to see it, and make it easy to identify. Then use themes to convey your proposal message and discriminators to separate yourself from the rest of the competition. Integrate features and their benefits to the customer to equip evaluators with more reasons to select you for the contract.

Use ghosting to undermine your competitor's approach and take specific actions to ensure that your proposal receives a favorable risk rating. Edit the final proposal so that it is easy to read, communicates clearly, and fits within any page-count restrictions. Apply graphics appropriately to enhance the effectiveness of your message.

A well-written proposal that effectively addresses all RFP requirements and clearly communicates your sales message to the customer is a powerful weapon on the battlefield of competitive procurements. It will positively distinguish you from the rest of the pack. This alone enables you to overcome the "sameness of proposal" problem government evaluators complain about. Given two proposals of equal technical merit, the one that is better written and communicates more effectively captures competitive advantage.

Chapter 12

Tips for Effective Proposal Writing

Pose the question "What is a proposal?" to ten people and you will likely get ten different answers. Some will say that a proposal is a sales document. Others will argue that a proposal is a technical document with a sales message. Those remaining will suggest some variation of these two themes or profess ignorance.

However you slice it, a proposal is the means we use to communicate with our prospective government customers. The medium is written narrative. The purpose is to secure new business. Through a well-structured series of written narratives and figures, we must convince the customer to award us the contract. Communication is the key. Words are the vehicle.

If you fail to communicate clearly and unambiguously, you will lose. It does not matter if you have the best technical solution, vast relevant experience, and a superior project team. These do not matter unless the customer understands what you propose. Only by reading your proposal can the customer conclude that you have the best technical solution, relevant experience, or a superior project team. You may believe that you have said those things in your proposal. But unless the customer agrees, it is all for naught.

Effective proposal writing is an uphill challenge. Two factors make good proposal writing especially problematic.

First, good writing skills are hard to acquire. Except for the gifted few, such skills grow out of lots of practice obtained in an environment where critical feedback is provided. Few ever get (or want) this experience. People assigned to a proposal team typically are selected because they possess the necessary technical or subject matter expertise, not because they are in danger of writing the great American novel. In short, proposal team members seldom get the opportunity or quality feedback they need to truly hone their writing skills.

Second, the writing required of technical personnel usually is limited to communicating with their technical peers and general business correspondence. Proposal writing is very different. It requires a strange blend of writing ability. On one hand, it must clearly explain complex technical material to a broad audience of lay people and technical experts. On the other hand, it must contain a powerful sales message capable of convincing government evaluators that your organization is the best choice for the contract. Writing easy-to-understand text that fully responds to RFP requirements and integrates themes and discriminators, while highlighting features and benefits, is a tall order to fill. Even the best of writers struggle to accomplish this feat.

There is no easy solution to the proposal-writing dilemma. You want the best available technical expertise applied to your proposal. Yet you will need to submit a proposal that captures this expertise while reading like a *New York Times* bestseller. No magic wand exists to instantly transform mere technical mortals into talented proposal writers. However, a handful of basic writing tips can be applied effectively by anyone to improve his or her proposal writing. A final edit still will be required. But having the original authors work out the rough spots first will make final editing more efficient. It also will enable authors to sharpen their writing skills.

The bidder who submits a well-written proposal that communicates clearly and effectively gains competitive advantage. Take two proposals with equivalent technical content. Both are responsive to RFP requirements. One is well written and easy to understand. The other is poorly written, confusing, and difficult to understand. Which proposal will receive the higher score? Everything else being equal, which will win the contract? Do not imagine that government evaluators will take the time required to understand a poorly written proposal. They will not!

Great technical solutions proposed by perfectly capable companies lose every day because they fail to communicate those solutions effectively. Do not yield the advantage to your competitors by submitting a poorly written proposal. Instead, deliver one that responds to RFP requirements concisely and clearly and that communicates your message effectively.

The remainder of this chapter contains some basic tips for effective proposal writing and editing. They can be used by anyone regardless of writing ability. Yet, a word of caution is required. Do not try to incorporate these tips in your first draft or focus on them as you prepare your original narrative. Doing so will distract you from your primary objective. It is more important to get your thoughts on paper. Then come back and apply these tips to edit your writing. Otherwise, you will drive yourself crazy trying to remember and apply these tips and write at the same time.

PRESENT TENSE

Proposals refer to events that will occur in the future. Therefore, proposal authors naturally tend to adopt the future tense in their writing. Despite the apparent logic of this practice, it is less effective than using the present tense. Too many "we will" phrases in a proposal suggests a "trust me" attitude. It also can create the impression that you have not done this before or that you will wait until after contract award to complete your planning. Neither of these creates a favorable impression with the customer.

TIP: Use present verb tense except for those cases where you *must* refer to the future. Consider the following example of future tense:

> *Our program manager will be responsible for the entire program. He will direct all program members and will issue work authorizations. Team members will be responsible for their portion of the program and will supervise the daily work of their team.*

Here is the same information written in present tense:

> *Our program manager is responsible for the entire program. He directs all program members and issues work authorizations. Team members are responsible for their portion of the program and supervise the daily work of their team.*

Overall, present tense provides a more forceful proposal presentation.

ACTIVE VERSUS PASSIVE VOICE

Passive-voice sentence structure is appropriate whenever the person responsible for the act cannot be identified or is unimportant. For example:

> *Equal amounts of HCl and H_2O were mixed as the first step of the experiment.*

Passive voice also applies to cases where the action is more important than the actor. Alternatively, active voice identifies and emphasizes the actor. For example:

- Passive voice: The ball was hit by John.
- Active voice: John hit the ball.

Passive voice is an outgrowth of scientific writing and finds its way into some journalism. For these applications, the doer of the action is either irrelevant or unimportant. Government documents tend to adopt passive-voice writing, as do many business publications. However, the active voice is much preferred for proposal writing.

TIP: Adopt an active-voice writing style for proposal narrative.

Using the passive voice weakens proposal writing. It makes sentences longer, and it may confuse readers. Active voice adds strength to proposal presentations. Depending on font size, it can reduce space compared to passive voice, an important benefit for page-limited proposals. Some additional advantages of active voice include:

- More readable
- More accurate, closer to the event
- More economical (words)
- Livelier style
- More aware of verbs
- More concerned with the doer of an action or event
- More conscious of the details of an action
- Better fits proposal requirements—who, what, when, where, and how.

Some simple examples illustrate the difference between the active and passive voices:

Passive voice: The design document has been completed.
Active voice: The *team* has completed the design document.
Passive voice: Meeting schedules will be coordinated between the customer and Delta Corporation.
Active voice: The *program manager* coordinates meeting schedules between the customer and Delta Corporation.
Passive voice: The interrelationship of all tasks, consultant interfaces, and manpower alignments will be coordinated and approved.
Active voice: Mr. Smith *coordinates and approves the interrelationship of all tasks, consultant interfaces, and manpower alignments.*
Passive voice: Necessary flow times and milestones are plotted and coded to correlate with a work breakdown structure and are the result of interaction among manufacturing, engineering, test, and material personnel.
Active voice: Manufacturing, engineering, test, and material personnel interact to plot and code necessary flow times and milestones to correlate them with a work breakdown structure.

Look for sentences where the doer is absent or shows up at the end of the sentence. Rewrite those sentences using active voice. Simple sentences structure works best for this purpose: subject–verb–object. In the active voice, the subject is the doer of the action or the focus of interest in the sentence.

The passive voice also transforms perfectly outstanding verbs into unassuming nouns. This robs writing of its vitality and zip. Using active verbs in your writing helps bring life and power to otherwise uninspiring prose. The first step is to identify those cases where you have adapted a good solid verb to serve as a noun. Here are a couple of examples:

Noun	Verb
Administration	Administer
Employment	Employ
Development	Develop

In sentence form, the comparison looks like this:

Passive: Authorization of fund expenditures is granted by the program manager.
Active: The program manager *authorizes* fund expenditures.

Figure 12-1 lists some common nouns that were once healthy, active verbs. Take a minute and convert these nouns into their respective active-verb forms.
Two more examples further illustrate this tip:

Noun usage: Development of appropriate test standards is the responsibility of the test engineer.
Active verb: The test engineer develops appropriate test standards.
Noun usage: Implementation of the reliability program is accomplished by the ILS manager.
Active verb: The ILS manager implements the reliability program.

Looking for verbs that are used as nouns is another way to spot the passive voice. When you detect such usage, rewrite the sentence.

CONCISE WRITING

Everyone understands inflation. It is when your paycheck buys fewer goods or services than it did last month or last year. In a sense, it is paying

Figure 12-1. Change the Nouns into Usable Verbs

NOUN FORM	ACTIVE VERB FORM
Administration	Administer
Implementation	
Performance	
Documentation	
Illustration	
Authorization	
Identification	
Negotiation	
Employment	
Producibility	

more for less. Inflation also applies to writing. It is using more words than necessary to say something. Using more words often accomplishes less than a comparable concise statement.

A popular expression in the proposal world says that, "if you cannot dazzle them with brilliance, then bury them in BS." Unfortunately, this lighthearted comment is quite often true.

TIP: Practice concise writing by eliminating unnecessary words and phrases.

Word inflation is using a string of words or phrase when a single word will do. It results in imprecise writing. Too many words can give the impression that you are long-winded or pretentious. Avoid this malady by using concise expressions that are economical and clear.

Some examples of word inflation include the following:

Inflated	**Concise**
In the event of	If
Submitted his resignation	Resigned
Within the realm of possibility	Possible
Due to the fact that	Because

We are all guilty of word inflation. Luckily, the solution is simple. Just replace the unnecessary string of words with a single word that conveys the same meaning. Figure 12-2 lists some common culprits and shows their one-word conversions.

Concise writing enhances direct communication and saves space. Again, this is especially important for page-limited proposals. Several examples demonstrate this point:

Inflated: At this point in time, it is our understanding that the new computer system will have the capability of processing 50 percent more information.

Concise: We now understand that the new computer system processes 50 percent more information.

Inflated: With regard to your recent memo, we cannot determine as to whether or not you will be in attendance at the meeting we have scheduled to be held on Tuesday.

Concise: Are you coming to the meeting on Tuesday?

In addition to normal word inflation, we sometimes inject unnecessary qualifiers into our sentences. The usual suspects include:

- There is, there are
- Who
- That
- Which.

Figure 12-2. Examples of Word Inflation and the Cure

INFLATED WORD	PREFERRED USAGE
1. Prior to	1. Before
2. Subsequent to	2. After
3. In the neighborhood of	3. Around
4. As to whether	4. Whether
5. At this point in time	5. Now, currently
6. In short supply	6. Shortage
7. Adjacent to	7. Beside
8. In the event of	8. If
9. During the time that	9. During
10. In a number of cases	10. Many
11. For the reason that	11. Because
12. Large in size	12. Large
13. Make an improvement in	13. Improve
14. Made an offer to	14. Offer
15. Provides for	15. Provide
16. With regard to	16. About
17. It has been brought to my attention	17. I know

These words can often be eliminated, as the following examples illustrate:

Inflated: There are several applicants *who* have the background for this position.
Concise: Several applicants have the background for this position.
Inflated: The broker *who* works in Chicago sent the file, *which* is incomplete, to the home office.
Concise: The Chicago broker sent the incomplete file to the home office.
Inflated: There are thousands of hours wasted because no one can use the files, which are out of date.
Concise: Thousands of hours are wasted because no one can use the out-of-date files.

However, do not pull out the word hatchet every time you see one of these words. Sometimes they are a necessary part of the sentence, or you may use them to vary sentence structure. Just remove them when they are unnecessary.

LONG SENTENCES

Proposals breed long sentences. Trying to explain complex concepts inevitably leads to sentence growth. Our attempts to be thorough foster long sentences. Unfortunately, long sentences can confuse readers, and run-on sentences often are connected incorrectly. This places a real hardship on the evaluator attempting to understand what you have written. Furthermore, reading a continual string of long sentences is wearisome. It may even prevent the reader from getting the message you intended. Key points get buried in an avalanche of words.

Every writer has an Achilles heel. I have several. Using long sentences is one. The good news is that most long sentences can be broken into two or more separate sentences to solve the problem. A long sentence may need reorganizing as well. For example, try to decipher the meaning of the following sentence:

> *To help Debra in her present position, we recommend that she be given the opportunity to participate, on a rotating basis, with the department supervisor, in these meetings to be held twice a month, with the specific purpose of discussing optional work methods for processing workflow.*

This monster of a sentence consists of several disjointed points. Hence, it will require a little surgery before it makes sense. Here is a post-surgical rendition:

> *To help Debra in her present position, we recommend she participate in meetings to discuss optional work methods for processing workflow. Starting in the first quarter of 2004, she can attend meetings twice a month on a rotating basis with the department supervisor.*

This rewrite makes two sentences out of one very long sentence. It is an improvement over the original, but the remaining sentences are still a little long.

Some tips on sentence length include:

- Keep average sentence length around 17–24 words (15–18 words for complex technical material, if you can).
- Vary sentence length to give writing variety and vitality.
- Count total words for a paragraph and divide by the number of sentences. Average sentence length should be in the 15–18 word range.

Most word processing software has a word counting function. Some will actually calculate average sentence length and reading level. But you do not need the talents of Sherlock Holmes to identify long sentences. As appropriate, divide long sentences into separate, shorter sentences. Not every long sentence requires dismantling. If you detect a string of long sentences, intentionally insert a short sentence to break the monotony. Varying sentence length will make your writing more palatable to evaluators. It also will enable them to digest the long-winded variety occasionally required to address complex topics fully.

AMBIGUOUS WRITING

Apart from politicians, few people are intentionally ambiguous. In proposal writing, ambiguous, unclear, or vague statements should be avoided like the plague. Such writing confuses the reader. Confused readers may conclude that you do not know what you are talking about, or your approach is so complex the reader can't understand it. Neither will create a favorable impression. If a proposal section must be read several times to be understood, then a language or communication problem exists.

TIP: Replace ambiguous writing with concrete, specific narrative that clearly communicates your point.

Several factors contribute to ambiguous writing. One arises from trying to describe complex or abstract concepts. Another comes from discussing future events, where it is difficult to be precise. Additional factors are poorly constructed sentences and the use of imprecise and nonspecific words. All are easily cured.

Ambiguity caused by sentence structure can be fixed by rearranging the sentence. How we arrange phrases within a sentence can affect its meaning. Consider the following sentence:

The director spoke to the manager with disturbing harshness.

Who is exhibiting the disturbing harshness? Is it the director or the manager? Here is the simple fix:

The director spoke with disturbing harshness to the manager.

A better fix still is:

The director spoke harshly to the manager.

Vague writing suggests you have nothing to say. Worse, it may appear that you are inventing information or exaggerating the truth. Rather than muddle along by saying:

A period of unfavorable weather set in.

Use concrete words to state:

It rained every day for a week.

As you review your initial proposal draft, look for abstract or vague words and replace them with more precise, specific words. For example:

Vague: Recently, we looked at a *structure* that might be suitable for our *needs.*

Specific: Yesterday, we looked at a *warehouse* that might be suitable for storing *our excess equipment.*

Note that by changing a few words we significantly increase the amount of information contained in the sentence. Proposals, especially the page-limited variety, should contain as much useful information per unit of space as possible. Using specific words:

- Limits the number of possible interpretations
- Conveys more precise meanings
- Reduces ambiguity and confusion
- Leads to clearer, more effective communication.

Figure 12-3 lists some common vague words that creep into our writing. Take the time to convert them into concrete, specific words.

Vague words are not inherently bad. They are an important part of communication. Their usage is appropriate where precision is not important or where only a qualitative difference is being made. For example, we use words like "some," "many," and "most" to distinguish increasing levels of magnitude without specifying the exact number.

The purpose of the communication and the intended audience determine the acceptability of using vague words. Chatting with a friend is very different from submitting your résumé to a prospective employer. Saying you have "lots of experience developing software code," may be okay in the first instance but would be inappropriate for the second.

Imagine you own a seven-year old Audi sedan with an automatic transmission. The transmission slips when it changes gears. You want to have it

---

Figure 12-3. Sample Vague Words

Vehicle	Many
Equipment	Significant
Traveled	Numerous
Contacted	In a timely manner
Personnel	Proper
Extensive	Some
Recently	
Small	

repaired. You live in a mid-western city of 200,000 and are concerned about finding an experienced, reputable repair shop. Here is your dialogue with the Ace Repair Shop:

> **You**: Do you have experience working on foreign cars, Audis in particular?
>
> **Shop**: We have extensive experience working on a vast array of car makes and models.
>
> **You:** How much experience do you having working on automatic transmissions?
>
> **Shop:** We can fix anything. Our experience includes providing a broad range of high-quality repairs, and all of our mechanics are certified.
>
> **You:** How much will it cost?
>
> **Shop**: We have the best prices in town. Our repair practices are especially cost-effective.
>
> **You:** How long will you need to keep my car?
>
> **Shop:** Our repair services are efficient and among the quickest in the industry. We pride ourselves in customer satisfaction.

Based on this information, would you take your car to the Ace Repair Shop?

On average, government evaluators are more discerning than consumers and far more suspicious. If you are unwilling to contract with a business that provides vague answers to your questions, why would you expect the government to act differently when far more is at stake?

The purpose of a proposal is to secure new business. For this purpose, clarity, precision, and the absence of ambiguity are paramount considerations. We cram our proposals full of claims, hoping they will convince the customer to award us the contract. However, vague or unsubstantiated proposal claims are worse than no claims at all. Consider the following proposal statements:

> *We have extensive experience performing contracts comparable to the ABC program, and our program team has years of relevant experience.*

> *Our proven maintenance practices have achieved high availability rates and saved our customers money by significantly reducing lifecycle costs.*

These statements look remarkably similar to those of the Ace Repair Shop. Unless we convert them into claims with more precise information, they will remain what I call "throw-away" sentences. That is, we can throw them away without any impact on the proposal. Actually, that is the best-case scenario. Such vague claims take up space and gain you no advantage. They may even create an unfavorable customer impression. Yet a little bit of work can transform these impotent word strings into powerful proposal claims. For example:

> *We have performed ten contracts with technical requirements comparable in scope and complexity to the ABC program. Three of these contracts—Contract 1, Contract 2, and Contract 3—had nearly identical technical requirements. Our program team possesses an average of 10 years' experience performing the same job they will perform on the ABC program.*

> *Our proven maintenance practices have achieved an average availability rate above 98% over the last five years on six separate contracts. These practices have reduced annual maintenance costs between 10 and 15%, with five-year average annual savings of 12.5%.*

Take two proposal sections, each written by bidders with the same experience and capability. One proposal uses vague language to state their experience and capability. The other adopts a specific communications style. Which proposal section will receive the higher score? How important is this? In a photo finish, it just might be enough to push your pony across the line ahead of the other competitors.

Gain competitive advantage by submitting well-written proposals that communicate your message clearly and effectively. Use the following tips to spruce up your writing and guide your editing efforts:

- Write in the present tense
- Use the active voice
- Vary sentence length and minimize long sentences
- Practice concise wording
- Use specific, concrete words and expressions
- Avoid vague or ambiguous words and phrases
- Be direct and write to the point.

Make the evaluator's job easy. Provide clear, concise, convincing responses to RFP instructions and questions. Include easy-to-understand reasons why the customer should select your organization for the contract. Effective writing is simple, not simplistic. Minimize the use of jargon, acronyms, and non-essential words. Be smart in your choice of words to provide clarity and precision of expression.

The purpose of proposal writing is to communicate and convince, not impress. Well-written proposals pack a punch. Use this information to knock out the competition.

Chapter 13

Preparing the Winning Cost Volume

Stating that cost is important in winning government contracts is equivalent to proclaiming that the Pope is Catholic. Of course cost is important! Sometimes it is the most important ingredient of a winning bid. Occasionally, it is practically the only consideration. Being the low bidder has its advantages regardless of the relative weight of cost in the overall source selection criteria. No matter what you read, hear, or think, cost is *always* important. Yet there is more to winning the cost war than just bidding the lowest number.

Winning means capturing a piece of new business *and* making money for your organization. Winning is easy if you are willing to lose money. The key is to bid low enough to win, yet high enough to satisfy contract requirements and still book a little profit. Moreover, in many instances, the government is just as interested in *how* you arrived at your bid as they are in its absolute value. Viewing the preparation of the proposal cost volume as simply a task of deriving cost estimates and plugging numbers into pricing forms could be a fatal mistake.

How well you present cost information and substantiate its basis can have a significant impact on the outcome of the source selection process. This is especially true for best-value procurements. Even government customers willing to award an auditory vigilance contract to the low-bidding deaf person may be concerned about how you arrived at your bid price. They know a low bid that cannot reasonably be executed is no bargain. Contractors who underbid programs likewise tend to underperform. Government customers and users most often bear the brunt of such bids. Consequences come in the form of slipped schedules, cost overruns, and lower-than-expected performance.

Admittedly, the outcome of government source selection often seems to defy reason. Sometimes the government awards contracts to lower-priced and less qualified, or unqualified, offerors. Other times they pick a more qualified and higher-priced bidder.

Some amount of mystery will always surround government source selection. It is an inherently subjective process implemented by fallible and biased humans. Nonetheless, understanding your customer and what they are attempting to achieve when they evaluate your cost proposal is the first step on the journey toward competitive advantage.

Adequately describing the full array of cost estimating techniques and addressing the intricacies of preparing a cost volume would require a separate book in its own right. Instead, this chapter attempts to shed some light on key variables that shape the cost proposal evaluation process. It also focuses on tips, guidelines, and recommendations that will enable you to step ahead of the competition and prepare a winning cost volume.

COMMON COST PROPOSAL MISTAKES

As you jockey for position in the cost race, it is important to avoid mistakes that could undermine the evaluation of your cost proposal. Just steering clear of these potholes might be sufficient to edge out the competition.

The following list of common cost proposal shortfalls is based on a briefing given by a major government procurement agency:

- Not responsive to RFP instructions
- Inadequate definition and description of the building blocks of the cost approach
- Failure to provide logical conclusions and illustrate that the cost estimate is realistic and reasonable
- Making good intention statements such as "we understand," "we are committed," "we are capable," "our experience ensures," "we comply," instead of showing how experience is applied, showing results and benefits, proving the level of capability, and providing the cost estimate basis and substantiating data
- Not following instructions to complete costing forms provided in the RFP
- Not showing the associated CLIN for each WBS, or a WBS to CLIN cross-reference
- Not providing cost subtotals for each higher level of WBS
- Failure to separately report prime/subcontractor indirect rates
- Failure to separately break out hardware/software requirements
- Not providing historical cost data for labor hours, staffing levels/labor mix, etc.
- Not providing required data for each major subcontractor (e.g., cost summaries, detailed substantiation, labor/overhead rates)
- Inadequately defining what work is/is not included in task descriptions
- Not providing an adequate trace from the lowest level of detailed substantiation to the cost summaries

- Referencing paragraphs that do not exist
- Failure to ensure accuracy of costs/hours at each higher level of cost summary
- Assuming that cost summaries are sufficient substantiation
- Not providing negotiated rates/rate agreements and a trace between calendar year rates and rates used in the proposal
- Not explaining changes from recent historical rates
- Not providing labor category definitions
- Classifying material as commercial off the shelf (COTS) or non-developmental item (NDI) when extensive modifications are required.

In this same briefing, the government presented its recommendations for preparing an adequate cost proposal, as follows:

- Demonstrate that you have a thorough understanding of the requirements and inherent risks, can devote the necessary resources, and have a solution to meet the RFP requirements.
- Support your statements with facts, analysis, and substantiating data to illustrate that your approach is realistic and reasonable.
- Provide clear and concise cost estimate descriptions/ justifications.
- Understand the evaluation criteria so you know where to place emphasis in your proposal.
- Ensure traceability throughout the proposal (bill of material to WBS; WBS to CLIN, WBS to statement of work, etc.).
- Ensure that technical and cost proposals are consistent.
- Show support for any proposed improvements to historical cost data (i.e., improved technology).
- The burden of proof for cost credibility rests with the offeror. Please substantiate the cost estimate!

In the words of the customer:

> *We want to accept your estimate—show us your work.* **BUT**—*provide only data and information that is relevant in a concise, direct manner explaining changes from recent historical rates.*

Most of this information represents the view of a single government agency. However, experience suggests that it is representative of most, if not all, government customers. Use it as a general checklist to prepare your cost proposal. Better still, arrange a meeting with your customer's head of contracts. Ask him or her to share with you the common shortcomings of cost proposals they receive. Also, ask what actions you can take to ensure that your cost proposals contain the information necessary for cost evaluators to perform their job effectively and efficiently. Use this information to build a checklist to guide the preparation of cost proposals to that customer.

Remember, "the government wants to accept your estimate." Make their job easy, and you gain competitive advantage. Make their job difficult, and you forfeit advantage and perhaps the bid opportunity. A poor cost proposal can completely neutralize a superior technical proposal.

Consider this scenario: Two bidders are scored as technically equivalent, and both bid about the same price. One bidder submits a cost proposal that lacks sufficient traceability and does a poor job of substantiating cost estimates. The other bidder provides the necessary cost traceability and does a good job of substantiating cost estimates. With few exceptions, the second bidder will win.

More often than you might imagine, contracts are lost because of an inadequate cost proposal. To reiterate: There is more to preparing a cost volume than developing and presenting cost estimates. It is possible to have the best technical approach, bid the lowest price, and still lose. In such cases, the likely culprit is a cost proposal that fails to convince government evaluators that your proposed price is reasonable, realistic, and complete.

COST VOLUME EVALUATION

Cost proposals, unlike technical proposals, are not scored. They do not receive a color rating or point count, but they are evaluated. Depending on the procuring agency, the cost volume also may receive a risk rating based on past contract cost performance and a cost risk based on your proposed technical approach and the corresponding cost information contained in the cost volume.

The role of cost evaluators is to ensure that the government pays a fair and reasonable price for the work being procured. They evaluate cost proposals to determine factors like the reasonableness, realism, and completeness of the cost estimate, the probable cost to the government, and the bidder's understanding of the required effort. To ensure that it receives a proper evaluation, your cost proposal must be accurate, complete, and well-documented.

The government contracting officer's primary concern is the overall price the government will actually pay. Hence, in evaluating cost proposals, two plus two does not necessarily equal four. If the government views your proposed cost as being risky, it may increase your bid cost to the "most probable cost to the government." You might propose the lowest price but be evaluated as the highest-priced bidder based upon the type of cost analysis performed.

To illustrate this point, carefully read the following Section M excerpt, which clearly states the government's intent to adjust the proposed price based on its cost analysis:

The Government will evaluate the realism and reasonableness of all the offeror's proposed costs and not-to exceed (NTE) prices. Cost realism refers to the ability of the offeror to project costs which are reasonable and which indicate the offeror's understanding of the nature and scope of work to be performed. The Government believes that realism and completeness are of paramount importance in its ability to evaluate a proposal. A proposal that is neither realistic nor justified may result in a higher evaluated price. The offeror's proposed costs may be adjusted up or down for purposes of evaluation based upon the results of the cost realism analysis. Costs (i.e., labor, material, rates, escalation, and any other predictable costs of performance) which do not reflect the probable cost at contract completion will be adjusted for evaluation purposes. Also the proposed program schedule will be evaluated for realism and reasonableness and could factor in the cost realism adjustments.

Pay close attention to the language contained in Section M concerning how cost will be evaluated. The government is supposed to inform prospective bidders about its intention to perform cost analyses. When in doubt, ask the government contracting officer.

CONTRACT TYPE AND COST

An important role of the customer's contracting officer is to manage risk to the government. To accomplish this role, contracting officers select a contract type appropriate to the scope and uncertainty of the work being procured. The amount and type of information requested in the cost volume normally reflect the type of contract that will be awarded. Other factors include the criticality and sophistication of the work to be performed, local procuring agency policies, and the recent cost performance of contracts managed by the agency.

Contract types fall into two broad categories: fixed-price and cost-reimbursement. They also vary in terms of how profit is awarded. Profit either is fixed at contract award or based on contract performance. This creates four general contract types; Figure 13-1 lists some general characteristics of each.

Under a fixed-price contract, you are completely responsible for contract cost performance. A fixed cost is bid and reimbursed by the government. If your actual costs exceed the amount bid, you will likely lose money. Only formal contract changes made and approved by the government result in additional money being allocated to the contract.

Cost-reimbursement contracts provide payment of incurred costs up to the maximum prescribed by the contract. Increases in work scope and government-directed or -approved changes lead to an increase in allowable cost. Under cost-type contracts, cost risk is shared between the government and the contractor.

Figure 13-1. General Characteristics of Different Government Contract Types

	FIXED FEE	INCENTIVE FEE
FIXED PRICE	• Highest risk to contractor • Contract cost predetermined • Profit predetermined • Normal profit range 12–15% • Product or service well-defined • Least risk to government • Normally requires least cost substantiation • Requires least amount of government contract administration • Referred to as firm fixed-price contracts	• Higher risk to contractor than cost-reimbursement contract • Contract cost predetermined • Profit based on contractor performance • Normal profit range 8–12% • Product or service well-defined • Less risk to government than cost-reimbursement contract • Normally requires less cost substantiation • Requires more government contract administration than firm fixed-price contract
COST REIMBURSEMENT	• Least risk to contractor • Contract cost not predetermined • Profit percentage predetermined • Normal profit range 6–9% • Highest risk to government • Product or service not well-defined • Requires most cost substantiation • Requires more government contract administration than fixed-price contacts	• Less risk than fixed price contracts • Contract cost not predetermined • Profit based on contractor performance • Normal profit range 7–10% • Product or service not well-defined • Less risk to government than cost plus fixed fee contract • Requires cost substantiation • Requires greatest amount of government contract administration

Under a fixed-fee contract, profit (normally expressed as a percentage) is determined at contract award and does not vary. If you bid a profit of 10 percent, that is the profit you receive for work performed. For incentive-type contracts, the amount of fee earned depends upon contract performance. Better performance earns higher fees. Performance can be geared toward achieving target contract costs or tied to technical contract performance.

Contract Type and Cost Risk

Considerations of cost risk, technical uncertainty, and type and complexity of the requirement determine the type of contract selected. Fixed-price contracts place the greatest risk on the contractor. They are appropriate when cost risk and technical uncertainty are low and where competition is adequate. Most service-type contracts fall into this category. Cost-type contracts place the greatest risk on the government. They are appropriate when cost risk or technical uncertainty is high, or where contract requirements are complex. Developmental contracts fall into this category. Incentive profit schemes are used to reward contract performance on both fixed-price and cost-reimbursable contracts.

Generally, the amount of cost information requested by the RFP is related directly to the amount of cost risk assumed by the government and the complexity or criticality of the procurement. A firm fixed-price contract places all the risk on the contractor. Hence, a formal cost proposal may not be requested for some firm fixed-price contracts. In these cases, the government assumes that sufficient competition exists to ensure cost reasonableness.

Alternatively, the government assumes the greatest amount of risk on cost-reimbursement contracts. Therefore, more cost information is required for cost-type contracts, and the government typically conducts a more thorough cost analysis. In fact, procuring agencies are required to perform a cost realism analysis on cost-reimbursement contracts.

To assess cost realism, government evaluators assess specific elements of each bidder's proposed cost estimate to determine:

- Whether the estimated cost elements are realistic for the work to be performed
- Whether costs reflect a clear understanding of the requirements
- If proposed costs are consistent with the technical proposal.

The outcome of such cost analyses can have a profound effect on the evaluation of your cost proposal. You may lose the contract or be eliminated from the competition if the government views your proposed cost as risky or inadequately substantiated, or if they have difficulty understanding your proposed cost. The primary information evaluators use to determine the cost realism of your bid is the information contained in your cost proposal. Do a good job here, and you gain competitive advantage. Fail here, and you may lose the contract.

Although cost analyses are required for cost-reimbursement contracts, evaluators may elect to perform similar analyses for fixed-price contracts if requirements are complex or when successful contract performance is critical. Therefore, do not assume that the cost volume is less important, or that the low bid price automatically wins, for fixed-price contracts. Pay close attention to information being requested by the RFP and the corresponding cost evaluation factors contained in Section M. Be especially sensitive to the fact that it is your job to convince evaluators that your proposed price is reasonable, realistic, and complete. Give them the information they need to manage cost risk and give your cost proposal high marks.

Contract Type and Profit

Contract type also influences how much profit you bid. A general rule of thumb is: The more risk you assume, the higher the allowable profit. This translates into higher allowable profit on fixed-price versus cost-reimbursement contracts. Similarly, higher potential profit is allowed on incentive-type contracts because profit is at risk, based on contract performance. However, things are not always this simple. The government may expect you to bid a lower profit margin on a fixed-price contract if contract requirements are well-defined and uncertainty is low.

Do not assume that the government just looks at the bottom-line price and ignores profit. They often scrutinize your direct and indirect costs and profit in evaluating price. Two bidders may propose the same overall price but differ in the proposed amount of direct effort or profit.

For cost-reimbursement contracts, profit margin may represent the deciding factor if the total proposed price is similar among bidders. Consider the case where two bidders propose similar direct costs and total price, but where one bidder proposes a profit margin of 7 percent and the other bids a profit of 10 percent.

	7% Profit	**10% Profit**
Total proposed cost:	$10,000,000	$9,700,000
Profit margin:	700,000	970,000
Total proposed price:	$10,700,000	$10,670,000

The bidder with 10 percent profit is the lower bidder in this case but may lose the competition. Why? Suppose the customer expects a 20 percent ($2 million) growth in total contract cost. This amounts to a price increase of $2,140,000 for the 7 percent profit bidder and $2,200,000 for the 10 percent profit bidder. Probable total cost to the government is now $12,840,000 for the low-profit bidder and $12,870,000 for the high-profit bidder. If everything else is equivalent between these two bidders, the one with the lower profit margin—but higher proposed cost—may win.

This may appear to be a trivial difference. Yet contracts often are won and lost on less meaningful differences. Note that blindly bidding the lowest percentage profit for a cost-reimbursement contract does not ensure that you will win or even receive an advantage. It only ensures that percentage profit may be a consideration on a cost-reimbursement contract.

Within the constraints of the Federal Acquisition Regulation, selecting profit margin should be the outcome of careful deliberation. Bidding a standard profit margin for fixed-price contracts and another for cost-type contracts is the essence of simplicity. It is an approach, however, that occasionally will yield competitive advantage to a more astute bidder. Weigh factors like contract type, customer expectations, perceived contract risk, competitors, and your own organization's profit goals to arrive at a reasonable and competitive profit margin for each bid.

MAJOR COST COMPONENTS

Three components are necessary to arrive at a bid price for government procurements: direct costs, indirect costs, and profit or fee.

Direct costs consist of both labor and material. Direct labor is the salaries of the people who will charge their time directly to the contract. Direct material is the cost of parts, equipment, raw materials, etc., that will be purchased to perform the contract. Another part of direct costs is referred to as "other direct costs (ODC)." These are costs that are directly charged to the contract but do not fit easily into either direct labor or direct material categories. For example, travel cost charged to the contract is a typical ODC. So is the cost to lease or rent equipment or acquire special services that will be used on the contract.

Indirect costs are not charged directly to the contract. However, they are added to direct costs to determine the cost of your bid before profit is added. Indirect costs include overhead and general and administrative (G&A) components. Overhead costs include items like employee benefits, payroll taxes, paid time off, facility costs, salaries and benefits of indirect employees whose time is not charged directly to a specific contract, and other miscellaneous costs. G&A costs typically include salaries and benefits for accounting and finance personnel, marketing expenses (including B&P costs), and salaries and benefits for senior management. Many organizations also have a material burden, which is an indirect cost added to all direct material purchases.

Indirect costs are expressed as a percentage. They are calculated separately for overhead, G&A, and material burden. Indirect costs are added to direct costs to calculate total cost. For example, an overhead rate of 150 percent means that you will add 150 percent of the cost of direct labor to calculate your total labor cost.

Profit, expressed as a percentage, is then added to the total cost to arrive at your bid price:

Price = Total Direct Cost + Total Indirect Cost + Profit

Total price, based on $1 million of direct labor, an indirect rate of 150 percent, and a profit of 10 percent, is:

Price = ($1,000,000 + 1,500,000) = 2,500,000 + 250,000 = $2,750,000

Determining which personnel are classified as direct versus indirect is part of an organization's business model. It can vary enormously between companies. In addition, companies may vary regarding which costs they allocate to overhead and which they capture as part of G&A. Within reason, you can allocate costs as you choose as long as you are consistent and follow government cost accounting standards.

Understanding the Relationships among Cost Categories

Understanding the relationships among cost categories is a vital prerequisite to preparing a competitive cost proposal. Of the three price components, two (direct cost and profit) are variable and one (indirect cost) is fixed.

Direct costs reflect your proposed technical solution and cost to perform the contract. They vary based on your approach. Profit likewise can vary within the range allowed by the government and what it takes to be cost-competitive.

Indirect costs are set. Normally, they do not vary from proposal to proposal. They are based on an organization's total direct revenue generated by all existing contracts compared to its total indirect costs. (Overhead, G&A, and material burdens are calculated separately.) Indirect rates are recalculated periodically to reflect changes in revenues and indirect costs. However, the government must approve your indirect rates. They conduct audits to ensure that you comply with generally acceptable cost accounting standards and to verify your indirect rates.

If you want to reduce bid price for a specific proposal, you must reduce direct costs, profit, or both. Part of gaining cost advantage is developing creative solutions that minimize direct cost while meeting RFP requirements, as well as understanding how to set profit margins.

As noted, the government generally is willing to allow higher profit margins for contracts where you assume more risk. Within this context, you must still know what the customer expects. A 10 percent profit margin may be allowable for a cost-plus fixed-fee contract, but the customer may be expecting the winner to bid a 7 percent fee. You also must be aware of what your competitors are likely to bid and what is competitive for the market niche within which you are competing. For example, firm fixed-price contracts allow the greatest potential profit margin. Yet, many large service contracts are won with bid profits of 5 percent or less.

Value of Managing Indirect Costs Effectively

Another part of gaining cost advantage involves managing indirect costs. These costs routinely account for more than half of your bid price. Normally, you cannot arbitrarily change indirect rates for a specific bid. But you can and should actively manage indirect costs to minimize their impact over the long haul.

The best way to reduce indirect costs is to increase the amount of direct revenue generated while holding total indirect costs constant or allowing indirect costs to grow at a slower pace than direct revenue. Another way is to reduce indirect costs while maintaining direct revenue constant. These are easier said than done. Nevertheless, I heartily recommend that you initiate a program to review indirect costs periodically and look for ways to improve the cost-effectiveness of indirect functions. Few activities have the potential to contribute more to the cost-competitiveness of your organization.

Concurrently, use the information provided in this book and your organization's creative talents to improve your percentage of winning bids. B&P costs are among an organization's largest manageable indirect expense. Reducing your unit B&P costs per bid contract—by winning more often—will reduce your indirect cost. It also will increase your direct revenue and improve your cost-competitiveness. Becoming more cost-competitive means either winning more bids or making more profit—or both. Nothing begets success like success.

Here is an example of the impact of indirect bid rates. Two bidders propose the same direct cost and profit margin. Bidder A's total indirect rate is 100 percent, while Bidder B's indirect rate is 120 percent.

	Bidder A	**Bidder B**
Direct Cost	$10,000,000	$10,000,000
Indirect Cost	$10,000,000	$12,000,000
Profit (10%)	2,000,000	2,200,000
Price	$22,000,000	$24,200,000

This causes Bidder B's price to be $2.2 million, or about 10 percent, higher than Bidder A's price. If total proposed price is key to winning this procurement, then Bidder A is the hands-down winner. Even under a best-value procurement, a 10 percent price differential will be difficult to overcome. To bid the same price, Bidder B must either reduce direct cost by $2.2 million (22 percent) or bid zero profit. Reducing direct cost by 22 percent, while proposing an equivalent technical solution to other competitors, is not a likely scenario. Clearly, bidding zero profit (with few rare exceptions) is not an acceptable alternative.

Under most circumstances, differences in competitor indirect rates are less than shown in this example, but the point remains. Everything else being even, maintaining lower indirect rates than your competitors affords a significant competitive advantage.

STARTING POINT

The starting point in any cost competition is to know your customer. You must be knowledgeable about how your customer evaluates cost and the role cost plays in contract award. If your customer always, under every circumstance, awards to the low bidder, then you know the rules of the game. The second piece of information for this part of the equation is knowledge about the cost-competitiveness of other bidders.

Given these two bits of data, can you reasonably expect to win? If cost is king, can you be the low bidder? If not, will you be able to overcome any cost disadvantage? These considerations should have been part of your bid/no bid decision and integrated into your bid strategy. Even so, it is worth reviewing them before going too far down the road of developing a proposal. Better to cut your losses while you can.

You also should know how much money the customer has. Some RFPs provide funding information, including a spending profile for each contract year and category of funds. If this information is not available in the RFP, you must make every effort to determine the customer's budget. The easiest way in the world to lose is by bidding more than the customer has to spend—or to overbid the funding profile for any given year. Sometimes getting your bid to fit within the customer's funding profile requires some near superhuman costing gymnastics.

PREPARING COST ESTIMATES

The work effort necessary to prepare a cost volume comprises two major activities. The first is deriving cost estimates. The second involves preparing any required cost narrative, filling out customer-required pricing forms, and organizing the cost volume according to Section L instructions and your proposal outline.

The cost volume manager is responsible for preparing the cost volume and overseeing the development of cost estimates. The program manager should work closely with the cost manager to oversee costing efforts and to ensure that they match the proposed technical approach.

Work Breakdown Structure

The first step in preparing an initial cost estimate is to create a work breakdown structure (WBS). The WBS is a hierarchical division of the work effort into manageable parts. To illustrate, Figure 13-2 shows a customer-provided WBS based on a contract to build a military flight simulator and provide one year of contractor logistics support.

Assign cost estimating responsibility for each WBS element to an individual person. If a WBS element requires multiple inputs, pick a lead person to be responsible. Use this information to create a cost-estimating responsibility matrix. Then develop a completion schedule for each WBS element that coincides with Tier 1 and Tier 2 proposal schedules (see Chapter 9).

Use the WBS provided in the RFP as a starting point. Expand it as necessary to support your pricing efforts, but do not change the upper-level structure. Otherwise, you may confuse government cost evaluators. Figure 13-3 demonstrates how you might expand WBS elements 1.8.1 and 1.8.2 from Figure 13.2. If the RFP does not provide a WBS, create one yourself.

The WBS creates a cost structure for collecting and organizing your cost estimates. It also is the basis for allocating, monitoring, and reporting cost expenditures after contract award. As such, it is a critical component of program management. Every cost proposal should be based on a WBS, regardless of whether or not it is required by the RFP. Also, plan to prepare a WBS dictionary.

A dictionary defines which costs are contained in each WBS element. It helps cost evaluators understand your cost proposal, and it can be an invaluable asset after contract award. Cost allocations and adjustments performed during the heat of battle often are forgotten by the time the contract is awarded. Maintaining an up-to-date WBS dictionary helps overcome this potential problem.

Quick-Look Cost Estimate

Use your knowledge of the customer's budget to perform a "quick-look" cost estimate. The purpose of this estimate is to determine if you can meet all RFP requirements and still make money while remaining within the customer's budget constraints. This is vital information you need early in the proposal development phase. It might lead to you deciding not to bid the program. Or, it might highlight the need to drastically alter your technical approach. The following scenario illustrates the value of performing a quick-look estimate.

You know the customer's budget but allow cost estimates to be developed using a "bottoms-up" technique. Cost estimates are made by functional organizations starting at the lowest WBS level. Once all costs are

Figure 13-2. Sample Work Breakdown Structure

1.0 TRAINING SYSTEM
   1.1 Flight Simulator Development
      1.1.1 Visual System
         1.1.1.1 Hardware
         1.1.1.2 Software
         1.1.1.3 HSI and Test
         1.1.1.4 Visual Database
      1.1.2 Motion System
         1.1.2.1 Hardware
         1.1.2.2 Software
         1.1.2.3 HSI and Test
      1.1.3 Instructor Operator System
         1.1.3.1 Hardware
         1.1.3.2 Software
         1.1.3.3 HSI and Test
      1.1.4 Student Station
         1.1.4.1 Hardware
         1.1.4.2 Software
         1.1.4.3 HSI and Test
      1.1.5 Computational system
         1.1.5.1 Hardware
         1.1.5.2 Software
         1.1.5.3 HSI and Test
      1.1.6 Other Systems/Subsystems
         1.1.7.1 Hardware
         1.1.7.2 Software
         1.1.7.3 HSI and Test
      1.1.7 Systems Integration
      1.1.8 Systems Engineering/Program Management
         1.1.9.1 Program Management
         1.1.9.2 Systems Engineering
      1.1.9 Deployment
   1.2 Contractor Logistics Support
      1.2.1 Training System Support Center
      1.2.2 Logistics Support Package
      1.2.3 Trainer Maintenance
   1.3 Program Data

---

summed to arrive at a total price, you discover that your total is three times greater than the customer's budget. Unfortunately, completing the bottoms-up estimate has consumed most of the time available to prepare a cost proposal. Initially, you struggle trying to trim your estimates, but

Figure 13-3. Sample Expansion of WBS 1.1.8.1 and 1.1.8.2

1.1.8 SYSTEMS ENGINEERING/PROGRAM MANAGEMENT
    1.1.8.1 Program Management
        1.1.8.1.1 Integrated Product and Process Development
        1.1.8.1.2 Integrated Master Plan
        1.1.8.1.3 Integrated Master Schedule
        1.1.8.1.4 Contract Management
        1.1.8.1.5 Earned Value Management
        1.1.8.1.6 Risk Management
        1.1.8.1.7 Associate Contractor Agreements
        1.1.8.1.8 Subcontractor Management
        1.1.8.1.9 Program Management Reviews
    1.1.8.2 Systems Engineering
        1.1.8.2.1 Requirements Analysis
        1.1.8.2.2 Specification Analysis and Generation
        1.1.8.2.3 Flight Test Program
        1.1.8.2.4 Software Development
        1.1.8.2.5 Hardware Development and Manufacturing
        1.1.8.2.6 Configuration Management
        1.1.8.2.7 Data Management
        1.1.8.2.8 Test
        1.1.8.2.9 Logistics Support Development

eventually you realize that the only way to stay within budget is to radi-cally alter your technical approach. This results in major revisions to your technical proposal and a frantic scramble to prepare a cost proposal for the new approach.

The clock is ticking. Insufficient time remains to develop a reliable cost estimate. Consequently, the technical and cost proposals do not match, and internal cost reviews to verify a reasonable bid are skipped. The most probable outcome in such a situation is a losing proposal or a bid that cannot be executed.

Conducting a quick-look cost estimate offers an opportunity to avoid this scenario. It also can be a key weapon in your arsenal to capture com-petitive advantage by preparing a winning cost proposal.

One way to accomplish a quick-look estimate is to perform a "top-down" cost analysis. Using the customer's budget, allocate a percentage of the total to each major part of the work effort as defined by the WBS. Then further allo-cate the budget of each major WBS to its component parts in a top-down fashion. Continue this process until you have allocated the total budget to a manageable size, but keep things at a fairly high level. Then ask functional managers (or the responsible person) to review the cost estimate for each area and determine if they can perform the contract within these costs. This is a rough order of magnitude (ROM) estimate, so do not try to carry it out to four decimal points. Its purpose is to decide if you can accomplish your proposed technical approach within customer budget constraints.

At this point, you are probably okay if you are close to the customer's budget. Subsequent cost trimming normally will allow you to achieve a reasonable cost target that fits within the customer's budget. However, a prudent cost bid will be something less than what the customer has to spend.

If the quick-look estimates show a huge discrepancy between what it will take to execute your proposed technical approach and the customer's budget, you have two options: overhaul your approach to match the budget or pull the plug on the bid effort. Conducting a quick-look cost estimate maximizes the time remaining to adjust your technical approach if an adjustment is required.

Initial Cost Estimates

Starting early is a cardinal rule for all proposals. Nowhere is this rule more important than for the cost proposal. Cost estimates lag the development of the technical approach upon which they are based. Hence, they tend to be shoved to the end of the proposal development cycle and often get shortchanged. To the extent practical, avoid this potentially disastrous scenario. Hastily prepared cost proposals rarely have a happy ending.

Many costing activities can be performed ahead of or in parallel with the technical proposal effort. At the earliest time possible, build the cost structure required to fulfill RFP costing requirements and meet your organization's plan to allocate, track, and report costs after contract award. Identify potential labor categories, direct labor rates, any known direct material costs, applicable indirect rates, escalation factors, required travel, and anything else required to develop your cost estimates. Determine the likely start dates and time spans for each WBS. Start preparing any required subcontractor statements of work. Begin assembling historical cost data and structure from past contracts comparable to the one you are bidding. This information may save time later, and it will be required to develop your basis of estimates. If applicable, start preparing a bill of material to support subsequent material cost estimates.

Piecemeal this information to your cost team so they can get timely vendor quotes. Build cross-reference matrices to relate individual WBS elements to CLINs, lots, or any other RFP pricing requirement. Verify that you have a place in your cost model for every RFP requirement. Test your initial cost structure to ensure that it accurately sums individual WBS costs and that costs are allocated and collected at the right level.

Look for every conceivable opportunity to jump-start your cost estimating effort. Collect estimates for costs that are not likely to change. For example, travel required to attend customer reviews and meetings, or other travel required by the contract, can be estimated early. Recognize that some early costing efforts will need to be discarded or altered due to subsequent decisions or changes. The gains in competitive advantage by starting early will more than compensate for any effort "wasted" by starting the process before the technical effort is perfectly defined.

Your proposed technical solution ultimately will be used to populate the cost structure to derive initial cost estimates for each WBS, CLIN, lot, and the entire program.

Scrubbing Initial Cost Estimates

Plan to "scrub" initial cost estimates to arrive at the best bid price. The "best" price is the least amount necessary to fulfill program requirements, comply with your cost bid strategy, cover program risks, and achieve target profit goals. Arriving at the best price is a serious and difficult balancing act. On one side, you must identify and adjust cases where costs are underestimated. On the other side, you must strive to trim every possible cost element.

Most initial estimates are too high. This is especially true if you use a bottoms-up cost estimating approach, which tends to include the same cost in multiple WBS elements.

Start by identifying the major cost drivers. These are cost elements that make up a significant percentage of the entire program cost. Then search for ways to reduce cost without impacting your proposed technical solution or diluting your bid strategy.

Every program is different. Be innovative. Look for functions or tasks that can be combined. Can one person perform two jobs or functions? Can one long trip replace three individual trips? Are there cases where equipment commonality could reduce development or logistics support costs? Find tasks or functions where a qualified subcontractor is cheaper. Look for opportunities to substitute a less expensive solution that offers nearly the same performance. Minimize management and oversight costs. Remove any double-counted costs.

Apart from major cost drivers, review all remaining cost elements to complete the cost-scrubbing exercise. Trimming a few dollars here and a few dollars there may amount to enough cost savings to win a close competition. Throughout the entire process, ask yourself if you are taking a reasonable amount of risk. Every cost estimate entails an element of risk. Being too conservative improves the comfort level of those charged with program execution but may take you outside the competitive range. Assuming too much risk may enhance your cost-competitiveness but will probably undermine successful program performance. It might even cause you to be eliminated from the competition if the customer feels your bid is too low. Again, the key is balance.

PREPARING THE COST VOLUME

Section L of the RFP provides instructions about the content and organization of the cost volume or section. Follow these instructions absolutely. However, cost volume instructions do not always specify all the information that cost evaluators require to perform their job effectively. In fact, cost volume instructions often are sparse bordering on deficient. The guiding rule in such cases is to include whatever information you deem necessary to fully substantiate the realism and reasonableness of your proposed cost. If you must err, then err on the side of providing more information than requested. Just be sure to explain the information and its relevance to your bid.

Remember, one of your goals, in addition to presenting your cost estimates, is to satisfy the government's need to manage risk. I therefore also recommend that you include the following information whether or not it is requested:

- Executive summary
- Work breakdown structure and dictionary
- Explanation of costing approach
- Cost summaries
- Basis of estimate
- Risk management
- Groundrules and assumptions.

If you provide information beyond what is requested by the RFP, make sure you integrate it into the proposal outline and the list of topics specified by Section L. Otherwise, you may confuse the evaluators and make it difficult for them to find what they are looking for. Do not bury evaluators in a pile of meaningless costing information. Include only those data necessary to explain clearly and substantiate your cost estimates.

Executive Summary

Cost evaluators do not read the technical volume of your proposal. They also may be relatively unaware of the RFP technical requirements. Therefore, plan to include a brief (two- to four-page) executive summary of your approach to meet RFP requirements. Include major highlights of your technical approach and any relevant experience upon which your cost estimates are based. If this is a best-value procurement, then showcase what you are proposing that provides "best value" to the government.

WBS and WBS Dictionary

Always include a WBS and a WBS dictionary with your cost proposal. Use the customer-provided WBS included with the RFP, expanded as necessary to meet RFP costing requirements or your own plan to manage the program. Develop your own WBS if one is not included with the RFP.

If the work effort is divided into CLINs or lots, prepare a WBS-to-CLIN matrix and include it with the cost proposal. If it makes sense, also include a WBS-to-SOW matrix.

Explanation of Costing Approach

Provide a high-level explanation of your approach to developing cost estimates. At a minimum, explain your overall approach to estimating direct labor, direct material, and other direct costs, provide a brief explanation of your indirect cost categories and how they are applied to determine cost, and specify the number of hours contained in a person-year of labor. If applicable, include an explanation of how you determined the proposed labor categories and skill mix, how you escalated costs for multiyear contracts, or the application of any forward-pricing rate agreements you have negotiated with the government. The key is to provide and briefly explain data that allow cost evaluators to understand how you prepared your cost proposal and the major ingredients of your bid.

The following sample illustrates the level of detail for topics in this section:

> *Other Direct Costs: Other direct costs include travel and relocation. Travel is based on two trips per year, from City A to City B, to attend program meetings specified by SOW 1.2.3. Program relocation costs are estimated at $12,000 per contract year and included in CLIN 0001. This covers an average of two relocations per year, based on the average number of personnel relocations experienced on our other similar programs for the last three years, factored by program size. These other programs include: Program 1, Program 2, and Program 3.*

Cost Summaries

Section L typically specifies how to present cost estimates and the level of cost information that should be provided. Within these instructions, plan to present cost information from general to specific. That is, present cost information at the higher levels first, followed by a more detailed breakout for each major cost (WBS) division.

Figure 13-4 shows a sample cost summary at the CLIN level, which also provides insight into the division of cost for each major cost category. Figure 13-5 provides another example. It displays total program price presented by major WBS but does not segregate cost into separate categories. At the total program level, you could easily include both types of cost summaries. Each provides a different view of the same cost information.

Subsequent presentation of cost information should be a more detailed breakout for each major WBS. For example, Figure 13-6 shows subordinate prices for WBS 1.1.1 from Figure 13-5. Whether you present prices below

Figure 13-4. Cost Summary at the CLIN and Program Level for Each Major Cost Category

PROGRAM SUMMARY				
Cost Elements:	CLIN 001	CLIN 002	CLIN 003	Total Program
Direct Labor	500,000	1,200,000	250,000	**1,950,000**
Labor Overhead 100%	500,000	1,200,000	250,000	**1,950,000**
Total Labor	1,000,000	2,400,000	500,000	**3,900,000**
				0
Direct Material				**0**
A) Purchased Parts	8,000	20,000	40,000	**68,000**
B) Subcontracted Items	2,000			**2,000**
C) Other	0			**0**
Total Direct Materials	10,000	20,000	40,000	**70,000**
Material Overhead @ 5%	500	1,000	2,000	**3,500**
Total Material	10,500	21,000	42,000	**73,500**
				0
Other Direct Costs				**0**
Travel	1,500	0	0	**1,500**
Other	0	3,000	5,000	**8,000**
Total OCD	1,500	3,000	5,000	**9,500**
Total Direct Cost and Overhead	1,012,000	2,424,000	547,000	**3,983,000**
G&A @10%	101,200	242,400	54,700	**101,200**
				0
Total Cost	1,113,200	2,666,400	601,700	**4,381,300**
Fee @10%	111,320	266,640	60,170	**438,130**
TOTAL PRICE	**1,224,520**	**2,933,040**	**661,870**	**4,819,430**

this level depends on several factors: pricing instructions provided in the RFP (which often specify the WBS level for pricing), how much visibility you want to provide evaluators, and whether the next level of pricing provides any meaningful insights into your price buildup.

The WBS level you use to develop cost estimates is determined both by RFP requirements and the level at which you plan to track and report actual program costs. Some RFPs require that costs be presented in the cost

Figure 13-5. Sample Cost Summary at the Program and Major WBS Level

WBS and Category	Price	CLIN
1.0 TRAINING SYSTEM	11,104,761	
1.1 Flight Simulator Development	**9,794,929**	CLIN 0001
1.1.1 Visual System	2,408,250	CLIN 0001
1.1.2 Motion System	750,259	CLIN 0001
1.1.3 Instructor Operator System	225,032	CLIN 0001
1.1.4 Student Station	3,138,387	CLIN 0001
1.1.5 Computational system	249,003	CLIN 0001
1.1.6 Other Systems/Subsystems	689,742	CLIN 0001
1.1.7 Systems Integration and Assembly	886,687	CLIN 0001
1.1.8 Systems Engineering/Program Management	1,097,697	CLIN 0002
1.1.9 Deployment	349,872	CLIN 0001
1.2 Contractor Logistics Support	**1,097,300**	CLIN 0003
1.2.1 Training System Support Center	324,222	CLIN 0003
1.2.2 Logistics Support Package	311,099	CLIN 0003
1.2.3 Trainer Maintenance	461,979	CLIN 0003
1.3 Program Data	**212,532**	CLIN 0004

proposal at one level but specify a lower level for cost reporting. In addition, you may plan the program at a much lower WBS level than you present in your cost proposal.

For illustration purposes, the examples used here are fairly simple. Many procuring agencies require elaborate cost breakouts, like segregating recurring and nonrecurring costs, and presenting cost data for each major cost category and labor division for every WBS element. Nonetheless, the key in all instances is to ensure traceability between different cost-estimate levels and to supply the cost information that government evaluators need to perform cost analyses. In addition, plan to prepare and present your basis of estimate at the same WBS level at which you provide cost estimates.

Figure 13-6. Pricing Data for WBS 1.1.1

WBS	Price	Subtotal
1.1.1 Visual System	2,398,299	
1.1.1.1 Hardware		1,625,414
1.1.1.2 Software		241,826
1.1.1.3 HSI & Test		62,123
1.1.1.4 Visual Database		468,936

Basis of Estimate

The basis of estimate is perhaps the most critical portion of the cost volume narrative. It is where you explain the method you used to develop your cost estimate and the source information upon which it is based. This is where you *must* convince evaluators you have a sound basis for your cost estimates. Otherwise, they may assign risk to your estimates or add cost to your bid to arrive at a "most probable cost to the government."

The government recognizes three general cost estimating methods: parametric, analogous systems, and detailed (grassroots) engineering estimates.

Parametric Estimates

Parametric estimates are based on cost estimating relationships (CERs). CERs are equations that relate one or more characteristics of an item to some element of its cost. They can consist of complex formulas based on extensive statistical analysis, or they may simply be a relationship between two variables. In addition, CERs can be established for major systems or subsystems or for specific program components. For example, a CER might relate avionics unit cost to the weight of the avionics system or the cost per mile for a paved highway of specified dimensions over defined terrain.

The value of a CER depends upon its specificity and historical validation. Typically, they are derived from historical data. Here are two examples:

1. Number of hours, by labor category, to produce one hour of run-time computer-based training based on the required level of lesson interactivity
2. Number of labor hours to perform systems integration based on the total number of engineering hours required to design and develop the system.

Formal estimating models, like those available to estimate the number of hours required to produce a line of software code, qualify as parametric models. These models consist of a series of CERs. For a model to be accepted as a reliable basis of estimate, you must demonstrate that you have used it previously to estimate cost accurately. In the absence of valid historical cost data, a formal model is still better than no model at all. In such cases, carefully and thoroughly explain how you derived inputs for the model.

Government evaluators tend to like parametric cost estimating methods because they potentially remove human bias from the process and produce precise estimates. However, to be believable, such estimates must be validated by historical data that attest to their accuracy. One way to achieve this is to show initial cost estimates for past programs and the actual values achieved after contract award. This is easily done in a table that can be included as part of your basis of estimate. However, it does require that you collect and maintain actual cost performance data.

Analogous System Estimates

With this technique, cost estimates are based on your experience developing a comparable system or performing analogous requirements on other past or current programs. The estimated cost of the proposed system is determined by comparing it to comparable systems previously developed and adjusting the estimate to account for any differences between the systems.

Three elements are required to use this technique. First, you must have historical cost data based on your actual experience with the system or requirements you plan to use as a baseline. Second, you must carefully demonstrate that the system being proposed is comparable to the baseline system. Third, you must convince evaluators that the method you used to determine system differences (the basis of your adjustment) is rational and reliable.

The "value" of an analogous cost estimate is directly related to the amount of relevant experience you can present and the believability of how you determined the difference between the proposed and baseline systems.

Engineering Estimates

This method uses estimates of cost or labor hours based on the experience and expertise of your technical staff. It is based on a specification of the work effort and schedule typically associated with a "bottoms up" cost estimating approach. Cost estimators may use factors like equipment reliability, maintainability, and component cost characteristics to develop estimates from the "bottom up" for each cost category.

Engineering estimates are viewed as the most subjective. Hence, they carry the highest risk. To offset this potential negative, you must carefully explain the cost estimating process and the data you used to derive the estimate. You also should reference any previous and successful cost performance based on engineering estimates and emphasize the experience and expertise of the people performing the cost estimate.

Different cost estimating methods carry more or less weight with cost evaluators. The more precise and objective your estimation methodology, the better. In addition, cost estimates tied to historical data for comparable requirements are viewed favorably. Some key characteristics of an effective and believable basis of estimate include the following:

- Uses a systematic and repeatable process
- Is based on objective characteristics of the task or product being estimated
- Is related to historical data for comparable requirements
- Is related to successful past cost and schedule performance
- Is clearly and thoroughly explained.

For hardware estimates, include a bill of material, where practical, and use actual vendor quotes as your basis of estimate for those costs. Likewise, for ODC such as travel, use actual airfare and hotel room rates quotes. If you have any undefined travel destinations, make an assumption or select a baseline destination city on which to base quotes. Then include this information in your basis of estimate and in the "groundrules and assumptions" section of your cost proposal (see below).

Cost estimates are developed according to the WBS. For consistency, also present your basis of estimate according to the WBS. Basis-of-estimate formats rarely are specified by the RFP. So, you are free to build your own. Just make sure you include enough information to convince evaluators that you know what you are doing and to enable them to follow the logic you applied to derive the cost estimate. The following is a sample basis of estimate for WBS 1.2.3 (from Figure 13-5) (dollar values are for illustration purposes only):

WBS 1.2.3 Trainer Maintenance (CLIN 0003)

WBS prices includes all direct labor and material required to provide trainer maintenance for the Flight Trainer for a 16-hour operational day, five days per week, at an availability rate of 95%. CLIN prices include indirect costs and profit.

Labor Rationale:

Staffing levels and skill mix are based on current and past experience maintaining other flight simulators of comparable complexity to the Sample Flight Simulator. Over the last five years, Alpha Company has maintained over 50 flight simulators at an average availability rate of 98.4% using the same skill mix as proposed here. Table 1.2.3 (not shown) lists the specific program, number of flight simulators maintained, and the average availability rate achieved.

Maintenance staffing is derived from the number and type of training devices to be supported, plus the necessary maintenance shift coverage required to support a 16-hour operational day, five days per week. The number of personnel and labor categories required to staff a three-shift maintenance operation for a single flight simulator is as follows:

- *One (1) Site Manager to perform managerial duties, provide customer interface, perform maintenance, and coordinate maintenance priorities.*
- *Two (2) Shift Supervisor to coordinate and perform flight simulator maintenance activities. One Shift Supervisor for the second maintenance shift and one for the third maintenance shift. (Shift Supervisor duties are performed by the Site Manager for the first maintenance shift).*
- *Four (4) Contract Maintenance Technicians to perform maintenance on Training Devices. One Contract Maintenance Technician for each of the first two maintenance shifts and two Contract Maintenance Technicians for the third shift.*

Direct Labor Calculations:

Direct labor rates are the average labor rate for current Alpha Company employees for each specific labor category. A direct labor year consists of 1,908 hours per year or 159 hours per month. Direct labor calculations for WBS 1.2.3 are as follows:

Title	Labor Category	No. Personnel	Total Direct Hours	Direct Labor Rate	Direct Labor Cost
Site Manager	Field Engineer I	1	1,908	20.50	39,114
Shift Supervisor	Technician III	2	3,816	17.75	67,734
Contract Maintenance Technician	Technician II	4	7,632	16.00	122,112
Total Direct Labor:					**$228,960**

Direct Material:

Direct material includes cost to repair and replace spare components and test equipment, cost of bench stock and consumable items, equipment calibration costs, and cost of packaging, handling, shipping, and transportation.

Alpha Company's direct material estimate is based upon our experience maintaining comparable flight simulators and a five-year historical database of actual material costs. This database is updated once per quarter, and we use the most current 24-month average to estimate material costs per hour of flight simulator utilization. Costs for repair and replacement of visual system components are calculated separately based on the type of visual system and the number of channels provided.

Direct Material Calculations:

To calculate direct material costs we first estimated the expected number of hours the flight simulator would be operated per year. Then we multiplied this number times the rate per hour derived from historical cost data. To estimate expected flight simulator utilization we multiplied student throughput numbers contained in SOW 3.2.1 times the number of simulator hours contained in the training syllabus. Then we added 10% to this number to cover student remedial training and other miscellaneous use. Expected operating hours were derived as follows:

100 students x 32 hours per student = 3,200 hours + 10% = 3,520 hours expected utilization

Based on the most recent historical cost data, direct material costs are as follows:

- Average material cost for flight simulator maintenance: $10.00 per operating hour

- *Visual system costs are $8.25 per simulator operating hour for a five-channel projector system*
- *Total Material Costs = $10.00 x 3,520 + $8.25 x 3,520 (visual system = $64,240*

Total Direct Cost: *Total direct cost consists of Direct Labor and Direct Material as follows: $228,960 (Direct Labor) + 64,240 (Direct Material) = $293,200.*

Risk Management

Risk management is an important part of your technical approach (see Chapter 10). It also is a valuable component of your cost proposal. If you have taken measures to mitigate risk, which includes cost, then include this information in the cost proposal. If possible, quantify the dollar value of potential risks, both before and after you have applied your risk mitigation strategy. Also, include an explanation and the dollar amount of any risk management funds included in your cost proposal.

Explaining your risk management approach and identifying any contingent risk funds contained in your cost estimates may offset the potential of evaluators to assign an unfavorable risk rating to your cost volume. Doing so also may highlight a potential shortcoming of one of your competitors that does not include a risk management explanation in its cost proposal.

Groundrules and Assumptions

Groundrules and assumptions are an other important part of your cost proposal. Some elements of your cost estimate are conditional upon each of the groundrules and assumptions being true. Therefore, they must be documented in the cost proposal as completely as practical.

Groundrules are the basic parameters you used to prepare cost estimates. They include things like whether costs are presented in now (current) year dollars or "then" year dollars or whether you used a constant escalation rate for cost beyond the first year of the contract. Groundrules are provided so that cost evaluators can better understand your cost proposal.

Assumptions generally need to be made in cases where RFP guidance is either absent or vague concerning some program aspect upon which your cost estimate is based. Some simple examples may involve assumptions about undefined schedule events, like the start date of the contract, the start date of contract options, or the timing of government-provided assets (e.g., people, data, equipment). Because your cost estimate is based on these assumptions, failing to meet them could jeopardize your ability to perform the contract for the amount proposed.

Include any assumption you made to estimate cost that is not contained in the RFP or where the RFP is vague. In addition, if you have interpreted an RFP requirement to your advantage, then you must include this assumption in your cost proposal.

Chapter 7 described a case where computer installation costs could be interpreted as being part of development, which was covered under a cost-type contract, or as part of operations, which were covered under a fixed-price contract. To avoid risk, we interpreted installation as a development task and bid it as part of the cost-type contract. Then we clearly explained this as an assumption in our cost proposal and included it as part of our WBS dictionary.

Here is another example of the prudent use of a documented cost-estimate assumption. We were bidding for a service contract being performed by another contractor. Employees at one of the work sites were covered by a collective bargaining agreement that was scheduled to expire between the time we submitted our proposal and the expected contract award date. We were afraid that the incumbent would renegotiate the collective bargaining agreement at higher salaries than those being paid when the contract was bid, which was the basis of our labor cost estimate. To protect ourselves, we included an assumption in our cost proposal that our proposed labor rates were based on salaries in effect when we submitted our proposal and that the same salaries would be in effect at contract award.

In essence, assumptions serve as insurance against those cases, after contract award, where your cost estimates are no longer valid because the assumptions upon which they are based have not proven true. However, your assumptions cannot contradict RFP guidance or requirements. Also, do not include every conceivable assumption. Limit assumptions to events that could have a meaningful impact on your actual incurred cost.

MAINTAINING GOOD COST PERFORMANCE RECORDS

Few activities will pay a higher return on investment than maintaining good records concerning your cost performance on past and current contracts and the method used originally to estimate those costs. Creating and maintaining a database of past basis of estimates and the actual cost incurred on the subsequent contract pay dividends in several areas.

First, past basis of estimates can be used to reduce the effort of preparing future cost proposals. They probably will need to be amended to fit the specific requirements of each bid, but this is still far more efficient than starting from scratch. Second, you can use actual contract cost data to adjust your basis of estimate. Over time, this should enable you to make more efficient and accurate cost estimates.

Finally, correlating your basis of estimate with actual contract cost performance is just the type of data the government is looking for in your cost proposal. Historically validated basis of estimates are worth far more than you will spend collecting and maintaining the data necessary to derive them.

Keeping good cost performance records, along with basis of estimates, potentially will enable you to reduce B&P costs, improve subsequent program cost performance, and enhance the customer's evaluation of your cost proposal. These are all ingredients of gaining competitive advantage.

BEST-VALUE PROCUREMENTS

Over the last decade, many government agencies have made a concerted effort to award contracts based on best value rather than low price. The application of such initiatives, however, has been uneven across agencies. Some agencies have done a good job of making awards based on value. Others pay lip service to value yet remain fixated on cost.

Despite considerable cynicism among contractors, best-value awards are real. Government customers really do award contracts based on best value. However, you must fulfill several prerequisites if you plan to prance into the winner's circle based on a best-value solution.

First, you must know your customer well enough to discern whether they actually will award to other than the lowest bidder. Second, you must have a sense of the "cost bandwidth" within which a best value award will be made. This bandwidth is the percentage difference between the cost of the best-value solution and the next lower qualified bidder. My experience suggests that the bandwidth in most cases is a cost difference of no more than about 10 percent. Cost differences greater than this become very difficult for the customer to defend.

Third, value is in the eyes of the beholder. Hence, you must ensure that the customer values the features of your technical solution enough to pay for them. Otherwise, they will pick a less expensive, technically compliant solution. Fourth, your technical proposal must clearly and effectively communicate the value of your technical solution and its benefit to the customer.

Finally, I recommend that you include a best-value section in your cost proposal. Highlight those aspects or characteristics of your technical solution that provide value to the customer. To the extent possible, show the dollar value of your solution compared to a lesser, but technically compliant, solution. Oftentimes, value comes in the form of future cost savings or the ease with which a system can be modified to accommodate new requirements. In such cases, provide an estimate of the cost savings the customer can expect to achieve, or illustrate the "value" of an easily modifiable system. This is exactly the type of information source selection teams need to justify making a best-value award.

One of the chief reasons contracts are awarded on the basis of cost is that there is no discernable difference in the technical solutions proposed by competing bidders. If you hope to win based on value, then you must convince evaluators that your solution has "value," and supply them with the ammunition necessary to support a best-value award.

Being the lowest-priced qualified bidder affords an inherent advantage. For procurements where cost is the primary consideration, it is an advantage not easily overcome. Even for procurements where cost is the least important factor, being the low bidder is still an enviable position. Nonetheless, in many instances, being the low bidder is not enough.

Sometimes the government is as interested in the basis of your cost estimates as they are in their absolute value. Other times they weigh the value of your proposed technical solution against its cost. Hence, how you prepare and present cost information can have a significant impact on the evaluation of your cost proposal and ultimately on whether you win the contract.

Gain competitive advantage by recognizing that there often is more to winning than bidding the lowest cost. Avoid common cost proposal mistakes. Know your customer and the true role cost will play in the overall source selection process. Formulate your cost strategy accordingly and make sure your technical solution fits within the customer's budget. Understand the role that risk plays in the selection of contract type and the type and amount of cost information required to support government cost analyses.

Prepare and present your cost proposal in a way that enables evaluators to easily understand how you derived your cost estimates. Provide strong basis of estimates based on historical data and previously completed contracts where you successfully fulfilled comparable contract requirements. Maintain good cost performance and basis of estimate records to support future proposal efforts. Ensure that each level of your cost estimate is traceable to higher-level WBS elements (e.g., CLINs, lots, SOW).

Avoid having evaluators assign high-risk ratings to your cost proposal or increase your proposed cost to determine most probable cost to the government. Make sure your cost proposal is thorough, complete, and accurate, and that estimated costs correspond with the solution and effort described in your technical proposal. If you undertake to win on value, then understand and be able to meet the key prerequisites necessary to capture a best-value procurement.

Chapter 14

Proposal Reviews

Proposal reviews are conducted during the proposal development phase to assess progress and make any necessary course corrections. Progress in this sense is not about how much you have accomplished but what you have accomplished. Is your proposal responsive to RFP requirements? Is your bid strategy being implemented effectively? Are themes and discriminators clearly articulated and integrated into the proposal narrative? Is your proposal well written and organized?

Proposal reviews are intended to answer questions like these. They also should provide clear directions about how to remedy identified shortcomings. No one would expect to hike across Antarctica or through the Amazon without periodically checking to ensure that they were on course. Likewise, no one should expect to prepare a winning proposal without performing comparable course checks. So, the issue is not whether or not you will conduct proposal reviews, but how and when.

Gain competitive advantage by integrating timely, effective proposal reviews into your proposal process. Use review information to correct deficiencies and improve proposal quality. Those who stumble through the review process risk slipping behind the competition.

DIFFERENT TYPES OF REVIEW

Proposal reviews typically are referred to by color. Different "color" reviews occur at different stages of proposal development. The best-known review is the red team review, which seems to get its name from those glory days when proposals were prepared on typewriters and evaluated in hardcopy format. Proposal reviewers marked up the draft proposal with red pens. Hence the term "red team." (Some argue that the term "red" comes from the spilt blood of the proposal team). Since then we have added other reviews, each with its own color designation. These various reviews are summarized below, although not everyone is consistent in how they use the color labels or in their review focus.

Storyboard Review

Storyboard reviews are not assigned a color and are applicable only when storyboards are part of the proposal development process. Normally conducted by the proposal manager or technical volume manager, they consist of a check of completed storyboards. These checks focus on verifying that the author has a solid outline to work from and one that clearly addresses the relevant RFP requirements.

Pink Team Review

Logic says that if there is a red team, then a review before this should probably be a pink team. Pink team reviews generally are early course correction reviews. They identify areas inconsistent with the basic proposal architecture and organization established by approved proposal outlines and author guides.

Pink team reviews also identify cases where proposal narrative is not responsive to RFP requirements. For those cases, they identify the deficiency and define the necessary corrective action. Pink teams generally avoid minor issues of proposal format, page count, or things likely to be corrected during the normal revision process.

Red Team Review

The red team review is a formal evaluation of your proposal. It should be conducted using the same evaluation methods and criteria that your customer will use to select the winner.

Red team reviewers evaluate your proposal for compliance with RFP instructions, requirements, and evaluation criteria. They also assess the extent to which you have effectively conveyed your proposal sales messages and bid strategies, and check for the presence and substantiation of themes, clarity of text and artwork, and overall proposal persuasiveness.

Red team members identify proposal deficiencies and define corrective actions. They also list proposal strengths and weaknesses to help guide subsequent revision efforts.

Gold Team Review

The gold team (sometimes called the blue team) conducts a final review of the proposal. This is the last opportunity to identify areas for improvement and to make those improvements before the proposal is submitted. Typically, gold team membership is limited to just the proposal manager and a few hand-picked individuals who have extensive proposal experience. They provide the final "polishing" to ensure that the proposal communicates the bid strategy clearly and effectively and is well written. In some cases, gold team members perform final proposal proofreading and quality assurance checks as well.

Black Team Review

Black teams, or black hat teams, perform a detailed assessment of all major competitors, or just your major competitor. The purpose of a black team review is to determine the most likely bid strategies of your competitors. In some cases this might be a "straw man" proposal, intended to represent what your competitor is expected to submit. This information is then used to develop offsetting strategies. To be effective, black team reviews must be conducted during the pre-proposal phase to allow enough time to use the results. They are restricted to strategically important contracts. They also typically are conducted by outside consultants who possess in-depth knowledge of competitors or a consulting group that can investigate the competition without involving your company directly.

FORMAL VERSUS INFORMAL REVIEWS

Proposal reviews may be either formal or informal.

Formal proposal reviews are conducted by people who have not worked on the proposal. They review the entire proposal at one time, formally document their findings, and debrief the whole proposal team and other interested parties on the results.

An informal review, or in-process review, is one conducted by a small team, sometimes just the proposal manager. They are conducted as individual proposal sections become available. Feedback concerning deficiencies and corrective actions is given to individual authors on a section-by-section basis. For an in-process gold team review, the final changes may be made by the proposal manager or a small group appointed specifically for that purpose.

Determining which proposal reviews to conduct, and whether or not they should be formal reviews, depend on a host of variables. These include:

- Time available to prepare your proposal
- Number of draft proposals planned
- Experience and capability of proposal capture team members to perform reviews
- Proposal budget (if consultants will be used)
- Importance or value of the contract
- Availability of people to serve on formal review teams.

In some cases, pink, red, and gold teams all are conducted as formal reviews. However, this is usually the case only for contracts with a value in the multi-hundred million or billion-dollar range and when you have 60 to 90 days to prepare your proposal. More routine are cases where a formal pink and red team review are conducted, or only the red team review is a formal review.

For contracts with a 30- to 45-day response time, consider limiting your formal review process to the red team. Add a formal pink team review only when it can be completed prior to final RFP release or if the program is extremely important. Trying to cram too many reviews into the proposal development process will likely undermine proposal quality, not improve it. Proposal authors must have adequate time to develop and edit their sections.

Here is a typical scenario. After losing a string of proposals, or one very significant bid, management becomes convinced that the problem lies in failing to detect problems early in the development cycle. To avoid this, they schedule earlier reviews. Authors faced with insufficient time to prepare their sections then submit nonresponsive material for review. Management's suspicions are confirmed. So, they schedule earlier and more frequent reviews—with predictable results.

Proposal success, like most things in life, is a matter of balance. For proposal reviews, the balance is between giving authors enough time to complete their writing assignment effectively and conducting a timely assessment of proposal progress. As a baseline, I recommend that you plan to conduct informal storyboard and pink team reviews, a formal red team review, and an informal gold team review. Ideally, this will include: pink team reviews of a draft proposal written in response to a draft RFP and the first draft proposal after receiving the final RFP; a red team review after the second draft has been edited; and a gold team review after red team corrections have been made. You can adjust the suggested baseline to accommodate individual circumstances.

INFORMAL STORYBOARD REVIEW

The purpose of a storyboard review is to ensure that authors have a good foundation before they start writing the first draft. Either the proposal manager or the technical volume manager should check sheet 1 of the author guide to verify that it is thorough and appears to address the required topics adequately. They also should check to ensure that paragraph numbering and headings are consistent with the proposal outline. Once sheet 2 is complete, it should be checked to ensure that themes are consistent with the bid strategy and that any suggested features, benefits, and risk mitigation strategies meet basic criteria.

IN-PROCESS PINK TEAM REVIEW

The purpose of initial or pink team reviews is to check the proposal to ensure that it complies with and is responsive to all RFP requirements. We are just trying to "bake the cake" at this stage. Therefore, do not worry about themes or your sales message yet.

The proposal manager or other capture team leaders can conduct initial in-process reviews. To check compliance, use the proposal requirements matrix discussed in Chapter 10. Recall that this matrix lists Section L preparation instructions and shows corresponding evaluation criteria and other relevant RFP requirements. The matrix conveniently provides all the information required to perform a compliance check. It saves reviewers the hassle of looking up all the relevant RFP sections. Moreover, it is the foundation for your proposal outline and author guides and hence provides the perfect reference for assessing your first draft narrative.

Read each proposal section and compare it against the requirements contained in the proposal requirements matrix. Identify areas where the proposal narrative is either nonresponsive to instructions or noncompliant with RFP requirements. Note these deficiencies along with the necessary corrective actions.

You can use any reasonable format to record the results of the pink team review and communicate them to authors. My preference is to make an electronic copy of the proposal section. Then I embed my comments and recommendations within the proposal section itself using a different-colored font. This is efficient, and it works well for me. However, you can build an evaluation form or adapt the one used for red team reviews.

RED TEAM REVIEW

The red team review should always be conducted as a formal review. A properly conducted red team review can be an invaluable asset and an important ingredient of a winning proposal. A poorly conducted red team review can be worse than no red team review at all.

Conduct the red team review using the same methods, procedures, and evaluation criteria the government will use to evaluate your proposal. Evaluate your proposal at the subfactor level as defined in Section M of the RFP. If your customer assigns color scores as an evaluation method, use colors to score your proposal. If the customer uses a point system for evaluation, use a point system. If the customer will evaluate proposal risk, then you also must assess proposal risk. Whatever the customer does is exactly what you should do. The value of the red team review results will be directly proportional to the extent to which you mirror your customer's source selection process. Of equal importance are the people assigned as members of the red team.

In the mid 1980s, I was hired as the proposal director to establish and manage a proposal process for a company that was not winning much new business. Red teams consisted primarily of company vice presidents and directors who were using the red team reviews to familiarize themselves with proposals they would eventually have to approve before they were submitted to the government. Unfortunately, they practically never read the RFP, did not understand government source selection, were frequently interrupted during the review, and generally gave terrible advice to the proposal team. To help solve this problem, I scheduled red team reviews on weekends and set as prerequisites for *all* red team members a thorough reading of the RFP and red team training. This solved the problem, and I have used this strategy ever since.

With few exceptions, the people who wrote the proposal should not serve as red team members. They know too much about the proposal and hence are not representative of government evaluators. In addition, to the extent that it is within your power, keep senior management off the red team. In general, they make terrible reviewers. They normally do not have enough time to prepare for the review properly or give it their full attention. Perhaps worse, because they are *senior management*, few people on the proposal team will be willing to oppose their advice, even if it is wrong.

Of course, there are exceptions to this general rule. Furthermore, if the president or vice president of your company wants to be a red team member, it could be career-limiting to refuse his or her request.

Organize the red team according to the organization of evaluation criteria—areas and factors—contained in Section M. This is how the government's source selection will be organized. Have a separate group of red team evaluators for each evaluation area and factor. If possible, have at least three people read and score each proposal section.

Some reviewers should be knowledgeable about the proposal area they will review, and a few should be experts. Whenever possible, use people with past red team experience who understand government source selection. A key characteristic of an effective reviewer is someone who can read proposal material, compare it with requirements, and give clear directions about how to fix shortcomings. If you have major subcontractors who helped prepare the proposal, then consider asking them to contribute a member to the red team.

The leader of the red team is responsible for training and organizing the team, structuring the review process, managing the review, assimilating review results, and preparing and presenting the red team debriefing to the proposal team. For small proposals, the proposal manager can serve as the red team leader. If it is within your budget and justified by the value of the contract, I highly recommend that you use an outside red team consultant to serve as the red team leader.

For major proposals, consider having outside consultants lead the evaluation of proposal areas or key factors. If the normal scope of your proposals does not justify an outside consultant, consider having one come in and evaluate your proposal review process. This can be a one-time event, which you can use to build an effective review process or modify the one you already have in place.

Whenever schedule constraints permit, I prefer to schedule red team review for weekends. Allow one full day to prepare and format the proposal for review. Most red teams can be conducted in two days (three days for larger, complex proposals if you have the time). Schedule a debriefing session for the proposal team either at the end of the second day or the beginning of the third day.

Red team reviewers must be familiar with the RFP. Before the red team review begins, make sure all team members have read at least RFP Sections L and M, plus the statement of work and any other pertinent RFP attachments. Plan on conducting a brief training session for red team members before they start their review, preferably the day before. Minimum topics for the training session include:

1. An overview of your customer's source selection process—do not assume reviewers already know this
2. A schedule of red team events (review, assimilation of results, proposal team debriefing)
3. An overview of the red team review process
4. Instructions to reviewers about the purpose of the review and what you want the review to accomplish
5. A review of red team documents and evaluation forms and how they should be used.

Plan about two hours to complete the training session.

Good planning and organization will contribute mightily to the effectiveness of your red team review. Provide each reviewer with a document package that includes the following:

- Written instruction about how to conduct the review
- Proposal sections to be reviewed
- RFP Sections L and M (access to a complete RFP)
- RFP requirements matrix
- Relevant author guides
- Proposal evaluation forms.

Red Team Instructions

Provide reviewers a secure, quiet, comfortable work environment. Have an administrative or clerical person available to help the review team organize and collate evaluation forms and prepare the final proposal debriefing. If you are under a schedule crunch or reviewers expect to work long hours, plan to bring in nutritious meals for them. If your customer plans to evaluate your proposal electronically, then I highly recommend that you conduct the red team review electronically.

Written instructions provide reviewers with specific direction about how to conduct the review. They state the review's purpose and set some boundaries concerning appropriate ways to evaluate the proposal and provide feedback to authors. Reviewers need to be mindful of the hard work of the proposal team, regardless of how bad the proposal may appear. Derogatory, rude, or distasteful reviewer comments are uncalled for and should not be permitted. They only discourage and inflame those tasked to fix the problem.

The reviewer's task is to identify deficiencies and areas for improvement and then clearly communicate that information to the author. No one likes a critic, but nearly everyone appreciates definitive instructions that will enable them to improve the quality of their product. That should be the focus of red team reviewers. Accordingly, corrective actions captured on evaluation forms should be specific and detailed. Otherwise, the author will be unable to determine the recommended solution to an identified deficiency. Comments like, "This section is vague," "What are you trying to say?" or "Fix it" will be of little help to the author. Ask reviewers to be specific in identifying proposal deficiencies and explicit in defining the necessary corrective actions.

Consider keeping a collection of past evaluation forms, both good and bad, to use as examples for red team training. Finally, ask reviewers to refrain from marking typographical, spelling, or grammatical errors. They need to focus on more substantive issues. Furthermore, these types of errors are easily fixed during the next rewrite and edit cycle.

Conducting the Red Team Review

Equipped with the RFP requirements matrix and relevant author guides, the reviewer's task is to read the proposal section to determine if each requirement is adequately addressed. Deficiencies are noted on the proposal evaluation form, along with the recommended corrective actions. Sample evaluation forms are provided in Figures 14-1 and 14-2. In addition, the reviewer also checks to see if sales messages and themes contained in the author guide made their way into the proposal. If not, or if they are ineffective, then a deficiency is noted.

Figure 14-1. Sample Proposal Evaluation Form (Sheet 1)

Proposal Evaluation Form (Sheet 1 of 2)		
Control Number:		
Volume:	**Section:**	**Pages:**
RFP Reference:		
Deficiency Description:		
Recommended Corrective Actions:		

Use a separate evaluation form for each deficiency. This will help track the subsequent resolution of deficiencies. Sheet 2 of the evaluation form includes space to list proposal strengths and weaknesses. For identified weaknesses, reviewers should provide their recommended corrections. Strengths are listed to ensure that they are preserved during the next revision cycle and to potentially enhance their effectiveness. The "control number" on sheet 1 is used to keep track of deficiencies. Assign each reviewer a unique alpha identifier—A, B, C, etc. The reviewer assigns each deficiency a control number using his or her alpha code as a prefix, and sequentially numbers each deficiency (e.g., A-1, A-2, A-3).

To complete their evaluation task, reviewers assign each proposal section a score according to the method the customer will use to evaluate proposals. For Department of Defense contracts, government evaluators use color codes—red, yellow, green, and blue—to designate the extent to which the proposal meets requirements. Red denotes an unacceptable section; blue a section that exceeds requirements (see Chapter 2 for more details). Other

Figure 14-2. Sample Proposal Evaluation Form (Sheet 2)

Proposal Evaluation Form (Sheet 2 of 2)		
Major Weaknesses and Recommendation		
Major Weakness	**Reference**	**Recommendation • Correct**
Major Strengths and References		
Major Strengths Reference		

agencies use either a numerical score or a point system. Use the appropriate scoring system and the same standards your customer will use. If appropriate, have reviewers assign a proposal risk rating—high, moderate, low—to every proposal section using the risk criteria and definitions contained in the RFP.

Reviewers will need a form of some type to record their scores and risk ratings. Some of the documents developed during proposal planning can be adapted easily for this task. In Chapter 10, we described how to prepare a proposal outline and a corresponding proposal responsibility matrix (see Figure 10-14). Changing some of the column headings of the responsibility matrix produces a convenient recording form, as shown in Figure 14-3.

Combine scores and risk ratings for individual proposal sections to arrive at a score for each evaluation subfactor, factor, and area, as defined by Section M of the RFP. Remember to apply relative importance weights of subfactors to

Figure 14-3. Sample Evaluation Recording Form for One Subfactor

Proposal Section	Proposal Score	Proposal Risk Rating
VOLUME I:		
2.2 Subfactor 2 Training System Support Center (TSSC)		
Introduction		
2.2.1 XYZ Approach and Proposed Resources to Operate and Maintain the TSSC		
2.2.2 Overview of XYZ Maintenance Approach to Meet the 95% Availability Requirement		
2.2.3 XYZ Methods to Maintain LSP, ICS, MDC at the Site and System Level		
2.2.3.1 Ability of XYZ's LSP to Support Logistics Functions		
2.2.3.2 Capability of XYZ's Inventory Control System (ICS)		
2.2.3.3 XYZ Approach to Maintenance Data Collection		
2.2.4 XYZ Approach and Capability to Support Equipment for the Aging ATS		
2.2.5 XYZ Approach to Integrate and Maintain Multiple Baselines		
2.2.6 XYZ Approach to Develop and Maintain All Aspects of C-141 ATS Configuration		
2.2.7 XYZ Approach to Ensure a First-time Quality Delivery of Courseware		
2.2.8 XYZ's Maintenance Plan for the ABC System		

determine factor scores. The final evaluation score/risk rating should be the consensus of all the reviewers who scored the section. This is the score that will be presented to the proposal team at the red team debriefing.

Likewise, all the proposal strengths and weakness should be agreed upon by the relevant reviewers and listed for each evaluation subfactor or factor. All the reviewers for each proposal section should collaborate and agree upon the corrective action contained in the evaluation forms. Otherwise, authors may receive inconsistent or contradictory directions about how to correct a noted deficiency.

Debriefing of Red Team Results

Assemble the entire proposal team and summarize the results of the red team review. Start with an overview of the entire proposal evaluation and highlight any general concerns or areas that need to be addressed. Explain how the review was conducted and what the proposal scores and risk ratings mean. Then present scores and risk ratings for each evaluation area and factor. Work from general to specific. Provide a separate presentation for each subfactor, including a list of strengths and weaknesses.

Try to maintain a positive tone during the debriefing. The evaluation scores will speak for themselves, good or bad. Emphasize the actions necessary to correct the proposal's deficiencies and transform it into a winner. Avoid language or comments that assign blame or otherwise demean the efforts of the proposal team. The debriefing should be an objective presentation of red team results with a clearly defined roadmap for recovery and improvement.

Once the red team has completed its evaluation, have the assigned administrative assistant make copies of all evaluation forms. Organize them according to proposal section and log them into a deficiency tracking form or electronic database using the control number as an identifier. Figure 14-4 shows a sample tracking form. Use the tracking log to record and track the resolution of each deficiency identified by the red team.

After the red team debriefing, distribute copies of evaluation forms to the relevant author or person assigned to respond to evaluation results. Each author then reviews the evaluation forms and determines how to respond to the recommendations of the red team. The red team is a recommending body. They do not provide direction, nor should all their recommendations be followed absolutely. If the author disagrees with a red team recommendation, the proposal manager determines the final course of action.

After reviewing the evaluation forms, each author builds a plan and schedule to revise his or her proposal sections accordingly. Plan to revise

Figure 14-4. Sample Proposal Deficiency Tracking Form

Control Number	Person Assigned	Resolution			Resolved
		Ignore	Incorporate	Amend	

those proposal sections that require the least amount of rework first to leave more time available for the most difficult ones. Every evaluation deficiency must be resolved and recorded in the deficiency tracking form. Resolution can be to ignore the recommendation, incorporate it, or amend it. The proposal administrator should maintain the tracking form and report progress to the proposal manager. Tracking deficiency resolution provides traceability between the red team results and the next revision cycle. It also ensures that each deficiency has been addressed.

GOLD TEAM REVIEW

Except for major proposals with ample preparation time, gold team reviews should be conducted informally as individual proposal sections are revised. The proposal manager should conduct the gold team review, with assistance from selected members of the capture team. Its primary purpose is to verify that deficiencies discovered by the red team have been corrected and that themes, discriminators, and strengths are presented effectively. Any deficiencies or further improvements identified during the gold team review usually will be corrected by the proposal manager and capture team during the final revision of the proposal. However, individual proposal authors can be used for this task provided that they have the requisite proposal experience and writing skills.

A Tier 3 schedule is developed for each proposal section with completion dates for revisions. The in-process gold team review is conducted on a section-by-section basis as soon as each section becomes available.

Strategically positioned and effectively conducted proposal reviews offer an excellent opportunity to gain competitive advantage. Seize this advantage. Use in-process reviews to provide timely course correction information to proposal authors. Schedule and manage reviews to maximize the time available to correct deficiencies and improve proposal quality. Conduct well-structured red team reviews with qualified and trained evaluators.

Provide clear, definitive guidance on how to correct deficiencies and enhance proposal strengths. Track deficiency resolution to completion and verify that all legitimate deficiencies have been corrected. Allocate proposal revision duties to optimize the individual talents and strengths of the proposal team. Use your best people to make the final revisions and put the finishing touch on the proposal.

Chapter 15

Proposal Production

Proposal production refers to the collective tasks necessary to format, edit, organize, publish, copy, package, and deliver a proposal to the customer. It is best performed by experienced, well-trained production professionals. Mistakenly viewed by some as a low-level clerical function, proposal production is a critical part of the overall proposal development process. A "well-oiled" and well-managed production capability staffed with experienced professionals can help you gain competitive advantage. At the other end of the spectrum, a poorly managed and inadequately staffed production team can be a burdensome millstone.

Two general factors contribute to the importance of proposal production. First, a good production team can maximize the amount of time proposal authors have to prepare, modify, and polish their final product. For proposals, time is more valuable than gold. Giving the proposal team more time to perform their tasks will contribute immeasurably to proposal quality.

Second, the production team is largely responsible for the overall "appearance" of the final product delivered to the customer. Submitting a proposal that looks like it was prepared by a group of disinterested teenagers will not win you any points with government evaluators. Sloppy format; failure to follow RFP instructions; typographical, spelling, or grammatical errors; inaccurate references, page numbers, or figure references; missing information; wrong file formats, etc., all contribute to the overall appearance of your proposal.

The statement that you only have one chance to make a good first impression is trite, but true. In fact, it may be doubly true for proposals.

It is the role of the production team to ensure that you make a good first impression with the customer. However, as you work to maximize the time available for the proposal team, you must also ensure that production personnel have sufficient time to perform their jobs.

PRODUCTION ORGANIZATION AND MANAGEMENT

The proposal administrator is responsible for proposal production. He or she works directly for the proposal manager. In small companies, or on small proposals, the administrator may perform most of the formatting and production tasks, with assistance from other trained staff. If your organization has a separate publications department or production group, then the administrator will serve as the primary interface between the proposal team and the production team.

The size and composition of the production team will vary according to the size and complexity of the proposal, the proposal schedule, and other competing production projects. At a minimum, you will need someone to help format and produce the proposal, an editor, and a graphic artist.

To develop a production approach and staffing plan, consider the following production tasks that must be performed:

- Proposal formatting to comply with Section L instructions
- Preparation of graphs, illustrations, and photographs
- Electronic and hardcopy configuration management and version control
- Word processing to integrate text and graphics
- Preparation or acquisition of proposal covers, spines, and tabs for hardcopy proposals
- Development of tables of contents, figures, and tables, plus acronym or other lists
- Proofreading of text and graphics
- Reproduction of hardcopy proposal material
- Collation and assembly (such as three-ring binders), including placing covers, spines, and tabs into binders
- Final quality assurance check for hardcopy material
- Preparation of electronic version of proposal and electronic quality assurance check
- Packaging of proposal for delivery to customer
- Completion of specific bid forms and packaging labels
- E-mail delivery, overnight shipping, or hand-delivery of proposal.

Completing all these tasks in the shortest time possible, while maintaining a high-quality product, can be a formidable challenge. Take too much time for production, and you shortchange the proposal team. Squeeze production time too hard, and you run the risk of delivering a shoddy product. Neither outcome is acceptable. So the key is balance and disciplined management. Here are some guidelines for managing this process.

During the first draft, authors should not worry about formatting or other production issues. They need to concentrate on their assigned tasks.

Identify required graphics early and have them prepared concurrently with the first draft (at least before the red team review). Use "waterfall" schedules for each individual proposal section to maintain the fluidity of proposal production. As the author completes each section, it is passed to production for formatting, integration, and editing.

After the red team review, again build individual schedules for each proposal section. Based on the red team results, you will be able to determine which sections need the most work and which need the least. Schedule those sections that require the least amount of work to be completed first. Those that require significant rework are scheduled last. As the author completes each proposal section, that section moves to production, where it undergoes all the steps necessary to produce a final document. This enables each proposal section to be processed and produced individually. It also allows the greatest amount of time to work on those sections that require the most work. As authors complete their proposal assignments, they can help with production tasks.

There are some limits on how far you can go with this approach. In most cases you will not be able to number the pages until a major portion or volume is complete. If you are fighting page-count problems, you may need to leave a major section, or the entire volume, open until you solve the problem. Nonetheless, you can perform all the editing, proofreading, and quality assurance checks for each section. Also make sure you leave at least one full day (24 hours) to complete the final quality checks, assemble the proposal, and package it for shipping.

Another potential barrier to using a waterfall scheduling approach comes from organizations that have a separate publications department. Such departments often perform the production and publication services for the entire company. To manage their workload, they require that a complete product be delivered before they start production. In such cases, it is not unusual for the production group to ask for five to seven days to produce your proposal. This makes great sense for the production group, but it could spell disaster for your proposal. Using 15 percent or more of the time available to produce your proposal gives the competitive advantage to bidders that are more efficient.

Several solutions are possible. First, you can start your proposal early enough and manage it so that you have ample time left over to meet the production group's schedule. Personally, I would rather eat a grub worm than let the production group dictate proposal schedule, but you probably do not have that option.

A second option is to create a special proposal production group apart from, or as a subset of, the company's production group. This group would work alongside your proposal team and support a waterfall production schedule. They would receive special training in proposal production and be assigned to the proposal team to accomplish production tasks. Such a group can be assembled or supplemented with outside personnel. In fact, I recommend that you maintain a cadre of qualified and experienced freelance production personnel to help supplement your in-house capability. Maintain a list of prequalified local freelance graphics artists, word processing operators, editors, and proofreaders to call upon during peak periods.

Some will argue that a separate proposal production group undermines the cost-effectiveness of having a centralized publication capability. That is a vacant argument, however. Spending a few extra dollars to improve proposal win probability will prove to be one of the most cost-effective moves your company ever makes.

PROPOSAL CONFIGURATION MANAGEMENT

Configuration management covers both the control of different versions of proposal documents and authorized changes to those documents. Everyone on the proposal team must be able to identify the most current version of each proposal section. Few things are more disheartening than to work all day on a proposal section only to find out that it is last week's version.

Having computers networked via a local area network or comparable system simplifies proposal configuration management. It also is an absolute necessity for preparing government proposals. No one can afford *not* to work on networked computers. Therefore, this section assumes that you have a computer network with individual access to centralized file directories.

There are undoubtedly many ways to implement proposal configuration management. The following is a system I have found to be effective.

Create a separate file directory for the proposal. Limit directory access to people assigned to the proposal or via password. Build subdirectories for each proposal volume and major proposal section. You can use the paragraph number derived from the proposal outline and contained in the author guide to identify each individual proposal section or subsection. Save the first-draft proposal write-up by using a file name consisting of the proposal paragraph number, a short heading, and a version number. For example:

1.2.3 Program Management v.1
Structure all the files in the proposal directory as "read only" files. When a change is made to the original file, it is saved with the next higher version number. For example:

1.2.3 Program Management v.2
Because the files are read-only, no one can make a change and then save the file with the original file name. The version number lets you know the

latest version. If you wish, you can ask authors to add their initials to the end of the version number:

1.2.3 Program Management v.2 SRO

This system lets you know which is the latest version. It also maintains all previous versions so you can go back and see what has been changed.

To further help with version control, put a time and date stamp in the header or footer of draft documents. This is a simple process and is a selectable feature of word processing software.

Separate subdirectories can be created to store and manage proposal documents through the different phases or milestones of proposal development and production. Here is a candidate list of proposal subdirectories:

01 1st Draft
02 1st Draft Edited
03 2nd Draft
04 2nd Draft Edited
05 Ready for Red Team
06 Post-Red Team
07 Post-Red Team Edited
08 Final Edit
09 Final Proposal.

Numbering each subdirectory will enable you to maintain the order in which subdirectories occur in the file listing if you use a Microsoft Windows operating environment. Also, plan to create a separate set of subdirectory files for each proposal volume. You can develop a similar scheme to handle configuration management of proposal documents like the proposal requirements directive or the proposal outline.

First draft proposal documents are stored in the "first draft" subdirectory. Once a first draft proposal document has been edited, it can be stored in the "1st draft edited" subdirectory. Older versions of the document are moved to an archived directory to avoid confusion. Version numbers continue to be changed each time the document is changed so the highest version number is always the most recent version. Eventually, each proposal section will end up in the "final proposal" subdirectory.

Limiting access to the proposal during its final stages of development is an important configuration control technique. You do not want everyone to be able to make changes. Some network systems have the ability to limit directory access according to user name. This is the easiest method. As the proposal nears completion, limit access to those authorized to make changes. If your network system does not have this capability, then you will need to devise a password system to limit access. You also can tell the proposal team not to make any changes unless the proposal manager specifically authorizes them, but this does not always work.

CONFIGURATION MANAGEMENT OF GRAPHICS

The same method can be used to control the configuration of proposal graphics. Create a separate read-only graphics directory for each proposal volume. Assign each graphic a unique control number and version number. Each time the graphic is changed, it will be stored in the graphics directory with the next higher version number. Include the control number within the graphic itself using a very small font.

When authors reference a graphic in the proposal, have them include the graphic control number. For example:

Figure 1.2.3-1 (*00181*) depicts our systems engineering process.

The italicized number in parentheses is the control number. This number remains constant despite changes to the figure reference caused by proposal revisions. The control number can be removed from the proposal once all final revisions are complete.

INTERNAL DOCUMENTATION STANDARDS

It is worthwhile to develop and maintain a standard proposal publication guide that defines basic style and format for company proposals. This guide can be derived from your company publications handbook if one exists. Otherwise, you can develop your own. The production group, working with the business development staff, should develop and maintain format and style standards. This will ensure consistent presentation of a uniform company image.

Several writing, editorial, and proofreading standards can be used to develop a format and style guide. These include the United States Government Printing Office *Style Manual* and the Supplement to the United States Government Printing Office *Style Manual*. Both documents are available online.

The formatting instructions provided in Section L of the RFP define basic format. However, a standard style and format guide can be used to assist proposal authors, proposal reviewers, and production staff in working toward a consistent style and presentation structure. In addition, the proposal administrator should develop a list of RFP-specific terms to be used in your proposal. Proposal writers and publication staff can use this list to capitalize, hyphenate, and abbreviate terms according to a set of predefined standards consistent with the style and format your customer uses.

HARDCOPY AND ELECTRONIC PROPOSAL SUBMITTAL

Many federal agencies now require bidders to submit both hardcopy and electronic (e.g., e-mail, diskette, CD-ROM) versions of their proposal. These same agencies also evaluate proposals electronically. Eventually, hardcopy proposals will disappear, and we will deliver all our proposals over the Internet. Until then, here are some tips to help you avoid costly mistakes:

- Provide your proposal in the specific version of the software application requested by the RFP, on the requested medium, and in the correct format. Government agencies often use older versions of software that are not capable of opening documents prepared with later versions.
- Use filenames specified by the RFP and do not submit both your technical and cost proposals on the same diskette or CD-ROM unless specifically authorized by the government contracting officer.
- If your proposal contains complex or color graphics, make sure they will not bog down the government's computers. I know of an instance where government evaluators were using antiquated computers with limited memory to evaluate proposals. One of the bidders submitted a proposal with graphics that routinely took three to five minute to open. Not good!
- Be mindful of how your proposal will look on a computer monitor versus a hardcopy version. This may affect some basic proposal formatting decisions and how you construct graphics. If possible, avoid using oversized pages for illustrations. They are practically impossible to view on standard monitors. Personally, I do not like using a two-column text format if proposals will be evaluated electronically.
- If you are delivering your proposal via overnight mail, then send two separate packages, each with a different carrier. This is cheap backup protection against a late delivery that could eliminate you from the competition. Just let the contracting officer know in advance and advise them to either return or destroy the backup copy of your proposal.
- Verify the delivery address for overnight mail deliveries. Sometimes they are different from the address for hand deliveries or regular mail deliveries. Bidders have been eliminated because they failed to deliver their proposal by the time and date specified by the RFP because they sent their proposal to the wrong address.

FINAL QUALITY ASSURANCE CHECK

Plan to conduct a final quality assurance check before submitting your proposal to the customer. If time permits, perform a final proofreading of the entire proposal to detect and correct any remaining typographical and spelling errors. Also, have someone check each copy of the proposal to:

- Verify the number of hardcopy proposals to be submitted.
- Check files names to verify that they correspond to those specified by the RFP if an electronic copy is being submitted. Label the CD or diskette. Verify that the electronic copy "opens" properly.
- Proof volume cover pages and spines.
- Verify that each volume has a table of contents, table of figures and tables, plus any other required information, such as an acronym list.
- Check each page for overall appearance. Look for improperly printed pages, smudges, and consecutive page numbers. Make sure that no pages are missing.
- Verify that all required attachments are included and submitted in the proper proposal volume.
- Verify that any RFP-required binding or proposal assembly instructions have been followed, such as submitting each volume separately in a three-ring binder.
- Check anything that could affect the appearance of your proposal and verify that all RFP instructions concerning proposal organization and packaging have been followed.

Allot one day of your proposal schedule to perform a final quality assurance check and to package the proposal for delivery to the customer.

Use proposal production as a vehicle to gain competitive advantage in an area that generally receives very little attention. Establish and maintain a proposal production capability to maximize the time available to work on your proposal and to prepare a professional-looking document that will favorably impress your customer. Prequalify and maintain a cadre of contract production personnel to fill staffing shortfalls and to supplement the talents of in-house production capability. Implement a disciplined process to manage the configuration of proposal preparation documents and proposal material. Conduct a final quality assurance check of the proposal before it is submitted to your customer.

Avoid the common pitfall of viewing proposal production personnel as simple clerks or low-level administrative hacks. They make up an important part of the proposal team and play a critical role in the proposal development process.

Part 4

Post-Proposal Submittal Phase

Chapter 16

Post-Proposal Submittal Phase

The post-proposal submittal phase begins officially when the customer receives your proposal. The first order of business once this happy day arrives is to express your and the company's gratitude to the proposal team. Take them to dinner, buy them a drink, or take them to a ballgame. Do whatever is appropriate for your organization and the members of the proposal team. Submitting a proposal is an event to be celebrated regardless of the ultimate outcome. Just do something meaningful, and do it shortly after the proposal is submitted.

Give the proposal team and yourself a few days off, if possible, to recharge your collective batteries. Then review the entire proposal to identify any omissions, critical errors, or areas that require improvement. This will prove to be valuable information if the procurement cycle includes customer discussions or a best and final offer (BAFO) request.

In addition, have each member of the capture team prepare a written lessons-learned of the entire proposal effort. Note those things that worked well and those that did not. Include observations, suggestions, and recommendations to improve your company's proposal process. If appropriate, provide the lessons-learned to senior management so they can review and respond to the recommendations. If not, maintain a file of lessons-learned to help guide future proposal activities.

If your organization gives bonuses for proposals, then complete the process to recommend those who went beyond the call of duty. If not, consider writing letters of commendation for those people. Send the letters to the appropriate managers in your organization and try to get a copy placed in each employee's personnel file. Few people are amply rewarded for their proposal participation. Do what you can to recognize their efforts.

After the euphoria of finishing the proposal has worn off, prepare for the next phase of the proposal process. The road from here to contract award can be especially treacherous. A lapse in focus during this phase could lead to unpleasant consequences. An excellent proposal effort can turn to ruin if you fail to prepare adequately for any required oral presentations or if you slip in responding to customer inquiries about your proposal.

These are two rich areas where you can recover from a less than spectacular proposal and potentially gain competitive advantage. Alternatively, they represent opportunities to transform an otherwise winning proposal into a losing effort. Many contracts are won and lost during this important proposal phase.

ORAL PRESENTATIONS

Many procuring agencies require an oral presentation as part of the proposal response. In other cases, customers may request an oral presentation of your overall proposal or in response to questions they have about your proposal. In some instances, your entire technical proposal may consist of an oral presentation.

Section L or M of the RFP will identify those cases where an oral presentation is considered to be part of your proposal submittal. Regardless of their origin, always take seriously the opportunities and dangers involved in making an oral presentation to your customer. Most contracts are won or lost by a narrow margin. The quality of your presentation and the people who give it may well represent that margin. Two stories with vastly different outcomes will help illustrate this point.

The first procurement was a two-phase affair where three bidders were selected to design an entire integrated system. One bidder would then be selected to implement their design during the second phase of the program. At the end of the first phase, each bidder was given the opportunity to present its design and program approach during a four-day, system-level design review. The audience consisted of the people who would select the winner.

To prepare, we worked with authors to script their presentation. Then we brought in a communications consultant. Each presenter delivered his or her presentation in front of a small audience while it was being videotaped by the consultant. Through repeated rehearsals, critiques, and practice, each presentation was honed to perfection. Our presentation to the customer was a smashing success, and we won a major contract.

The second story involves a situation where an oral presentation was part of our technical proposal. We delivered our presentation slides with the proposal and made the presentation several weeks later. Presenters were limited to those people who would execute the program. Despite all my urgings, I was unsuccessful in convincing management to script our presentation or practice it beforehand. We traveled to the customer's site the day before our scheduled presentation to prepare. Unfortunately, several of our presenters experienced travel problems. Consequently, we went through our presentation for the first time the night before.

Our lack of preparation was painfully obvious. One speaker, who was presenting an especially critical aspect of our program, got stage fright and froze at the podium. The results were disastrous. Everyone who attended experienced that uncomfortable embarrassment that comes from watching someone sweat, stammer, and generally struggle through a presentation. Needless to say, we lost this important contract.

Was either of these contracts won or lost solely on the basis of our oral presentation? Probably not, but it likely contributed significantly to the balance that tilted the scales to a win in one case and a loss in the other. Use oral presentations as yet one more opportunity to wrestle advantage away from your competitors.

Oral Presentations As Part of Formal Source Selection

Since 1994, various agencies have experimented with selecting contractors on the basis of oral presentations instead of hardcopy or electronic technical and management volumes. Beginning in 1997, oral presentations were covered by FAR 15.102. A variant of this approach is to use oral presentations as a supplement to an offeror's written proposal. In either case, there are some important guidelines for preparing and delivering your oral presentation. Good presentations are the result of planning, development, organization, and practice.

Review Section L carefully to determine the details concerning the oral presentation. These include where, when, time allowed, and presentation content. Note whether or not copies of your presentation have to be included with your submitted proposal. Find out as soon as possible what type of projection equipment will be available at the customer's location. This will determine your presentation medium.

Build the content of your oral presentation concurrent with the development of your written proposal, if both are required. This will ensure that the two complement each other. Based on the content requirements of the oral presentation, decide what information to include with your written proposal and what to include in the presentation. Plan to include copies of the oral presentation as part of your red team review.

Analyze the details of the required technical content and prepare an author guide for each separate requirement of the oral presentation. Normally, Section M will not list separate evaluation criteria for the oral presentation. However, you can correlate the content required by the Section L instructions with the Section M evaluation criteria to determine which are relevant to the presentation. Prepare a detailed outline for each separate requirement. Likewise, develop themes, conduct a feature/benefit analysis, and identify potential strengths to emphasize.

I recommend that you prepare a written response for each oral presentation requirement, just as if you were going to submit it with your proposal. Then transform it into an oral presentation.

Organize the presentation according to the order it is asked for in Section L. Start by allocating an equal amount of time for each topic requested. Then adjust this allocation based on the relative importance of the corresponding evaluation criteria. Translate this into the number of slides per topic. Be careful not to build too many slides. Oral presentations are time-limited, and overrunning one topic will shortchange another. This could negatively impact the evaluation of your presentation. Allocate at least two to three minutes per slide, except for introductory or title slides. You will be able to fine-tune the specific timing when you practice the presentation.

We refer to presentations with visual aids as *oral* presentations, but they really are *visual* presentations with an oral narration. The information contained on the slide and its appearance may be more important than what you say. Some experts claim that an effective presentation is primarily made up of vocal (38 percent) and visual (55 percent) elements, while the verbal content accounts for 7 percent. This means that the visual information and how you deliver your presentation are critical elements. Keep this firmly in mind as you develop your presentation slides.

Because the presentation is so visually oriented, graphics can play an important role in making key points and helping evaluators remember them. Key points of your presentation and important themes should take center stage, normally as bulleted or numbered items on your slides. Your oral narrative serves to fill in the details and emphasize themes. That is not to imply that your presentation should resemble a sales pitch. Your oral presentation, like your written proposal, is primarily a technical presentation with a persuasive message.

Here is a simple checklist to help guide your planning:

- If your customer is located out of town, plan to arrive the day before your scheduled presentation. Devise one or two alternate routes to the customer's location or alternate forms of transportation that can be used if the unexpected happens. Plan to arrive early, and leave enough time for unforeseen contingencies. Being late, regardless of cause, gets you off on the wrong foot with your customer.
- Find out as much as possible about the room, the seating arrangements, and the location of the overhead projector at the customer's facility.
- Find out how soon you can get into the room before the presentation to set up. Once you know the room layout, decide where each team member will sit.
- Know the dress code of your customer audience and wear clothes that are appropriate. This is the wrong time to have your key technical

person show up wearing a plaid suit, striped shirt, and paisley tie, or in a neon mini-skirt with hot-pink glasses. Discuss what each team member will be wearing. The best approach is to dress conservatively.
- Plan the role of the team leader and each participant.

Organizing Your Team

Many government procurements limit presenters to people who will work on the program. In these cases, your proposed program manager must be the team leader and lead presenter. Other members of the proposed management team can present selected topics based on the technical requirements of the presentation.

Even if it is not a requirement, having the program manager lead the team is most often the best choice. Under no circumstances should you allow marketing to lead the oral presentation. Except as an observer, marketing should not attend oral presentations when they are part of your formal proposal submittal. On more than one occasion, I have heard government personnel complain about receiving a sales pitch when they expected a technical presentation covering the details of the bidder's proposed approach.

Marketing plays an important role in business acquisition. They can even participate in preparing the presentation, where their knowledge of the customer can be especially valuable. Just keep in mind that customers want to see and interact with members of the program team proposed to perform the contract and with whom they will be interacting in the future.

Each team member should know exactly what they are supposed to do for the presentation and when and how they are to do it. Plan to choreograph the entire presentation. Create a responsibility matrix to show team member assignments. Be sure to have backup team members available among your staff in case a team member is unable to perform his or her part of the presentation due to illness, accident, or family emergency.

Find out beforehand whether the customer will ask questions during the presentation, after the presentation, or not at all. Decide which team member will be responsible for handling customer questions. The program manager should field each customer question and then direct it to the person on your team most qualified to answer. This helps create a favorable customer impression that you are conducting an effective, well-coordinated team effort.

Practicing the Presentation

Practice may *not* make perfect, but it certainly affords an opportunity to work out the bugs and deliver an effective customer presentation. The amount of required practice depends upon the presentation skills of the speakers. If possible, practice early versions of the presentation as it is being developed. This will enable speakers to gain familiarity with presentation content early, which should reduce downstream practice time.

Have individuals practice in front of a small audience until they are comfortable with their presentation and can give it in the allotted time. Then practice the whole presentation at least three times with the entire team present.

The first presentation should be given to a group capable of critiquing your performance and scoring it. Practice looking like a cohesive team and making transitions between speakers. If the customer will ask questions during your presentation, then have the audience ask questions during practice. The second presentation should incorporate the comments from the first presentation. The third presentation is a dress rehearsal. Schedule additional presentations as required. If practical, plan a final dress rehearsal the day before the scheduled presentation.

Have speakers memorize their opening and closing remarks. Delivering an important presentation to the customer can be an anxiety-laden experience, especially for inexperienced speakers. Similarly, having a video camera pointed at you, which is a common practice at oral presentations, can be very unnerving. Memorization is good preventive medicine to overcome a fear-induced blank mind, which can plague even the most practiced speakers. Having recited the opening from memory, most people will be calm enough to gain control over the rest of their presentation.

Scripting each presentation also is a good safeguard against speaker anxiety. Under pressure, speakers tend to ad lib. Without a script, they may engage in verbal meandering, causing them to overrun their allotted time, miss making the key points of their presentation, or make inappropriate statements. Alternatively, anxious speakers may freeze up and be incapable of delivering their presentation. Avoid disaster through practice, memorization, and scripting presentations.

Team presentations should be conducted exactly as they will be given to the customer. This includes introductions, closing remarks, transitions between speakers, and presentation slides. Do not let a speaker "talk" through a presentation where he or she tells you what he is going to say. Have him deliver the entire presentation just like he will at the real presentation.

Assign a timekeeper within the team. Keep time for each presentation during both practice and the actual presentation. Work out subtle signals to alert speakers when they appear to be going over their allotted time.

Presentation Tips

The manner in which a presentation is delivered and the conduct of the presenter affect the perceived quality of the presentation. It can even impact the perceived competence of the presenter. The "presence" of the speaker can be as important as what he or she has to say; sometimes it is even more important.

An oral presentation is not the time to try and transform the entire program organization into gifted public speakers. Nonetheless, it is worth reviewing some presentations *dos* and *don'ts* and having your team incorporate as many of them as possible into their presentation style.

As a starting point, do everything you can to appear relaxed. Speakers who appear tense or anxious cause the audience to tense, which can be an uncomfortable experience.

When speaking, *do*:

- Look calm and confident
- Sound positive
- Complete each word clearly and articulately
- Project your voice
- Vary your rate of speech
- Pause after a key point for emphasis
- Make direct eye contact with audience members
- Move purposefully
- Be aware of your posture
- Allow your hands to fall to your sides when you are not using them
- Remember to breathe; smile if you can
- Pay attention to other team members who are speaking.

As you make your presentation, *do not*:

- Speak too softly or in a monotone voice
- Use non-words like "umm," "ahh," or "er"
- Clear your throat too often
- Use qualifiers like "maybe" or "perhaps"
- Roll your eyes, frown, or make expressions of exasperation
- Lean on the podium or projector
- Slouch, stand too still, or appear stiff
- Keep your hands in any one place for too long
- Hold an object in your hands unless you plan to use it
- Look expressionless or unhappy.

If you will be using an overhead projector, bring along some tape and use it to mark where to place transparencies. This will enable you to place each overhead without fidgeting. Cover or turn off the overhead projector when you are not projecting an image on the screen. Remember to bring along a spare projector bulb.

If you are going to project slides electronically, bring along a back-up presentation to use in case the primary medium fails to work. Murphy's law says that if anything can go wrong, it will. I think Murphy was an optimist. Plan ahead and be ready to cope with unforeseen contingencies.

From the moment you arrive at the customer's facility until you are safely driving away, everything you do and say is important. When interacting with the customer, be cordial and polite. Act friendly, and suppress any visible signs of frustration or anger.

Relative Importance of Oral Presentations

There is a tendency to relax and let down your guard once the written proposal is submitted. This is a deadly mistake. Whenever an oral presentation is part of your proposal submittal, it should be accorded the same diligence and attention to detail you give the written portion. You would not consider submitting your written proposal without a red team or some comparable review. Similarly, you would not willingly release a proposal without editing the final copy. Nor would you submit it on the back of an old envelope.

Preparing and delivering an effective oral presentation is difficult and time-consuming. In some respects, it is more difficult than preparing the written portion. Yet, if you attempt to follow the presentation guidelines contained in this section, eventually someone will ask, "How much is enough?" The answer is: When you are absolutely, positively convinced that your presentation is superior in every way to all the competitors. Anything less may permit the competition to steal away an advantage that could belong to you. Your goal is to gain competitive advantage, not to forfeit it.

Other Oral Presentations

Sometimes customers ask for an oral presentation of your proposal as a verbal executive summary. Such presentations are not part of the formal source selection process. So your presentation will not be scored. Nor will it officially contribute to the overall evaluation of your proposal. Nonetheless, do not take these presentations lightly. They afford an opportunity to make a favorable impression with your customer. Everything counts.

To determine presentation content, follow any customer instructions contained in the RFP. In the absence of specific direction, organize your presentation around the evaluation criteria contained in Section M of the RFP. You can also call the customer's contracting officer to ask for specific instructions. Use the guidelines presented above to prepare and practice your presentation. This type of presentation need not be as polished as when it is a part of your evaluated proposal. But why not put in the extra effort? It might be the best opportunity you have to distinguish yourself from the competition.

Oral executive summaries typically are an hour or less in duration. So one person can make the entire presentation, unless you choose to showcase the proposed team. The proposed program manager usually is the best person to make the presentation, unless he or she is an abysmal speaker. In these cases, the better part of valor is to let another credible person give the presentation.

Again, avoid the temptation to let marketing take the lead. The customer is not looking for a sales pitch, but a summary of your proposed program solution and technical approach. Marketing personnel will not be viewed as credible for this type of presentation regardless of their actual capability.

Occasionally, customers will send each bidder a set of questions based on an initial review of their proposal. Each bidder is asked to prepare and present orally their answers to these questions. To prepare for this type of presentation, read the following section describing how to respond to customer inquiries. Then use the presentation guidelines already discussed to prepare and practice your presentation.

Customer inquiries about the contents or intent of your proposal contribute to its final score. Treat them accordingly. Ask the contracting officer for clarification if you are unsure about how an oral presentation fits into the source selection process. Ignorance is not bliss in this situation.

RESPONDING TO POST-PROPOSAL CUSTOMER INQUIRIES

The first phase of government source selection is to conduct an initial assessment of each bidder's proposal. Based on this assessment, the customer will decide whether or not they require any additional information to clarify their understanding of what is being offered. If so, they have several avenues available to solicit information from bidders.

First, the government can elect to award the contract without discussions. However, they must declare this intent in the RFP. "Discussions" is a somewhat vague term. In general it means giving each bidder a chance to change its proposal. An award without discussions limits exchanges between the government and offerors to situations where a bidder may be given the opportunity to clarify certain aspects of its proposal. The magnitude of the allowable clarification is where the definition of discussions blurs. The government is not supposed to permit a bidder to make material changes to its proposal, but only to clarify minor points.

For example, the government may ask a bidder to clarify the relevance of its past performance information and adverse past performance information to which the bidder has not previously had an opportunity to respond, or to resolve minor or clerical errors. Under an award without discussions, the government does not have to solicit clarification information from all bidders.

The second condition under which the government can ask for additional information occurs when they decide to conduct discussions with all bidders in the competitive range. Based on the initial ratings of each proposal against all evaluation criteria, the contracting officer establishes a competitive range comprising all the most highly rated proposals. Proposals outside the competitive range are eliminated from further consideration, and the contracting officer notifies the unfortunate bidders. The remaining bidders then receive written inquiries from the customer concerning their proposals.

Exchanges between the government and bidders within the competitive range can take the form of oral discussions, written questions, or both. The intent of these exchanges, or "discussions," is to allow bidders to change their proposals. Discussions are tailored to each offeror's proposal. The stated objective of discussions is to maximize the government's ability to obtain best value, based on the requirements and the evaluation factors defined in the RFP.

Discussions most often consist of written questions. Evaluators write questions to identify significant weaknesses, deficiencies, and other aspects of your proposal (e.g., cost, price, technical approach, past performance, terms and conditions). They represent areas that could, in the opinion of the contracting officer, be altered or explained to enhance materially your proposal's potential for award. On the flip side, they are areas that, if improperly addressed, will result in your losing the contract. Keep this important piece of information firmly in mind: You can be dropped from the competitive range and eliminated from the competition at any time during discussions. One fatal slip, and you are out!

Some agencies refer to written questions as "deficiency reports" and "clarification requests," and others simply refer to them as "evaluation notices." Regardless of title, customer inquiries generally point out a deficiency in your proposal or an area where they are not sure what you are proposing. If you fail to fix a perceived deficiency, then your response for this portion of the proposal will be scored as "unsatisfactory," and you run the risk of being eliminated.

Other cases involve a situation where the customer is requesting more information to understand what you are proposing. How you respond will determine the final score, assessed risk, or both for that proposal section. The wrong response can turn a satisfactory score into a deficient or marginal rating. A good response can transform a marginal score into a satisfactory or higher rating or reduce the level of assessed proposal risk.

On the battlefield of competitive proposals, wars frequently are won and lost in the trenches of responding to customer inquiries. To say this phase is critical to proposal success would be a monumental understatement. Like other pivotal points throughout the proposal lifecycle, this area represents a significant opportunity to capture competitive advantage.

By this stage of the process, you have made the competitive range. You are a serious contender. The customer has flagged some areas where they perceive some deficiencies, omissions, or potential shortcomings in your proposal. You now have the chance to fix these sins. Moreover, with some perceptive hard work, you have the potential to transform your final proposal into a powerful and effective document that will secure a nice piece of new business for your organization. Take advantage of this opportunity.

Developing Written Responses to Customer Inquires

For planning purposes, ensure that you have ready access to key members of the proposal team. This should be coordinated well in advance so you don't have to scramble for resources at the last minute. Proposal team members may be reassigned to new jobs after the proposal is submitted.

Responding effectively to customer inquires requires that you perform a miniature proposal development activity. Key activities include developing a schedule; analyzing customer questions; preparing, reviewing, and editing responses; and producing and delivering those responses to the customer by the due date.

On page-limited proposals, your response may be similarly limited. So, plan accordingly. In addition, responses to customer inquiries are time-limited. Make sure you plan enough time for preparation, review, final production, and delivery to the customer. Customers often allow only a short time period to respond. You must be prepared to move quickly.

If the customer requires change pages to your proposal, then you must develop these concurrent with your written response. Pay close attention to customer instructions concerning how to mark and submit proposal change pages. If the customer wants an oral presentation of your answers, then use the information in this chapter to prepare one.

The first and most critical step in preparing your response is to fully understand what precipitated the question. Why is the customer asking this question? What information does the customer need to give this section a good score or a low risk rating? Start by reading and rereading the section of your proposal referenced by the customer's question. Compare what you said in your proposal to all of the associated RFP requirements in the proposal requirements matrix. What is missing? What needs to be added? Why doesn't the customer understand what you proposed? If you fail to understand *why* the customer is asking this question, you run the risk of providing a wrong answer. Have marketing participate in the review. Their customer insight may help decipher the question.

Sometimes the proposal team is too familiar with the proposal to grasp an evaluator's inability to understand what you have proposed. If so, bring in someone fresh to review the customer question and your proposal response. Also, do not view any customer question as trivial. Every question is important no matter how straightforward it seems. If the customer thought it was important enough to ask, then it is important enough to take seriously.

Once you clearly understand the genesis of the customer's question, begin to formulate a response. Prepare a draft and subject it to a critical review. The focus of this review is to determine whether your response has addressed the customer question adequately. If the customer question identified a deficiency, have you fixed it to everyone's satisfaction? If the question was a clarification, have you provided ample information that will lead to a high score?

Edit your response to accommodate review comments and review it again if you have enough time. Repeatedly compare your response with the customer's question to ensure that you have completely and clearly dispelled any customer concerns.

Preparing a Best and Final Offer

Making material changes to your proposal will likely change your bid price. As you prepare responses to customer questions and change your technical proposal, you must assess the cost impact of any proposed changes. Clarifying your proposal response normally will not alter your cost. However, fixing a deficiency may significantly affect cost. In such cases, you will need to balance the merits of how you fix the deficiency against its impact on the overall cost evaluation. Moreover, you will need to update your cost proposal to reflect any changes that have a cost impact.

After a customer has opened discussions, bidders usually are afforded the opportunity to adjust their proposed price (but not always). Sometimes the customer will formally request an adjusted price by requesting a best and final offer (BAFO) for each bidder in the competitive range. In other cases, pricing adjustments are made along with responses to written questions or on the basis of pre-award negotiations. In either case, build and maintain a record that traces changes in your technical proposal to corresponding changes in cost. Annotate each change in cost with comments that briefly explain the adjustment. This will prove invaluable after contract award.

Make sure you understand whether any post-proposal inquiry from your customer constitutes discussions. If the customer does not consider an exchange to be discussions, then you will not be permitted to adjust your price. Theoretically, any changes that are not discussions should not require any cost adjustment. However, some agencies have liberally expanded the envelope of information they solicit under the guise of award without discussions. If inquiries do not stipulate whether they constitute discussions or not, ask the contracting officer for clarification.

Value of a Good First Impression

Awarding contracts without discussions is a growing trend among government agencies. This approach is consistent with acquisition streamlining initiatives, and it saves the government a lot of work. The advantage of submitting your very best product the first time out is obvious under these circumstances.

Making every effort to submit the best proposal initially is still important, even for procurements that include discussions. Under these circumstances, proposals are evaluated twice: once to determine the competitive range and once after discussions. The final evaluation is the most important, but the results of the first are carried forward. It is far better to be perceived as the apparent winner after the first round of evaluations than to try and come from behind. Moreover, if you submit a great proposal the first time, you may relieve the customer from the burden of having to enter into discussions with all qualified bidders.

In yesteryears, a bid strategy of saving the best for last dominated many bidders' BAFO approach. This mentality persists in some organizations. However, it is an ill-advised strategy for two reasons. First, by saving the best for last, you may never get a chance to show your best. Second, you may never overcome the initial view that your bid is a loser regardless of what you do during discussions. Use your initial submittal to make a favorable first impression with your customer. Continue to provide information to further enhance this view.

Resist the impulse to let down your guard, or you may get knocked out of the competition. The post-proposal phase is where the government attempts to separate the wheat form the chaff. Use this opportunity to gain advantage over other bidders. Prepare oral presentations and customer inquiries to better the competition and waltz your way into the winner's circle.

Treat the preparation of an oral presentation to the customer with the same diligence and attention to detail you used to prepare your written proposal. Develop author guides for the presentation. Prepare written scripts and practice the presentation until it is perfect. If the oral presentation is part of formal source selection, it may be the pivotal event that determines the winner. Make sure that everyone knows his or her role. Prepare the presentation as a team. Practice as a team. Win as a team.

In responding to written inquires from the customer, make certain you understand why the question or clarification is being asked. Otherwise, you may not respond properly. What information does the customer need to give you a high score? Prepare your response to address the inquiry clearly. Review it. Critique it. Prepare a compelling response that gives the customer all the information necessary to dispel a noted deficiency, or clarify your proposed approach in a way that will lead to a favorable evaluation.

This is the final stretch. The finish line lies just ahead. Seize advantage and cross it ahead of the other bidders.

Chapter 17

Contract Award and Performance

The long road that defines the business acquisition lifecycle comes to an end at contract award. All the hard work and scheming, late nights at the office, and enormous expenditure of corporate energy either culminate in victory or end in defeat. You either win or you lose. There are no silver medals for a valiant effort. Few business experiences are more frustrating and disheartening than losing a proposal, especially major efforts where you have invested months or even years in its development. Alternatively, there is no substitute for the sense of exhilaration and accomplishment that comes from a winning effort.

The key is to win consistently. That has been the purpose of this book: to show you how to gain competitive advantage, maximize the application of your B&P resources, and dance in the winner's circle far more often than you experience the sting of defeat.

Contract award indeed terminates the acquisition lifecycle for the current opportunity. Yet there are still a few things you can do to gain advantage for the next time you step into the competitive arena.

The first order of business is to celebrate your victory. If you win a small contract, have a big celebration. If you win a big contract, have a bigger celebration. If you work in a small company, have a company-wide celebration. If you work in a large company, then at least have a division-wide celebration. Winning competitive proposals is the lifeblood of organizations that rely upon business from the federal government. I cannot think of a single business event that merits a celebration more than winning a new contract.

Actually, there are two good functional reasons for celebrating your proposal victories. First, they highlight the importance of proposal efforts to the whole organization. This can foster interdepartmental cooperation for future proposal efforts. I find that people on the periphery of proposals often fail to support proposals adequately because they neither understand their importance nor accept the sense of urgency demanded by proposal team members.

Second, people who work on proposals rarely receive just compensation for their efforts. Using a celebration party to publicly acknowledge the valiant efforts of the proposal team in front of their peers and managers helps overcome this shortcoming. Proposal team members cannot put praise in the bank nor use it to pay their mortgage. Nonetheless, it goes a long way toward enticing them back for a repeat performance in the future.

POST-AWARD DEBRIEFINGS

A cardinal sin in the proposal business is failing to understand clearly why you won or why you lost. There is a tendency to view winning proposals as exemplary efforts that need to be repeated and losing proposals as bad efforts to be avoided in the future. Such logic has surface validity but may betray the facts.

If you hearken back to your school days, you may recall an incident where you performed well but received less than a stellar grade because the teacher graded on a curve and the competition was tough. Alternatively, you may have an experience where your performance was not so great, yet you received a good grade because the class was full of dullards.

Proposals also are graded on the curve. You may submit a terrible proposal and still win because the competing proposals were even more terrible than yours. Or, you may submit a great proposal that loses to fierce competition. Retaining the winner as a future model or discarding the loser would be an error in either case. Gain competitive advantage for the future by knowing why you won or why you lost. The starting point is to ask the government for a debriefing of the source selection evaluation results.

Win or lose, always request a debriefing as soon as you have been notified of contract award or once you are eliminated from the competition. Make your request in writing to the contracting officer within three days of being notified. All bidders are entitled to a debriefing, at which the government will furnish the basis for the selection decision and contract award. Government debriefings may be done orally, in writing, or by any other method acceptable to the contracting officer. If the debriefing is oral, you still should be able to get a hardcopy of the briefing slides.

Making the Most of a Debriefing

Evaluation debriefings vary between government agencies and sometimes within the same agency. According to the FAR, the government is required to provide at least the following information:

- The government's evaluation of the significant weaknesses or deficiencies in the offeror's proposal, if applicable
- The overall evaluated cost or price (including unit prices) and technical rating, if applicable, of the successful offeror and the debriefed offeror, and past performance information on the debriefed offeror
- The overall ranking of all offerors, when any ranking was developed by the agency during source selection
- A summary of the rationale for award
- For acquisitions of commercial items, the make and model of the item to be delivered by the successful offeror
- Reasonable responses to relevant questions about whether or not the government followed source selection procedures contained in the solicitation, applicable regulations, and other applicable authorities.

The government is restricted from providing details of any competitor's technical approach or divulging any company proprietary information. If you won, you can piece this information together after contract award through future interactions with the customer. Also, use marketing to dig into the details of your competitors' bids. Persistent efforts to obtain this information generally will be successful. Few people are overly concerned with revealing the details of a losing effort. After all, what is there to protect?

If you lost the bid, immediately request a copy of the resulting contract. The contract will provide CLIN prices for the winning bid. You can request a copy of the winning proposal, but don't expect to receive anything of value. The winner is allowed to delete anything considered proprietary, which typically will cover its entire technical proposal.

Use the results of the debriefing along with a copy of the winning contract, plus whatever information you can assemble, to analyze your bid against those submitted by the other competitors. If you won, work to arrive at a clear understanding of how and why. What did you do that was better, cleverer, cheaper, faster, more reliable, etc., than the other competitors? What were your strengths and weaknesses compared to the competition? If you lost, you must determine how the winner was able to beat you. Did they bid a significantly lower price? If so, determine what they did to arrive at that price. If they did not win on price, then determine what they did and how they did it to win.

The best time to start the post-award analysis is as soon as you have enough data to reach some meaningful conclusions. You may need to continue collecting information for several months before you really know how you won or lost. Open a file for each award and maintain it until you are convinced that you clearly understand the reasons why you won or lost. This may sound like a lot of work, but it really is not. The key is to continue collecting information, most of which should come from your own marketing and program personnel. If you fail to understand why you won, you may not be able to repeat this feat in the future. If you fail to understand why you lost, then you risk repeating a losing strategy.

Gain competitive advantage. Invest the effort. Piece together the puzzle so you understand the key factors that led to contract award. Then use them to gain advantage on the next bid opportunity.

Proper Behavior at a Government Debriefing

Throughout this book I have provided guidance about proper conduct in front of the customer. Attending a debriefing after you lose can be a trying experience. So some pointers for this inauspicious occasion are in order. Recall that you should always attempt to leave the customer with a favorable impression of your organization.

Your purpose at a debriefing is to obtain as much information as you can about the evaluation. Demonstrating your displeasure with the evaluation or the customer's award decision will not accomplish that objective. In addition, you want to show your continued interest in future customer programs. Therefore, vent your anger and frustration before you attend the debriefing. Work through all the rationalization that accompanies losing. Reconcile yourself with the fact that you lost because another bidder did something better, smarter, cheaper, or took more risk than you did. Your job is to collect enough information to prevent a repeat performance.

Stay calm during the debriefing. Getting angry will only detract from your primary mission. Moreover, government attendees will be very reluctant to share more than the minimum information if you appear hostile. You should display a gracious attitude of wanting to find out what you did wrong and how you can do better in the future. This can be difficult. I have attended debriefings where I thought I would have to bite the end off my tongue to keep from saying something unpleasant.

Be prepared for the possibility that evaluators may have failed to understand or interpret accurately what you proposed, or erroneously attributed a shortcoming to your proposal that was not there. At this point it does not matter whether the error was yours or theirs. Try to create a comfortable atmosphere with the government evaluators. Get them talking and keep them talking for as long as you can. This will enable you to meet your objective of collecting information and will leave behind a good impression.

The same rules apply when you attend a debriefing after you win. Of course, it is much easier to be friendly and gracious under these circumstances. Your objective is still to collect as much information as possible. Find out what the customer liked and did not like about your proposal. Ask what you could do in the future to improve your proposal product or to make the customer's job easier.

CLOSEOUT

A few housekeeping chores are necessary to close out proposal activities for the current bid opportunity. First, archive the entire proposal file for future reference. If you maintain a proposal library (see Chapter 6), then add files from the current proposal to the appropriate areas of your proposal database library. Add the results of the evaluation debriefing to whatever file you maintain for this type of data. Update your competitor database with information you gain from the debriefing and your analysis of the contract award. If you are not finished with your post-award evaluation, keep this file open until the information is complete.

Finally, open a file for the new program win. Coordinate with the program manager to establish the basic information for the file and brief the program manager on his or her responsibility to update the file periodically. This will help support the preparation of subsequent past performance volumes.

The closeout portion of the proposal process may seem like an unlikely place to find opportunities to gain competitive advantage. Yet the post-evaluation assessment of why you won or lost can yield invaluable data to guide your next bid effort. Knowledge of why you lost is a critical prerequisite to building a winning strategy in the future. Likewise, use information about why you won to validate your bid strategy development process, improve your next effort, and prepare for a repeat performance.

When you win, the second aspect of gaining competitive advantage is performing well on the ensuing contract. Past performance is a key evaluation factor for many government procurements. Exemplary contract performance affords an obvious opportunity to delight your customer and gain the high road competitively for future bids.

Appendix A
Sample Capture Plan

CUSTOMER INFORMATION

Customer Name (Company, Division, Procuring Agency)

Customer Schedule (Draft RFP, Final RFP, Conferences, Proposal Due, Contract Award)

Contract Type:

Contract Value:

Customer Budget by Year (if known)

Customer Team:

Name	Position	Phone Number	Responsibility

Customer Decision-Makers:

Name	Position	Bias/Priority	Comments

Past Performance/History with Customer (Favorable, Unfavorable, Problems, Achievements)

Known Customer Biases That Could Affect Bid Outcome:

PROGRAM REQUIREMENTS

Program Title:

Program Description Summary:

Key Technical or Expertise Requirements:

Requirement	Priority	Metric	Comments

Proposed Technical Solution: (List key elements)

Technical Advantages or Shortcomings of Proposed Team:

COMPETITORS

Key Competitors:

Company Name	Product Offering	Likely Bid Strategy	Relationship with Customer

Competitor Advantages (List any known competitor advantages):

Competitor Strengths/Weaknesses: For each key program requirement, including cost, compare each competitor with the proposed team to determine if the competitor is better (+), equal to (=), or less (–) qualified than the proposed team.

Program Requirement	Competitor A	Competitor B	Competitor C

Plans to Counteract Competitor Strengths:

Competitor	Requirement	Strength	Plan to Counter

Plans to Exploit Competitor Weaknesses:

Competitor	Requirement	Weakness	Plan to Exploit

BID STRATEGY

Strategic Value of Bid Opportunity:

Risks/Opportunities: (List risks and opportunities associated with bidding or performing program)

B&P Funding Requirements:

IR&D Funding Requirements:

Statement of Overall Bid Strategy:

Customer Contact Plan:

Customer	L-3 Lead	Issue/ Requirement	Estimated Meeting Date	Meeting Objective

Action Plan:

Action No.	Action Item	Person Responsible	Action Due Date	Status/ Comments

Index

Z